# THE INTERNATIONAL JEW

# THE INTERNATIONAL JEW

## THE WORLD'S FOREMOST PROBLEM

BY

HENRY FORD

KALPAZ

ISBN: 978-93-5128-895-4(HB)

First Published in 1920
Indian Reprint in 2017

*Published by*

Kalpaz Publications
C-30, Satyawati Nagar,
Delhi – 110052
E-mail: kalpaz@hotmail.com
Website: kalpazpublications.com
Ph.: +91-9212142040

**Cataloging in Publication Data—DK**
Courtesy: D.K. Agencies (P) Ltd. <docinfo@dkagencies.com>

**The international Jew :** the world's foremost problem, being a reprint of a series of articles appearing in The Dearborn independent from May 22 to October 2, 1920.
pages cm
Reprint. Originally published: Dearborn, Michigan : Dearborn Publishing Co., November, 1920.
ISBN 9789351288954

1. Antisemitism—United States. I. Dearborn independent.

DS145.I58 2017 DDC 305.8924073 23

# FOREWORD
## to the Bi-Centennial Edition

In the year 1920 Henry Ford, Sr. published *The International Jew,* a comprehensive survey of Jewish power in the United States and throughout the world. This four-volume work was originally serialized in the *Dearborn Independent,* the house organ of the Ford Motor Company.

These books have been best-sellers in many parts of the world, and have been translated into the languages of most civilized countries. Sadly, there are many countries today where possession of these books has been made punishable by confiscation or worse. In Germany, for example, a person who wants to borrow *The International Jew* from a library must first prove that he needs it for historical research. In other words, an ordinary tax-paying member of the public who supports the public library with his hard-earned money is unable to further his knowledge or satisfy his curiosity in this regard.

It is therefore in the interest of spreading truth that we republish these books in full so that new generations shall see for themselves how our problems of today are the same problems which have "mysteriously" occured since the turn of the century. The fact that even the wealthy Henry Ford, Sr. could be forced to withdraw these books, starkly illuminates the power of the Jews, even in the 1920's. To reprint *The International Jew* now, when the Jews are so much more powerful, is some indication of the tremendous courage of the publisher.

Every American who loves his country should make it his duty to buy sufficient copies for donation to libraries, universities, business associations, etc. Most important, every American parent should have at least one set at home to pass on to his children.

In further support of the findings and conclusions of *The International Jew,* an excellent companion book, *The Dispossessed Majority,* by Wilmot Robertson, exposes the rapid increase of Jewish power since the first publication of Henry Ford's great work. No conscientious, thinking American should be without these amazing, fact-filled books.

*The Dispossessed Majority* ($4.95) is also available from this publisher.

*Christof Friedrich*

# Preface

WHY discuss the Jewish Question? Because it is here, and because its emergence into American thought should contribute to its solution, and not to a continuance of those bad conditions which surround the Question in other countries.

The Jewish Question has existed in the United States for a long time. Jews themselves have known this, even if Gentiles have not. There have been periods in our own country when it has broken forth with a sullen sort of strength which presaged darker things to come. Many signs portend that it is approaching an acute stage.

Not only does the Jewish Question touch those matters that are of common knowledge, such as financial and commercial control, usurpation of political power, monopoly of necessities, and autocratic direction of the very news that the American people read; but it reaches into cultural regions and so touches the very heart of American life.

This question reaches down into South America and threatens to become an important factor in Pan-American relations. It is interwoven with much of the menace of organized and calculated disorder which troubles the nations today. It is not of recent growth, but its roots go deep, and the long Past of this Problem is counterbalanced by prophetic hopes and programs which involve a very deliberate and creative view of the Future.

This little book is the partial record of an investigation of the Jewish Question. It is printed to enable interested readers to inform themselves on the data published in The Dearborn Independent prior to Oct. 1, 1920. The demand for back copies of the paper was so great that the supply was exhausted early, as was also a large edition of a booklet containing the first nine articles of the series. The investigation still proceeds, and the articles will continue to appear as heretofore until the work is done.

The motive of this work is simply a desire to make facts known to the people. Other motives have, of course, been ascribed to it. But the motive of prejudice or any form of antagonism is hardly strong enough to support such an investigation as this. Moreover, had an unworthy motive existed, some sign of it would inevitably appear in the work itself. We confidently call the reader to witness that the tone of these articles is all that it should be. The International Jew and his satellites, as the conscious enemies of all that Anglo-Saxons mean by civilization, are not spared, nor is that unthinking mass which defends anything that a Jew does, simply because it has been taught to believe that what Jewish leaders do is Jewish. Neither do these articles proceed upon a false emotion of brotherhood and apology, as if this stream of doubtful tendency in the world were only accidentally Jewish. We give the facts as we find them; that of itself is sufficient protection against prejudice or passion.

This volume does not complete the case by any means. But it brings the reader along one step. In future compilations of these and subsequent articles the entire scope of the inquiry will more clearly appear.

October, 1920.

# Contents

*"Among the distinguishing mental and moral traits of the Jews may be mentioned: distaste for hard or violent physical labor; a strong family sense and philoprogenitiveness; a marked religious instinct; the courage of the prophet and martyr rather than of the pioneer and soldier; remarkable power to survive in adverse environments, combined with great ability to retain racial solidarity; capacity for exploitation, both individual and social; shrewdness and astuteness in speculation and money matters generally; an Oriental love of display and a full appreciation of the power and pleasure of social position; a very high average of intellectual ability."*

*—The New International Encyclopedia.*

I.

# The Jew in Character and Business

THE Jew is again being singled out for critical attention throughout the world. His emergence in the financial, political and social spheres has been so complete and spectacular since the war, that his place, power and purpose in the world are being given a new scrutiny, much of it unfriendly. Persecution is not a new experience to the Jew, but intensive scrutiny of his nature and super-nationality is. He has suffered for more than 2,000 years from what may be called the instinctive anti-Semitism of the other races, but this antagonism has never been intelligent nor has it been able to make itself intelligible. Nowadays, however, the Jew is being placed, as it were, under the microscope of economic observation that the reasons for his power, the reasons for his separateness, the reasons for his suffering may be defined and understood.

In Russia he is charged with being the source of Bolshevism, an accusation which is serious or not according to the circle in which it is made; we in America, hearing the fervid eloquence and perceiving the prophetic ardor of young Jewish apostles of social and industrial reform, can calmly estimate how it may be. In Germany he is charged with being the cause of the Empire's collapse and a very considerable literature has sprung up, bearing with it a mass of circumstantial evidence that gives the thinker pause. In England he is charged with being the real world ruler, who rules as a super-nation over the nations, rules by the power of gold, and who plays nation against nation for his own purposes, remaining himself discreetly in the background. In America it is pointed out to what extent the elder Jews of wealth and the younger Jews of ambition swarmed through the war organizations—principally those departments which dealt with the commercial and industrial business of war, and also the extent to which they have clung to the advantage which their experience as agents of the government gave them.

In simple words, the question of the Jews has come to the fore, but like other questions which lend themselves to prejudice, efforts will be made to hush it up as impolitic for open discussion. If, however, experience has taught us anything it is that questions thus suppressed will sooner or later break out in undesirable and unprofitable forms.

The Jew is the world's enigma. Poor in his masses, he yet controls the world's finances. Scattered abroad without country or government, he yet presents a unity of race continuity which no other people has achieved. Living under legal disabilities in almost every land, he has become the power behind many a throne. There are ancient prophecies to the effect that the Jew will return to his own land and from that center rule the world, though not until he has undergone an assault by the united nations of mankind.

The single description which will include a larger percentage of Jews than members of any other race is this: he is in business. It may be only gathering rags and selling them, but he is in business. From the sale of old clothes to the control of international trade and finance, the Jew is supremely gifted for business. More than any other race he exhibits a decided aversion to industrial employment, which he balances by an equally decided adaptability to trade. The Gentile boy works his way up, taking employment in the productive or technical departments; but the Jewish boy prefers to begin as messenger, salesman or clerk—anything—so long as it is connected with the commercial side of the business. An early Prussian census illustrates this characteristic: of a total population of 269,400, the Jews comprised six per cent or 16,164. Of these, 12,000 were traders and 4,164 were workmen. Of the Gentile population, the other 94 per cent, or 153,236 people, there were only 17,000 traders.

A modern census would show a large professional and literary class added to the traders, but no diminution of the percentage of traders and not much if any increase in the number of wage toilers. In America alone most of the big business, the trusts and the banks, the natural resources and the chief agricultural products, especially tobacco, cotton and sugar, are in the control of Jewish financiers or their agents. Jewish journalists are a large and powerful group here. "Large numbers of department stores are held by Jewish firms," says the Jewish Encyclopedia, and many if not most of them are run under Gentile names. Jews are the largest and most numerous landlords of residence property in the country. They are supreme in the theatrical world. They absolutely control the circulation of publications throughout the country. Fewer than any race whose presence among us is noticeable, they receive daily an amount of favorable publicity which would be impossible did they not have the facilities for creating and distributing it themselves. Werner Sombart, in his "Jew and Modern Capitalism" says, "If the conditions in America continue to develop along the same lines as in the last generation, if the immigration statistics and the proportion of births among all the nationalities remain the same, our imagination may picture the United States of fifty or a hundred years hence as a land inhabited only by Slavs, Negroes and Jews, wherein the Jews will naturally occupy the position of economic leadership." Sombart is a pro-Jewish writer.

The question is, If the Jew is in control, how did it happen? This is a free country. The Jew comprises only about three per cent of the population; to every Jew there are 97 Gentiles; to the 3,000,000 Jews in the United States there are 97,000,000 Gentiles. If the Jew is in control, is it because of his superior ability, or is it because of the inferiority and don't-care attitude of the Gentiles?

It would be very simple to answer that the Jews came to America, took their chances like other people and proved more successful in the competitive struggle. But that would not include all the facts. And before a more adequate answer can be given, two points should be made clear. The first is this: all Jews are not rich controllers of wealth. There are poor Jews aplenty, though most of them even in their poverty are their own masters. While it may be true that the chief financial controllers of the country are Jews, it is not true that every Jew is one of the financial controllers of the country. The classes must be kept distinct for a reason which will appear when the methods of the rich Jews and the methods of the poor Jews to gain power are differentiated. Secondly, the fact of Jewish solidarity renders it difficult to measure Gentile and Jewish achievements by the same standard. When a great block of wealth in America was made possible by the lavish use of another block of wealth from across the seas; that is to say, when certain Jewish immigrants came to the United States with the financial backing of European Jewry behind them, it would be unfair to explain the rise of that class of immigration by the same rules which account for the rise of, say, the Germans or the Poles who came here with no resource but their ambition and strength. To be sure, many individual Jews come in that way, too, with no dependence but themselves, but it would not be true to say that the massive control of affairs which is exercised by Jewish wealth was won by individual initiative; it was rather the extension of financial control across the sea.

That, indeed, is where any explanation of Jewish control must begin. Here is a race whose entire period of national history saw them peasants on the land, whose ancient genius was spiritual rather than material, bucolic rather than commercial, yet today, when they have no country, no government, and are persecuted in one way or another everywhere they go, they are declared to be the principal though unofficial rulers of the earth. How does so strange a charge arise, and why do so many circumstances seem to justify it?

Begin at the beginning. During the formative period of their national character the Jews lived under a law which made plutocracy and pauperism equally impossible among them. Modern reformers who are constructing model social systems on paper would do well to look into the social system under which the early Jews were organized. The Law of Moses made a "money aristocracy," such as Jewish financiers form today, impossible because it forbade the taking of interest. It made impossible also the continuous enjoyment of profit wrung out of another's distress. Profiteering and sheer speculation were not favored under the Jewish system. There could be no land-hogging; the land was apportioned among the people, and though it might be lost by debt or sold under stress, it was returned every 50 years to its original family ownership, at which time, called "The Year of Jubilee," there was practically a new social beginning. The rise of great landlords and a moneyed class was impossible under such a system, although the interim of 50 years gave ample scope for individual initiative to assert itself under fair competitive conditions.

If, therefore, the Jews had retained their status as a nation, and had remained in Palestine under the Law of Moses, they would hardly have achieved the financial distinction which they have since won. Jews never got rich out of one another. Even in modern times they have not become rich out of each other but out of the nations among whom they dwelt. Jewish law permitted the Jew to do business with a Gentile on a different basis than that on which he did business with a brother Jew. What is called "the Law of the Stranger" was defined thus: "unto a stranger thou mayest lend upon usury; but unto thy brother thou shalt not lend upon usury."

Being dispersed among the nations, but never merging themselves with the nations and never losing a very distinctive identity, the Jew has had the opportunity to practice "the ethics of the stranger" for many centuries. Being strangers among strangers, and often among cruelly hostile strangers, they have found this law a compensating advantage. Still, this alone would not account for the Jew's preeminence in finance. The explanation of that must be sought in the Jew himself, his vigor, resourcefulness and special proclivities.

Very early in the Jewish story we discover the tendency of Israel to be a master nation, with other nations as its vassals. Notwithstanding the fact that the whole prophetic purpose with reference to Israel seems to have been the moral enlightenment of the world through its agency, Israel's "will to mastery" apparently hindered that purpose. At least such would seem to be the tone of the Old Testament. Divinely ordered to drive out the Canaanites that their corrupt ideas might not contaminate Israel, the Jews did not obey, according to the old record. They looked over the Canaanitish people and perceived what great amount of man-power would be wasted if they were expelled, and so Israel enslaved them—"And it came to pass, when Israel was strong, that they put the Canaanites to tribute, and did not utterly drive them out." It was this form of disobedience, this preference of material mastery over spiritual leadership, that marked the beginning of Israel's age-long disciplinary distress.

The Jews' dispersion among the nations temporarily (that is, for more than 25 centuries now) changed the program which their scriptures declare was divinely planned, and that dispersion continues until today. There are spiritual leaders in modern Judaism who still claim that Israel's mission to the nations is spiritual, but their assertions that Israel is today fulfilling that mission are not as convincing as they might be if accompanied by more evidence. Israel throughout the modern centuries is still looking at the Gentile world and estimating what its man-power can be made to yield. But the discipline upon Israel still holds; he is an exile from his own land, condemned to be discriminated against wherever he goes, until the time when exile and homelessness shall end in a re-established Palestine, and Jerusalem again become the moral center of the earth, even as the elder prophets have declared.

Had the Jew become an employe, a worker for other men, his dispersion would not probably have been so wide. But becoming a trader, his instincts drew him round the habitable earth. There were Jews in China at an early date. They appeared as traders in England at the time of the Saxons. Jewish traders were in South America 100 years before the Pilgrim Fathers landed at Plymouth Rock. Jews established the sugar industry in the Island of St. Thomas in 1492. They were well established in Brazil when only a few villages dotted the eastern coast of what is now the United States. And how far they penetrated when once they came here is indicated by the fact that the first white child born in Georgia was a Jew—Isaac Minis. The Jew's presence round the earth, his clannishness with his own people, made him a nation scattered among the nations, a corporation with agents everywhere.

Another talent, however, contributed greatly to his rise in financial power—his ability to invent new devices for doing business. Until the Jew was pitted against the world, business was very crudely done. And when we trace the origins of many of the business methods which simplify and facilitate trade today, more likely than not we find a Jewish name at the end of the clue. Many of the indispensable instruments of credit and exchange were thought out by Jewish merchants, not only for use between themselves, but to check and hold the Gentiles with whom they dealt. The oldest bill of exchange extant was drawn by a Jew —one Simon Rubens. The promissory note was a Jewish invention, as was also the check "payable to bearer."

An interesting bit of history attaches to the "payable to bearer" instrument. The Jews' enemies were always stripping them of their last ounce of wealth, yet strangely, the Jews recovered very quickly and were soon rich again. How this sudden recovery from looting and poverty? Their assets were concealed under "bearer" and so a goodly portion was always saved. In an age when it was lawful for any pirate to seize goods consigned to Jews, the Jews were able to protect themselves by consigning goods on policies that bore no names.

The influence of the Jew was to center business around goods instead of persons. Previously all claims had been against persons; the Jew knew that the goods were more reliable than the persons with whom he dealt, and so he contrived to have claims laid against goods. Besides, this device enabled him to keep himself out of sight as much as possible. This introduced an element of hardness into business, inasmuch as it was goods which were being dealt in rather than men being dealt with, and this hardness remains. Another tendency which survives and which is of advantage in veiling the very large control which Jews have attained, is of the same origin as "bearer" bills; it permits a business dominated by Jewish capital to appear under a name that gives no hint of Jewish control.

The Jew is the only and original international capitalist, but as a rule he prefers not to emblazon that fact upon the skies; he prefers to use Gentile banks and trust companies as his agents and instruments. The suggestive term "Gentile front" often appears in connection with this practice.

The invention of the stock exchange is also credited to Jewish financial talent. In Berlin, Paris, London, Frankfort and Hamburg, Jews were in control of the first stock exchanges, while Venice and Genoa were openly referred to in the talk of the day as "Jew cities" where great trading and banking facilities might be found. The Bank of England was established upon the counsel and assistance of Jewish emigrants from Holland. The Bank of Amsterdam and the Bank of Hamburg both arose through Jewish influence.

There is a curious fact to be noted in connection with the persecution and consequent wanderings of the Jews about Europe and that is: wherever they wandered, the center of business seemed to go with them. When the Jews were free in Spain, there was the world's gold center. When Spain drove out the Jews, Spain lost financial leadership and has never regained it. Students of the economic history of Europe have always been puzzled to discover why the center of trade should have shifted from Spain, Portugal and Italy, up to the northern countries of Holland, Germany and England. They have sought for the cause in many things, but none has proved completely explanatory. When, however, it is known that the change was coincident with the expulsion of the Jews from the South and their flight to the North, when it is known that upon the Jews' arrival the northern countries began a commercial life which has flourished until our day, the explanation does not seem difficult. Time and again it has proved to be the fact that when the Jews were forced to move, the center of the world's precious metals moved with them.

This distribution of the Jews over Europe and the world, each Jewish community linked in a fellowship of blood, faith and suffering with every other group, made it possible for the Jew to be international in the sense that no other race or group of merchants could be at that time. Not only were they everywhere (Americans and Russians are everywhere, too) but they were in touch. They were organized before the days of conscious international commercial organizations, they were bound together by the sinews of a common life. It was observed by many writers in the Middle Ages that the Jews knew more of what was transpiring in Europe than the governments did. They also had better knowledge of what was likely to occur. They knew more about conditions than the statesmen did. This information they imparted by letter from group to group, country to country. Indeed, they may be said thus to have originated unconsciously the financial news-letter. Certainly the information they were able to obtain and thus distribute was invaluable to them in their speculative enterprises. Advance knowledge was an immense advantage in days when news was scarce, slow and unreliable.

This enabled Jewish financiers to become the agents of national loans, a form of business which they encouraged wherever possible. The Jew has always desired to have nations for his customers. National loans were facilitated by the presence of members of the same family of financiers in various countries, thus making an interlocking directorate by which king could be played against king, government against government, and the shrewdest use made of national prejudices and fears, all to the no small profit of the fiscal agent.

One of the charges most commonly made against Jewish financiers today is that they still favor this larger field of finance. Indeed, in all the criticism that is heard regarding the Jew as a business man, there is comparatively little said against him as an individual merchant serving individual customers. Thousands of small Jewish merchants are highly respected by their trade, just as tens of thousands of Jewish families are respected as our neighbors. The criticism, insofar as it respects the more important financiers, is not racial at all. Unfortunately the element of race, which so easily lends itself to misinterpretation as racial prejudice, is injected into the question by the mere fact that the chain of international finance as it is traced around the world discloses at every link a Jewish capitalist, financial family, or a Jewish-controlled banking system. Many have professed to see in this circumstance a conscious organization of Jewish power for

Gentile control, while others have attributed the circumstance to Jewish racial sympathies, to the continuity of their family affairs down the line of descent, and to the increase of collateral branches. In the old Scriptural phrase, Israel grows as the vine grows, ever shooting out new branches and deepening old roots, but always part of the one vine.

The Jew's aptitude for dealing with governments may also be traced to the years of his persecution. He early learned the power of gold in dealing with mercenary enemies. Wherever he went there followed him like a curse the aroused antipathy of other peoples. The Jew was never popular as a race; even the most fervid Jew will not deny that, howsoever he may explain it. Individuals have been popular, of course; many phases of Jewish nature are found to be very lovable when known; but nevertheless one of the burdens the Jews have had to bear as a race is this burden of racial unpopularity. Even in modern times, in civilized countries, in conditions which render persecution absolutely impossible, this unpopularity exists. And what is more, the Jew has not seemed to care to cultivate the friendship of the Gentile masses, due perhaps to the failures of experience, but due more likely to his inborn persuasion that he belongs to a superior race. Whatever the true reason, he has always placed his main dependence on cultivating friendship with kings and nobles. What cared the Jew if the people gnashed their teeth against him, so long as the king and the court were his friends? Thus there was always, even through most of the severely trying times, "a court Jew," one who had bought by loans and held by the strangle-hold of debt an entrance to the king's chamber. The policy of the Jews has always been to "go to headquarters." They never tried to placate the Russian people, but they did endeavor to enlist the Russian court. They never tried to placate the German people, but they did succeed in permeating the German court. In England they shrug their shoulders at the outspoken anti-Jew reactions of the British populace—what care they? Have they not all of lorddom at their heels, do they not hold the strings of Britain's purse?

Through this ability of theirs to "go to headquarters" it is possible to account for the stronghold they got upon various governments and nations. Added to this ability was, of course, the ability to produce what the governments wanted. If a government wanted a loan, the Jew at court could arrange it through Jews at other financial centers and political capitals. If one government wanted to pay another government a debt without risking the precious metal to a mule train through a robber-infested country, the Jew at court arranged that too. He transferred a piece of paper and the debt was paid by the banking house at the foreign capital. The first time an army was ever fed in the modern commissary way, it was done by a Jew—he had the capital and he had the system; moreover he had the delight of having a nation for his customer.

And this tendency, which served the race so well throughout the troublous centuries, shows no sign of abatement. Certainly, seeing to what an extent a race numerically so unimportant influences the various governments of the world today, the Jew who reflects upon the disparity between his people's numbers and their power may be pardoned if he sees in that fact a proof of their racial superiority.

It may be said also that Jewish inventiveness in business devices continues to the present time, as well as Jewish adaptability to changing conditions. The Jew is credited with being the first to establish branch houses in foreign countries in order that responsible representatives of the home office might be on the ground taking instant advantage of every opening. During the war a great deal was said about the "peaceful penetration" which the "German Government" had effected in the United States by establishing here branch offices and factories of German firms. The fact that there were many German branch houses here is unquestionable. It should be known, however, that they were not the evidence of German enterprise but of Jewish enterprise. The old German business houses were too conservative to "run after customers" even in the hustling United States, but the Jewish firms were not, and they came straight to America and hustled. In due time the competition forced the more conservative German firms to follow suit. But the idea was Jewish in its origin, not German.

Another modern business method whose origin is credited to Jewish financiers is that by which related industries are brought together, as for example, if an electrical power company is acquired, then the street railway company using the electricity would be acquired too, one purpose being in this way to conserve all the profit accruing along the line, from the origination of the power down to the delivery of the street car ride; but perhaps the main purpose being that, by the control of the power house the price of current could be increased to the car company, and by the control of the car company the cost of a ride could be increased to the public, the controllers thus receiving an additional profit all down the line. There is much of this going on in the world today, and in the United States particularly. The portion of the business immediately next to the ultimate consumer explains that its costs have risen, but it does not explain that the costs were increased by the owners and not by outsiders who were forced to do so by economic pressure.

There is apparently in the world today a central financial force which is playing a vast and closely organized game, with the world for its table and universal control for its stakes. The people of civilized countries have lost all confidence in the explanation that "economic conditions" are responsible for all the changes that occur. Under the camouflage of "economic law" a great many phenomena have been accounted for which were not due to any law whatever except the law of the selfish human will as operated by a few men who have the purpose and the power to work on a wide scale with nations as their vassals.

Whatever else may be national, no one today believes that finance is national. Finance is international. Nobody today believes that international finance is in any way competitive. There are some independent banking houses, but few strong independent ones. The great masters, the few whose minds see clearly the entire play of the plan, control numerous banking houses and trust companies, and one is used for this while another is used for that, but there is no disharmony between them, no correction of each other's methods, no competition in the interests of the business world. There is as much unity of policy between the principal banking houses of every country as there is between the various branches of the United States Post Office—and for the same reason, namely, they are all operated from the same source and for the same purpose.

Just before the war Germany bought very heavily in American cotton and had huge quantities of it tied up here for export. When war came, the ownership of that mountainous mass of cotton wealth changed in one night from Jewish names in Hamburg to Jewish names in London. At this writing cotton is selling in England for less than it is selling in the United States, and the effect of that is to lower the American price. When the price lowers sufficiently, the market is cleared of cotton by buyers previously prepared, and then the price soars to high figures again. In the meantime, the same powers that have engineered the apparently causeless strengthening and weakening of the cotton market, have seized upon stricken Germany to be the sweatshop of the world. Certain groups control the cotton, lend it to Germany to be manufactured, leave a pittance of it there in payment for the labor that was used, and then profiteer the length and breadth of the world on the lie that "cotton is scarce." And when, tracing all these anti-social and colossally unfair methods to their source, it is found that the responsible parties all have a common characteristic, is it any wonder that the warning which comes across the sea—"Wait until America becomes awake to the Jew!"—has a new meaning?

Certainly, economic reasons no longer explain the condition in which the world finds itself today. Neither does the ordinary explanation of "the heartlessness of capital." Capital has endeavored as never before to meet the demands of labor, and labor has gone to extremes in leading capital to new concessions—but what has it advantaged either of them? Labor has heretofore thought that capital was the sky over it, and it made the sky yield, but behold, there was yet an higher sky which neither capital nor labor had seen in their struggles one with another. That sky is so far unyielding.

That which we call capital here in America is usually money used in production, and we mistakenly refer to the manufacturer, the manager of work, the provider of tools and jobs—we refer to him as the "capitalist." Oh, no. He is not the capitalist in the real sense. Why, he himself must go to capitalists for the money with which to finance his plans. There is a power yet above him—a power which treats him far more callously and holds him in a more ruthless hand than he would ever dare display to labor. That, indeed, is one of the tragedies of these times, that "labor" and "capital" are fighting each other, when the conditions against which each one of them protests, and from which each one of them suffers, is not within their power to remedy at all, unless they find a way to wrest world control from that group of international financiers who create and control both these conditions.

There is a super-capitalism which is supported wholly by the fiction that gold is wealth. There is a super-government which is allied to no government, which is free from them all, and yet which has its hand in them all. There is a race, a part of humanity, which has never yet been received as a welcome part, and which has succeeded in raising itself to a power that the proudest Gentile race has never claimed—not even Rome in the days of her proudest power. It is becoming more and more the conviction of men all over the world that the labor question, the wage question, the land question cannot be settled until first of all this matter of an international super-capitalistic government is settled.

"To the victor belongs the spoils" is an old saying. And in a sense it is true that if all this power of control has been gained and held by a few men of a long-despised race, then either they are super-men whom it is powerless to resist, or they are ordinary men whom the rest of the world has permitted to obtain an undue and unsafe degree of power. Unless the Jews are super-men, the Gentiles will have themselves to blame for what has transpired, and they can look for rectification in a new scrutiny of the situation and a candid examination of the experiences of other countries.

---

Issue of May 22, 1920.

# Germany's Reaction Against the Jew

HUMANITY has become wise enough to discuss those forms of physical sickness over which it formerly drew the veil of shame and secrecy, but political hygiene is not so far advanced. The main source of the sickness of the German national body is charged to be the influence of the Jews, and although this was apparent to acute minds years ago, it is now said to have gone so far as to be apparent to the least observing. The eruption has broken out on the surface of the body politic, and no further concealment of this fact is possible. It is the belief of all classes of the German people that the collapse which has come since the armistice, and the revolution from which they are being prevented a recovery, are the result of Jewish intrigue and purpose. They declare it with assurance; they offer a mass of facts to confirm it; they believe that history will provide the fullest proof.

The Jew in Germany is regarded as only a guest of the people; he has offended by trying to turn himself into the host. There are no stronger contrasts in the world than the pure Germanic and the pure Semitic races; therefore, there has been no harmony between the two in Germany; the German has regarded the Jew strictly as a guest, while the Jew, indignant at not being given the privileges of the nation-family, has cherished animosity against his host. In other countries the Jew is permitted to mix more readily with the people, he can amass his control unchallenged; but in Germany the case was different. Therefore, the Jew hated the German people; therefore, the countries of the world which were most dominated by the Jews showed the greatest hatred of Germany during the recent regrettable war. Jewish hands were in almost exclusive control of the engines of publicity by which public opinion concerning the German people was molded. The sole winners of the war were Jews.

But assertion is not enough; proof is wanted;

therefore, consider the evidence. What occurred immediately upon the change from the old regime to the new? The cabinet composed of six men, which substituted the Minister of State, was dominated by the Jews Haase and Landsberg. Haase had control of foreign affairs; his assistant was the Jew Kautsky, a Czech, who in 1918 was not even a German citizen. Also associated with Haase were the Jews Cohn and Herzfeld. The Jew Schiffer was Financial Minister of State, assisted by the Jew Bernstein. The Secretary of the Interior was the Jew Preuss, with the Jew Dr. Freund for his assistant. The Jew Fritz Max Cohen, who was correspondent of the Frankfurter Zeitung in Copenhagen, was made government publicity agent.

The kingdom of Prussia duplicated this condition of affairs. The Jews Hirsch and Rosenfeld dominated the cabinet, with Rosenfeld controlling the Department of Justice, and Hirsch in the Department of the Interior. The Jew Simon was in charge of the Treasury Department. The Prussian Department of Justice was wholly manned and operated by Jews. The Director of Education was the Jew Furtran with the assistance of the Jew Arndt. The Director of the Colonial Office was the Jew Meyer-Gerhard. The Jew Kastenberg was director of the Department of Art. The War Food Supply Department was directed by the Jew Wurm, while in the State Food Department were the Jews Prof. Dr. Hirsch and the Geheimrat Dr. Stadthagen. The Soldiers' and Workmen's Committee was directed by the Jew Cohen, with the Jews Stern, Herz, Lowenberg, Frankel, Israelowicz, Laubenheim, Seligsohn, Katzenstein, Laufenberg, Heimann, Schlesinger, Merz and Weyl having control of various activities of that committee.

The Jew Ernst is chief of police at Berlin; in the same office at Frankfurt is the Jew Sinzheimer; in Munich the Jew Steiner; in Essen the Jew Levy. It will be remembered that the Jew Eisner was President of Bavaria, his financial minister being the Jew Jaffe. Bavaria's trade, commerce and industry were in control of the half-Jew Brentano. The Jews Lipsinsky and Schwarz were active in the government of Saxony; the Jews Thalheimer and Heiman in Wurtemberg; the Jew Fulda in Hessen.

Two delegates sent to the Peace Conference were Jews and a third was notoriously the tool of Jewish purposes. In addition Jews swarmed through the German delegation as experts and advisors—Max Warburg, Dr. Von Strauss, Merton, Oskar Oppenheimer, Dr. Jaffe, Deutsch, Brentano, Bernstein, Struck, Rathenau, Wassermann and Mendelsohn-Bartholdi.

As to the part which Jews from other countries had in the Peace Conference, German observers declare that any candid student may discover by reading the accounts of impartial non-Jewish recorders of that event. Only the non-Jewish historians seem to have been struck by the fact; the multitude of Jewish writers apparently judged it wise to conceal it.

Jewish influence in German affairs came strongly to the front during the war. It came with all the directness and attack of a flying wedge, as if previously prepared. The Jews of Germany were not German patriots during the war, and although this will not appear a crime in the eyes of the nations who were opposed to Germany, it may throw some light on the Jew's assertion of patriotic loyalty to the land where he lives. Thoughtful Germans hold that it is impossible for the Jew to be a patriot, for reasons which will presently be given.

The point to be considered is the general claim that the persons already named would not have obtained the positions in which they were found had it not been for the Revolution, and the Revolution would not have come had not they brought it. It is true that there were unsatisfactory conditions in Germany, but they could and would have been adjusted by the people themselves; the conditions which destroyed the people's morale and were made impossible of reform were in control of the Jews.

The principal Jewish influences which are charged with bringing about the downfall of German order may be named under three heads: (a) the spirit of Bolshevism which masqueraded under the name of German Socialism; (b) Jewish ownership and control of the Press; (c) Jewish control of the food supply and the industrial machinery of the country. There was a fourth, "higher up," but these worked upon the German people directly.

As it is possible that German conclusions upon this matter may be received doubtfully by peoples whose public opinion has been shaped by Jewish influence, it may help to quote George Pitter-Wilson, of the London *Globe*, who wrote early in April, 1919, "Bolshevism is the dispossession of the Christian nations of the world to such an extent that no capital will remain in the hands of the Christians, that all Jews may jointly hold the world in their hands and reign wherever they choose." As early as the second year of the war, German Jews were preaching that Germany's defeat was necessary to the rise of the proletariat, at which time Strobel declared, "I openly admit that a full victory of the country would not be in the interest of the Social Democrats." Everywhere it was preached that "the exaltation of the proletariat after a won victory is an impossibility." These instances, out of many, are cited not to reopen the military question but to show how the so-called German Jew forgot loyalty to the country in which he lived and joined the outside Jews in accomplishing the collapse of Germany, and not merely, as we shall see, to rid Germany of militarism, which every thoughtful German desired, but to throw the country into such confusion as to permit them to seize control.

The press of Germany echoed this plan of the Jewish spokesmen, at first faintly, then boldly. The Berliner *Tageblatt* and the Munchner *Neuester Nachrichten* were during the whole war official and semi-official organs of the government. They were owned and controlled by Jews, as was also the Frankfurter *Zeitung* and a host of smaller papers that were their spiritual dependents. These papers, it is charged, were really German editions of the Jew-controlled press of the Allied countries, and their purpose was the same. One of the great pieces of research that ought to be undertaken for the purpose of showing the world how its thought is manufactured for it every day, and for what ulterior purposes, is this union of the Jewish press, which passes for the Public Press, throughout the world.

The food and supplies of the people quickly passed into Jewish hands as soon as the war emergency came, and then began a period of dishonesty which destroyed the confidence of the bravest. Like all other patriotic people, the German people knew that war meant sacrifice and suffering, and like other people they were willing to share the common lot. But they found themselves preyed upon by a class of Jews who had prepared everything to make profit out of the common distress. Immediately Jews appeared in banks, war companies, distribution societies, and the ministries of supplies—wherever the life of the people could be speculated in or taxed. Articles that were plentiful disappeared, only to reappear again at high prices. The war companies were exclusively Jewish, and although the government attempted to regulate the outgo of food in the interests of all the people, it became notorious that those with money could get all of anything they wanted, regardless of the food cards. The Jews simply trebled the price of the goods they let go without the cards, and so kept a stream of the nation's gold flowing into their private treasuries. None of the government's estimates of the food stocks could be depended on, because of the hidden hoards on which these speculators drew. This began to disturb the morale of the people, and complaints were made and prosecutions started; but as soon as the cases came up it was discovered that the prosecutor appointed to charge and the commissioner appointed to judge were also Jews, and so the cases usually wore themselves out without results. When, however, a German merchant was caught, great noise was made about it, and the penalty placed upon him was equal to what all the others should have had. Go the length and breadth of Germany today, say the reports, study the temper of the people, and you will discover that the abuse of power by the Jews has burned across Germany's memory like a hot iron.

While these influences were undermining the mass of the people, higher influences of Jewish origin were operating upon the government. The advisers of the Bethmann-Hollweg government were the great ship magnate, Ballin, a Jew; Theodor Wolff, of the Berliner *Tageblatt* and member of the Pan-Jewish press; Von Gwinner, director of the German Bank who is connected by marriage with the great Jew bankers, the Speyers; and Rathenau, the leader of Jewish industrial-financial activities. These men were at the source of things and were bending the government as the other influences were bending the people.

The rich German Jew could buy the recognition he desired by acquiring financial power over those interests which most directly affected the ruling class of Germany, but how was the poor Jew to gain the recognition he desired?—for all Jews are actuated by the same desire; it is in them; they feel the spur to mastery. Having explored the conquest of the higher circles by Jewish money-power, there is yet to explore the conquest of the body of the nation by Jews who had no money except what they could seize in the disorder which they caused. The analysis that is given, follows:

The Jew is not an anarchist. He is not a destructionist. All this is true, notwithstanding he is the world's Bolshevist and preeminently Germany's revolutionist. His anarchy is not ingrain, it is a device which he uses for a purpose. The rich Jew is not an anarchist, because he can achieve what he desires by more subtle methods. The poor Jew has no other recourse. But rich and poor go jointly for a long stretch; the bond of sympathy between them never breaks; for, if the anarchy is successful, then the poor Jew shall take his place with the rich Jew; and if the anarchy is not successful, it has nevertheless served to break up new fields in which the rich Jew may operate.

In Germany it was possible for the poor Jew to thrust himself up through the wall of Germanism above him only by breaking it up. In Russia the same was true. The social system had encrusted around the Jew, keeping him in a position where, as the nations knew by experience, he would be less harmful. As nature encysts the harmful foreign element in the flesh, building a wall around it, so nations have found it expedient to do with the Jew. In modern times, however, the Jew has found a means of knocking down the walls and throwing the whole national house into confusion, and in the darkness and riot that follows, seize the place he has long coveted. When Russia broke, who came first to light? Kerensky, who is a Jew. But his plans were not radical enough, and then came Trotsky, another Jew. Trotsky found the system too strong for him to break in America—he broke through the weak spot in Russia and would extend that weakness round the world. Every commissar in Russia today is a Jew. Publicists are accustomed to speak of Russia as if it were in disorder. It may be that Russia is, but the Jewish government of Russia is not. From a mass of underlings, the Jews of Russia came up a perfect phalanx, a flying wedge through the superinduced disorder, as if every man's place had been previously prepared for him.

That also is the way it was in Germany. The German ceiling had to be broken, as it were, before the poor Jews could realize their ambition. When the break was made they swarmed through and settled in places of control above the nation.

This may explain why Jews the world over supply the energy of disruptive movements. It is understood that the young Jews of the United States are propagandists of an ideal that would practically abolish the United States. The attack is aimed, of course, against "capitalism," which means the present government of the world by the Gentile. The true capitalists of the world are Jews, who are capitalists for capital's sake. It is hard to believe that they wish to destroy capital; they wish to obtain sole control of it, and their wish has long been in fair way to fulfillment.

In Germany, therefore, as in Russia, distinction is made between the methods of the rich and of the poor Jews, because one method affects the government and the other the morale of the people, but both converge on the same objective. It is not only desire to escape oppression that actuates the lower classes of Jews, but desire to gain control—for the spirit of mastery pulses strong within them. German convictions on this question have reached the place where they may be expressed thus: Revolution is the expression of the Jews' will to power. Parties such as the socialists, democrats and freethinkers are but tools for the Jewish plan to power. The so-called "dictatorship of the proletariat" is really and practically the dictatorship of Jews.

So suddenly have German eyes been opened, so stormfully wrathful has been the reaction, that the word has gone out through German Judaism to retire to the second trench. There has been a sudden and concerted abandonment of office wherever the office made direct contact with the public; there has, however, been no abandonment of power. What will happen in Germany is not now known. Some regrettable things have already happened. But the Germans will doubtless prove themselves equal to the situation by devising methods of control at once unobjectionable and effective. But as to Russia, it is hardly doubtful any longer what will happen there. When Russia turns, a shudder will run through the earth.

How Gentile Germany and Russia look at the entire question may be summarized as follows:

Judaism is the most closely organized power on earth, even more than the British Empire. It forms a State whose citizens are unconditionally loyal wherever they may be and whether rich or poor.

The name which is given in Germany to this State which circulates among all the states is "All-Judaan."

The means of power of the State of All-Judaan are capital and journalism, or money and propaganda.

All-Judaan is the only State that exercises world government; all the other States can and may exercise national government only.

The principal culture of All-Judaan is journalistic; the technical, scientific, literary performances of the modern Jew are throughout journalistic performances. They are due to the marvelous talent of the Jews for receptivity of others' ideas. Capital and Journalism are joined in the Press to create a political and spiritual medium of Jewish power.

The government of this state of All-Judaan is wonderfully organized. Paris was its first seat, but has now been moved to third place. Before the war London was its first, and New York its second capital. It remains to be seen whether New York will now supplant London—the drift is toward America.

As All-Judaan is not in a position to have a standing army and navy, other states supply these for it. Its fleet is the British fleet which guards from hindrance the progress of all-Jewish world economy, or that part of it which depends on the sea. In return, All-Judaan assures Britain an undisturbed political and territorial world rule. All-Judaan has added Palestine to British control. Wherever there was an All-

Judaan land force (whatever national uniform it might wear), it worked with the British navy.

All-Judaan is willing to entrust the government of various strips of the world to the nationalistic governments; it only asks to control the governments. Judaism is passionately in favor of perpetuating nationalistic divisions for the Gentile world. For themselves, Jews never become assimilated with any nation. They are a separate people, always were and always will be.

All-Judaan's only quarrel with any nation occurs when that nation makes it impossible for All-Judaan to control that nation's industrial and financial profits. It can make war, it can make peace; it can command anarchy in stubborn cases, it can restore order. It holds the sinews of world power in its hand and it apportions them among the nations in such ways as will best support All-Judaan's plan.

Controlling the world's sources of news, All-Judaan can always prepare the minds of the people for its next move. The greatest exposure yet to be made is the way that news is manufactured and the way in which the mind of whole nations is molded for a purpose. When the powerful Jew is at last traced and his hand revealed, then comes the ready cry of persecution and it echoes through the world press. The real causes of the persecution (which is the oppression of the people by the financial practices of the Jews) are never given publicity.

All-Judaan has its vice-governments in London and New York. Having wreaked its revenge on Germany it will now go forth to conquer other nations. Britain it already has. Russia it is struggling for, but the chances are against it. The United States, with its good-natured tolerance of all races, offers a promising field. The scene of operations changes, but the Jew is the same throughout the centuries.

---

Issue of May 29, 1920.

*"At first sight it would seem as if the economic system of North America was the very one that developed independently of the Jews . . . . Nevertheless I uphold my assertion that the United States (perhaps more than any other land) are filled to the brim with the Jewish spirit. This is recognized in many quarters, above all in those best capable of forming a judgment on the subject . . . .*

*"In the face of this fact, is there not some justification for the opinion that the United States owe their very existence to the Jews? And if this be so, how much more can it be asserted that Jewish influence made the United States just what they are—that is, American? For what we call Americanism is nothing else, if we may say so, than the Jewish spirit distilled."*

*—Werner Sombart, "The Jews and Modern Capital," pp. 38, 43.*

III.

# Jewish History in the United States

THE story of the Jews in America begins with Christopher Columbus. On August 2, 1492, more than 300,000 Jews were expelled from Spain, with which event Spain's prestige began its long decline, and on August 3, the next day, Columbus set sail for the West, taking a group of Jews with him. They were not, however, refugees, for the prophetic navigator's plans had aroused the sympathy of influential Jews for a long period previously. Columbus himself tells us that he consorted much with Jews. The first letter he wrote detailing his discoveries was to a Jew. Indeed, the eventful voyage itself which added to men's knowledge and wealth "the other half of the earth" was made possible by Jews.

The pleasant story that it was Queen Isabella's jewels which financed the voyage has disappeared under cool research. There were three Maranos or "secret Jews" who wielded great influence at the Spanish court: Luis de Santagel, who was an important merchant of Valencia and who was "farmer" of the royal taxes; his relative, Gabriel Sanchez, who was the royal treasurer; and their friend, the royal chamberlain, Juan Cabrero. These worked unceasingly on Queen Isabella's imagination, picturing to her the depletion of the royal treasury and the likelihood of Columbus discovering the fabulous gold of the Indies, until the Queen was ready to offer her jewels in pawn for the funds. But Santagel craved permission to advance the money himself, which he did, 17,000 ducats in all, about $20,000, perhaps equal to $160,000 today. It is probable that the loan exceeded the expedition's cost.

Associated with Columbus in the voyage were at least five Jews: Luis de Torres, interpreter; Marco, the surgeon; Bernal, the physician; Alonzo de la Calle, and Gabriel Sanchez. The astronomical instruments and maps which the navigators used were of Jewish origin. Luis de Torres was the first man ashore, the first to discover the use of tobacco; he settled in Cuba and may be said to be the father of Jewish control of the tobacco business as it exists today.

Columbus' old patrons, Luis de Santagel and Gabriel Sanchez, received many privileges for the part they played in the work, but Columbus himself became the victim of a conspiracy fostered by Bernal, the ship's doctor, and suffered injustice and imprisonment as his reward.

From that beginning, Jews looked more and more to America as a fruitful field, and immigration set in strongly toward South America, principally Brazil. But because of military participation in a disagreement between the Brazilians and the Dutch, the Jews of Brazil found it necessary to emigrate, which they did in the direction of the Dutch colony of what is now New York. Peter Stuyvesant, the Dutch governor, did not entirely approve of their settling among his people and ordered them to leave, but the Jews had evidently taken the precaution to assure their being received even if not welcomed, because upon revoking the order of Stuyvesant, the Directors gave as one of the reasons for the Jews being received, "the large amount of capital which they have invested in the shares of the Company." Nevertheless they were forbidden to enter public service and to open retail shops, which had the effect of driving them into foreign trade in which they were soon exercising all but a monopoly because of their European connections.

This is only one of the thousand illustrations which can be given of the resourcefulness of the Jew. Forbid him in one direction, he will excel in another. When he was forbidden to deal in new clothes, he sold old clothes—that was the beginning of the organized traffic in secondhand clothing. When he was forbidden to deal in merchandise, he dealt in waste—the Jew is the originator of the waste product business of the world; he was the originator of the salvage system; he found wealth in the debris of civilization. He taught people how to use old rags, how to clean old feathers, how to use gall nuts and rabbit skins. He has always had a taste for the furrier trade, which he now controls, and to him is due the multitude of common skins which now pass under various alluring trade names as furs of high origin. The idea of renovation gained commercial value through the Jew. In the "rag men" who blow tin horns through our cities and save the old iron, old bottles, old paper and old fabrics, we have the commercial descendants of those earlier Jews who turned adversity into success by converting the rubbish of the earth into material of value.

Unwittingly, old Peter Stuyvesant compelled the Jew to make New York the principal port of America, and though a majority of New York Jews had fled to Philadelphia at the time of the American Revolution, most of them returned to New York at the earliest opportunity, instinct seeming to make them aware that in New York was to be their principal paradise of gain. And so it has proved. New York is the greatest center of Jewish population in the world. It is the gateway where the bulk of American imports and exports are taxed, and where practically all the business done in America pays tribute to the masters of money. The very land of the city is practically the holdings of the Jews. A list of the property owners of the metropolis reveals only at rare intervals a Gentile name. No wonder that Jewish writers, viewing this unprecedented prosperity, this unchecked growth in wealth and power, exclaim enthusiastically that the United States is the Promised Land foretold by the prophets, and New York the New Jerusalem. Some have gone even further and described the peaks of the Rockies as "the mountains of Zion," and with reason, too, if the mining and coastal wealth of the Jews is considered.

The new waterways proposal, which will make an ocean port of practically every great city on the Great Lakes and take from New York the prestige she has maintained by being the gateway toward which the principal railways narrowed, is being strongly protested at this time. And the strongest motive in opposing this most obvious betterment is that so much wealth counted in New York is not wealth at all, but fictitious values depending solely on New York remaining New York. When anything comes which will make New York merely a city on the coast, and not the city where the great taxers sit to levy their tribute, much Jewish wealth will decrease. It was fabulous before the war. What it is now the statisticians will hardly undertake to say.

In fifty years the increase in the Jewish population of the United States has been from 50,000 to more than 3,300,000. In the British Isles there are only 300,000, in Palestine only 100,000. It is fortunate for the Jew himself that in Great Britain his numbers are not greater, for the large and evident control he exercises in great matters would sometimes make it inconvenient for the poorer Jew, if he were abroad in England in large numbers. An unusually well-informed Briton says that anti-Semitism is always ready to break out in England upon sufficient cause, but it cannot break out against the inaccessible rich Jews who control in politics and international finance. It is probably true that the commonest real cause of anti-Semitism is the action of the international Jew who is often unknown and always secure, but the innocent victim of it is the poor Jew. Anti-Semitism, however, will be considered in the next article.

The figures representing Jewish population in Great Britain and the United States indicate that the colossal power wielded by international Jewish financiers is neither consequent nor dependent upon their number. The arresting fact about the Jew is his world-wide unchallenged power, coupled with comparative numerical inferiority. There are only about 14,000,000 Jews in the world; they are about as numerous as the Koreans. This comparison of their numbers with the Koreans will illustrate still more vividly the phenomenon of their power.

In the time of George Washington there were about 4,000 Jews in the country, most of them well-to-do traders. For the most part they favored the American side. Haym Salomon helped the Colonies out with the loan of his entire fortune at a critical moment. But they never assimilated, they did not take up the usual employments nor farming, they never seemed to care for the worry of manufacturing things, but only for the selling of them after they were made.

It is only of recent years the Jew has shown any capacity for manufacturing, and most of what he now engages in has grown up as an adjunct to his merchandising plans. By manufacturing, he saves a profit. The result has not been a decrease in cost to the public, but an increase. It is characteristic of Jewish business methods that economies are for the sake of the business, not for the sake of the public. The commodities in which there have been the most inexcusable and exorbitant increases in prices to the public, and the lines of business which have been most quickly frightened into lower prices without any explanatory change in the general situation, have been those lines in which Jews exercise the widest control.

Business to the Jewish mind is money; what the successful Jew may do with his money after he gets it is another matter, but in the getting of it he never permits "idealistic slush" to interfere with the dollar. His dollar of profit is never "clipped" by any of the voluntary reforms by which a few men are trying to ameliorate the condition of the workers.

This is not by any means due to the hardness of the Jewish heart, but to the hardness of the Jewish view of business. Business is to it a matter of goods and money, not of people. If you are in distress and suffering, the Jewish heart would have sympathy for you; but if your house were involved in the matter, you and your house would be two separate entities; the Jew would naturally find it difficult, in his theory of business, to humanize the house; he would deal with it after a manner which other people would call "hard," but he would not feel the charge to be just; he would say that it was only "business."

It is probably this way that the Jewish "sweatshops" of New York may be explained. When the susceptible people of the nation commiserated the poor Jews of the New York sweatshops, they for the most part did not know that the inventors and operators of the "sweatshop" method were themselves Jews. Indeed, while it is the boast of our country that no race or color or creed is persecuted here, but liberty is insured to all, still it is a fact which every special investigator has noted that the only heartless treatment ever accorded the Jew in the United States came from his own people, his overseers and masters. And yet there is no evidence that either the "sweater" or the "sweated" ever thought of it as inhumanity or as "heartless." It was "business." The "sweated" lived in the hope of having a roomful of people sewing for him or her some day. Their endlessly vital interest in "business" and their unflagging ambition to get further up the ladder and become masters in their own sweatshop, enabled them to work without the slightest sense of oppression or injustice which, after all, is the sorest thing about poverty. The Jews never regard work as a calamity, but neither do they regard subordinate positions as permanently theirs. Thus, they spend their energies in getting up and out rather than in lamenting the inconveniences of the place where they are and trying to improve it.

All this is individually excellent but socially harmful. The result is that, until recently, the lower ranges of employment were wholly unsupervised, and the higher circles never felt the necessity of devising industrial reforms and benefits. The record of the great Jews in charity is very noble; their record in industrial reforms is nil. With commendable sympathy toward their own people they will donate a part of their profits to rectify some of the human need resulting from the method by which they made their profits, but as for reforming the method by which they get their profits in order that the resulting need might be diminished or prevented, apparently it has never occurred to them. At least, while there are many charitable names among the wealthier Jews, there are no names that stand for an actual, practical humanizing of industry, its methods and its returns.

This, of course, is unfortunate; but it is intelligible; more than that, it is explanatory of many things for which the Jew is blamed by those who do not understand his nature. The Jew will go part way in sharing the results of his prosperity; he has not gone any length, save upon outer compulsion, in sharing the processes, or sharing wealth in the making. And while the social effect is the same as if this were done out of cruel insensibility and inhumanity, still it must be said that mostly it is done not out of such feelings, but out of the Jew's ingrain conception of the game of business. Some proposals of industrial reform appear as crazy to him as would a proposal to credit one baseball batter's hit to his opponent's score, just as a matter of humanity.

The American Jew does not assimilate. This is stated, not to blame him, but merely as a fact. The Jew could merge with the people of America if he desired, but he doesn't. If there is any prejudice existing against him in America, aside from the sense of inquiry which his colossal success engenders, it is because of his aloofness. The Jew is not objectionable in his person, creed, or race. His spiritual ideals are shared by the world. But still he does not assimilate; he cultivates by his exclusiveness the feeling that he does not "belong." This is his privilege, and from one point of view it may indicate excellent judgment, but he must not make it one of the grounds of his complaint against Gentiles in general, as he has a tendency to do. It is better that he should make it clear to Gentiles once and for all where true Jews stand in the matter, as when a young Jew said—"There is all the difference in the world between an American Jew and a Jewish American. A Jewish American is a mere amateur Gentile, doomed to be a parasite forever."

The ghetto is not an American product but the Jews' own importation. They have separated themselves into a distinct community. Speaking of this matter the Jewish Encyclopedia says: "The social organization of the Jews resident in America has differed little from that in other countries * * * in the main, and without any compulsion, Jews preferred to live in close proximity to one another, a peculiarity which still prevails."

To make a list of the lines of business controlled by the Jews of the United States would be to touch most of the vital industries of the country—those which are really vital, and those which cultivated habit has made to seem vital. The theatrical business, of course, as everyone knows, is exclusively Jewish. Play-producing, booking, theater operation are all in the hands of Jews. This perhaps accounts for the fact that in almost every production today can be detected propaganda, sometimes glaringly commercial advertisement, which does not originate with playwrights, but with producers.

The motion picture industry.

The sugar industry.

The tobacco industry.

Fifty per cent or more of the meat packing industry.

Upward of 60 per cent of the shoemaking industry.

Men's and women's ready-made clothing.

Most of the musical purveying done in the country.

Jewelry.

Grain.

More recently, cotton.

The Colorado smelting industry.

Magazine authorship.

News distribution.

The liquor business.

The loan business.

These, only to name the industries with national and international sweep, are in control of the Jews of the United States, either alone or in association with Jews overseas.

The American people would be vastly surprised if they could see a line-up of some of the "American business men" who hold up our commercial prestige overseas. They are mostly Jews. They have a keen sense of the value of the American name, and when in a foreign port you stroll up to the office which bears the sign, "American Importing Company," or "American Commercial Company," or other similarly noncommittal names, hoping to find a countryman, an American, you usually find a Jew whose sojourn in America appears to have been all too brief. This may throw a sidelight on the regard in which "American business methods" are held in some parts of the world. When 30 or 40 different races of people can carry on business under the name "American," and do it legally, too, it is not surprising that Americans do not recognize some of the descriptions of American methods which appear in the foreign press. The Germans long ago complained that the rest of the world was judging them by the German-speaking Jewish commercial traveler.

Instances of Jewish prosperity in the United States are commonplace, but *prosperity*, the just reward of foresight and application, is not to be confounded with *control*. The prosperity of the Jews can be had by any one who is willing to pay the price which the Jews pay for it—a very, very high price, as a rule, all things considered—but it would be impossible for any Gentile coalition under similar circumstances to attain the control which the Jews have won, for the reason that there is lacking in the Gentile a certain quality of working-togetherness, a certain conspiracy of objective, and the adhesiveness of intense raciality, which characterizes the Jew. It is nothing to a Gentile that another man is a Gentile; it is next to everything to a Jew that the man at his door is another Jew. So, if instances of Jewish *prosperity* were needed, the case of the Temple Emmanu-el, New York, might be cited, which in 1846 could scarcely raise $1,520 for its budget, but in 1868, following the Civil War, raised $708,755 from the rental of 231 pews. And the rise of the Jewish clothing monopoly as one of the results of the same Civil War might be cited as an instance of prosperity plus national and international *control*.

Indeed, it might be said that the Jew has succeeded in everything he has attempted in the United States, except farming. The explanation usually made in Jewish publications is that ordinary farming is far too simple to engage the Jew's intellect and therefore he is not enough interested in it to succeed, but that in dairy and cattle farming where the "brain" is more necessary he has made a success. Numerous attempts have been made in various parts of the United States to start Jewish farming colonies, but their story is a series of failures. Some have blamed the failures on the Jew's lack of knowledge of scientific farming, others on his distaste for manual labor, others on the lack of the speculative element in agriculture. In any case, he stands higher in the non-productive employments than in this basically productive one. Some students of the question state that the Jew never was a man of the land, but always a trader, for which assertion one of the proofs offered is the Jews' selection of Palestine as their country, that strip of land which formed a gateway between East and West and over which the overland traffic of the world passed.

Issue of June 5, 1920.

*"'The Jewish Question still exists. It would be useless to deny it . . . . The Jewish Question exists wherever Jews live in perceptible numbers. Where it does not exist, it is carried by Jews in the course of their migrations. We naturally move to those places where we are not persecuted, and there our presence produces persecution . . . . The unfortunate Jews are now carrying anti-Semitism into England; they have already introduced it into America."*

*—Theodor Herzl, "A Jewish State," p. 4.*

IV.

# The Jewish Question—Fact or Fancy?

THE chief difficulty in writing about the Jewish Question is the supersensitiveness of Jews and non-Jews concerning the whole matter. There is a vague feeling that even to openly use the word "Jew," or to expose it nakedly to print, is somehow improper. Polite evasions like "Hebrew" and "Semite," both of which are subject to the criticism of inaccuracy, are timidly essayed, and people pick their way gingerly as if the whole subject were forbidden, until some courageous Jewish thinker comes straight out with the good old word "Jew," and then the constraint is relieved and the air cleared. The word "Jew" is not an epithet; it is a name, ancient and honorable, with significance for every period of human history, past, present and to come.

There is extreme sensitiveness about the public discussion of the Jewish Question on the part of Gentiles. They would prefer to keep it in the hazy borderlands of their thought, shrouded in silence. Their heritage of tolerance has something to do with their attitude, but perhaps their instinctive sense of the difficulty involved has more to do with it. The principal public Gentile pronouncements upon the Jewish Question are in the manner of the truckling politician or the pleasant after-dinner speaker; the great Jewish names in philosophy, medicine, literature, music and finance are named over, the energy, ability and thrift of the race are dwelt upon, and everyone goes home feeling that a difficult place has been rather neatly negotiated. But nothing is changed thereby. The Jew is not changed. The Gentile is not changed. The Jew still remains the enigma of the world.

Gentile sensitiveness on this point is best expressed by the desire for silence—"Why discuss it at all?" is the attitude. Such an attitude is itself a proof that there is a problem which we would evade if we could.

"Why discuss it at all?"—the keen thinker clearly sees in the implications of such a question, the existence of a problem whose discussion or suppression will not always be within the choice of easy-going minds.

Is there a Jewish Question in Russia? Unquestionably, in its most virulent form. Is it necessary to meet that Question in Russia? Undoubtedly, meet it from every angle along which light and healing may come.

Well, the percentage of the Jewish population of Russia is just one per cent more than it is in the United States. The majority of the Jews themselves are not less well-behaved in Russia than they are here; they lived under restrictions which do not exist here; yet in Russia their genius has enabled them to attain a degree of power which has completely baffled the Russian mind. Whether you go to Rumania, Russia, Austria or Germany, or anywhere else that the Jewish Question has come to the forefront as a vital issue, you will discover that the principal cause is the outworking of the Jewish genius to achieve the power of control.

Here in the United States it is the fact of this remarkable minority—a sparse Jewish ingredient of three per cent in a nation of 110,000,000—attaining in 50 years a degree of control that would be impossible to a ten times larger group of any other race, that creates the Jewish Question here. Three per cent of any other people would scarcely occasion comment, because we could not meet with a representative of them wherever we went in high places—in the innermost secrecy of the councils of the Big Four at Versailles; in the supreme court; in the councils of the White House; in the vast dispositions of world finance—wherever there is power to get or use. Yet we meet the Jew everywhere in the upper circles, literally everywhere there is power. He has the brains, the initiative, the penetrative vision which almost automatically project him to the top, and as a consequence he is more marked than any other race.

And that is where the Jewish Question begins. It begins in very simple terms—How does the Jew so habitually and so resistlessly gravitate to the highest places? What puts him there? Why is he put there?

What does he do there? What does the fact of his being there mean to the world?

That is the Jewish Question in its origin. From these points it goes on to others, and whether the trend becomes pro-Jewish or anti-Semitic depends on the amount of prejudice brought to the inquiry, and whether it becomes pro-Humanity depends on the amount of insight and intelligence.

The use of the word Humanity in connection with the word Jew usually throws a side-meaning which may not be intended. In this connection it is usually understood that the humanity ought to be shown toward the Jew. There is just as great an obligation upon the Jew to show his humanity toward the whole race. The Jew has been too long accustomed to think of himself as exclusively the claimant on the humanitarianism of society; society has a large claim against him that he cease his exclusiveness, that he cease exploiting the world, that he cease making Jewish groups the end and all of his gains, and that he begin to fulfill, in a sense his exclusiveness has never yet enabled him to fulfill, the ancient prophecy that through him all the nations of the earth should be blessed.

The Jew cannot go on forever filling the role of suppliant for the world's humanitarianism; he must himself show that quality to a society which seriously suspects his higher and more powerful groups of exploiting it with a pitiless rapacity which in its wide-flung and long drawn-out distress may be described as an economic pogrom against a rather helpless humanity. For it is true that society is as helpless before the well-organized extortions of certain financial groups, as huddled groups of Russian Jews were helpless against the anti-Semitic mob. And as in Russia, so in America, it is the poor Jew who suffers for the delinquencies of the rich exploiter of his race.

This series of articles is already being met by an organized barrage by mail and wire and voice, every single item of which carries the wail of persecution. One would think that a heartless and horrible attack were being made on a most pitiable and helpless people —until one looks at the letterheads of the magnates who write, and at the financial ratings of those who protest, and at the membership of the organizations whose responsible heads hysterically demand retraction. And always in the background there is the threat of boycott, a threat which has practically sealed up the columns of every publication in America against even the mildest discussion of the Jewish Question.

The Jewish Question in America cannot be concealed forever by threats against publications, nor by the propagandist publication of matter extremely and invariably favorable to everything Jewish. It is here and it cannot be twisted into something else by the adroit use of propaganda, nor can it be forever silenced by threats. The Jews of the United States can best serve themselves and their fellow-Jews all over the world by letting drop their far too ready cry of "anti-Semitism," by adopting a franker tone than that which befits a helpless victim, and by seeing what the Jewish Question is and how it behooves every Jew who loves his people to help solve it.

There has been used in this series the term "International Jew." It is susceptible of two interpretations: one, the Jew wherever he may be; the other, the Jew who exercises international control. The real contention of the world is with the latter and his satellites, whether Jew or Gentile.

Now, this international type of Jew, this grasper after world-control, this actual possessor and wielder of world-control is a very unfortunate connection for his race to have. The most unfortunate thing about the international Jew, from the standpoint of the ordinary Jew, is that the international type is also a Jew. And the significance of this is that the type does not grow anywhere else than on a Jewish stem. There is no other racial nor national type which puts forth this kind of person. It is not merely that there are a few Jews among international financial controllers; it is that these world controllers are exclusively Jews. That is the phenomenon which creates an unfortunate situation for those Jews who are not and never shall be world-controllers, who are the plain people of the Jewish race. If world-control were mixed, like the control, say, of the biscuit business, then the occasional Jews we might find in those higher financial altitudes would not constitute the problem at all; the problem would then be limited to the existence of world-control in the hands of a few men, of whatever race or lineage they might be. But since world-control is an ambition which has only been achieved by Jews, and not by any of the methods usually adopted by would-be world conquerors, it becomes inevitable that the question should center in that remarkable race.

This brings another difficulty: in discussing this group of world-controllers under the name of Jews (and they are Jews), it is not always possible to stop and distinguish the group of Jews that is meant. The candid reader can usually determine that, but the Jew who is in a state of mind to be injured is sometimes pained by reading as a charge against himself what was intended for the upper group. "Then why not discuss the upper group as financiers and not as Jews?" may be asked. Because they are Jews. It is not to the point to insist that in any list of rich men there are more Gentiles than Jews; we are not talking about merely rich men who have, many of them, gained their riches by serving a System, we are talking about those who Control—and it is perfectly apparent that merely to be rich is not to control. The world-controlling Jew has riches, but he also has something much more powerful than that.

The international Jew, as already defined, rules not because he is rich, but because in a most marked degree he possesses the commercial and masterful genius of his race, and avails himself of a racial loyalty and solidarity the like of which exists in no other human group. In other words, transfer today the world-control of the international Jew to the hands of the highest commercially talented group of Gentiles, and the whole fabric of world-control would eventually fall to pieces, because the Gentile lacks a certain quality, be it human or divine, be it natural or acquired, that the Jew possesses.

This, of course, the modern Jew denies. There is a new position taken by the modernists among the Jews which constitutes a denial that the Jew differs from any other man except in the matter of religion. "Jew" they say is not a racial designation, but a religious designation like "Episcopalian," "Catholic," "Presbyterian." This is the argument used in newspaper offices in the Jews' protests against giving the Jewish designation to those of their people who are implicated in crime—"You don't give the religious classifications of other people who are arrested," the editor is told, "why should you do it with Jews?" The appeal to religious tolerance always wins, and is sometimes useful in diverting attention from other things.

Well, if the Jews are only religiously differentiated from the rest of the world, the phenomenon grows stranger still. For the rest of the world is interested less in the Jew's religion than in anything else that concerns him. There is really nothing in his religion to differentiate the Jew from the rest of mankind, as far as the moral content of that religion is concerned, and if there were he would have overcome that by the fact that his Jewish religion supplies the moral structure for both of the other great religions. Moreover, it is stated that there are among English speaking nations 2,000,000 Jews who acknowledge their race and not their religion, while 1,000,000 are classed as agnostic—are these any less Jews than the others? The world does not think so. The authoritative students of human differences do not think so. An Irishman who grows indifferent to the Church is still an Irishman, and it would seem to be equally true that a Jew who grows indifferent to the Synagogue is still a Jew. He at least feels that he is, and so does the non-Jew.

A still more serious challenge would arise if this contention of the modernists were true, for it would necessitate the explanation of these world-controlling Jews by their religion. We should have to say, "They excel through their religion," and then the problem would turn on the religion whose practice should bring such power and prosperity to its devotees. But another fact would intervene, namely, that these world-controlling Jews are not notably religious; and still another fact would hammer for recognition, namely, the most devout believers and most obedient followers of the Jewish religion are the poorest among the Jews. If you want Jewish orthodoxy, the bracing morality of the Old Testament, you will find it, not among the successful Jews, who have Unitarianized their religion to the same extent that the Unitarians have Judaized their Christianity, but among the poor in the side streets who still sacrifice the Saturday business for their Sabbath keeping. Certainly their religion has not given them world-control; instead, they have made their own sacrifices to keep it inviolate against modernism.

Of course, if the Jew differs from the rest of mankind only when he is in full accord with his religion, the question becomes very simple. Any criticism of the Jew becomes sheer religious bigotry and nothing else! And that would be intolerable. But it would be the consensus of thoughtful opinion that the Jew differs less in his religion than in anything else. There is more difference between the two great branches of Christianity, more conscious difference, than between any branch of Christianity and Judaism.

So that, the contention of certain modernists notwithstanding, the world will go on thinking of the Jew as a member of a race, a race whose persistence has defeated the utmost efforts made for its extermination, a race that has preserved itself in virility and power by the observance of those natural laws the violation of which has mongrelized so many nations, a race which has come up out of the past with the two great moral values which may be reckoned on monotheism and monogamy, a race which today is before us as the visible sign of an antiquity to which all our spiritual wealth harks back. Nay, the Jew will go on thinking of himself as the member of a people, a nation, a race. And all the mixture and intermixture of thought or faith or custom cannot make it otherwise. A Jew is a Jew and as long as he remains within his perfectly unassailable traditions, he will remain a Jew. And he will always have the right to feel that to be a Jew is to belong to a superior race.

These world-controlling Jews at the top of affairs, then, are there by virtue of, among other things, certain qualities which are inherent in their Jewish natures. Every Jew has these qualities even if not in the supreme sense, just as every Englishman has Shakespeare's tongue but not in Shakespeare's degree. And thus it is impracticable, if not impossible, to consider the international Jew without laying the foundations broadly upon Jewish character and psychology.

We may discount at once the too common libel that

this greater form of Jewish success is built upon dishonesty. It is impossible to indict the Jewish people or any other people on a wholesale charge. No one knows better than the Jew how widespread is the notion that Jewish methods of business are all unscrupulous. There is no doubt a possibility of a great deal of unscrupulousness existing without actual legal dishonesty, but it is altogether possible that the reputation the Jewish people have long borne in this respect may have had other sources than actual and persistent dishonesty.

We may indicate one of these possible sources. The Jew at a trade is naturally quicker than most other men. They say there are other races which are as nimble at a trade as is the Jew, but the Jew does not live much among them. In this connection one may remember the famous joke about the Jew who went to Scotland.

Now, it is human nature for the slower man to believe that the quicker man is too deft by far, and to become suspicious of his deftness. Everybody suspects the "sharper" even though his sharpness be entirely honest. The slower mind is likely to conceive that the man who sees so many legitimate twists and turns to a trade, may also see and use a convenient number of illegitimate twists and turns. Moreover, there is always the ready suspicion that the one who gets "the best of the bargain" gets it by trickery which is not above board. Slow, honest, plain-spoken and straight-dealing people always have their doubts of the man who gets the better of it.

The Jews, as the records for centuries show, were a keen people in trade. They were so keen that many regarded them as crooked. And so the Jew became disliked for business reasons, not all of which were creditable to the intelligence or initiative of his enemies.

Take, for example, the persecution which Jew merchants once suffered in England. In older England the merchant class had many easy-going traditions. One tradition was that a respectable tradesman would never seek business but wait for it to come to him. Another tradition was that to decorate one's store window with lights or colors, or to display one's stock of goods attractively in the view of the public, was a contemptible and underhanded method of tempting a brother tradesman's customers away from him. Still another tradition was that it was strictly unethical and unbusinesslike to handle more than one line of goods. If one sold tea, it was the best reason in the world why he should not sell teaspoons. As for advertising, the thing would have been so brazen and bold that public opinion would have put the advertiser out of business. The proper demeanor for a merchant was to seem reluctant to part with his goods.

One may readily imagine what happened when the Jewish merchant bustled into the midst of this jungle of traditions. He simply broke them all. In those days tradition had all the force of a divinely promulgated moral law and in consequence of his initiative the Jew was regarded as a great offender. A man who would break those trade traditions would stop at nothing! The Jew was anxious to sell. If he could not sell one article to a customer, he had another on hand to offer him. The Jews' stores became bazaars, forerunners of our modern department stores, and the old English custom of one store for one line of goods was broken up. The Jew went after trade, pursued it, persuaded it. He was the originator of "a quick turnover and small profits." He originated the installment plan. The one state of affairs he could not endure was business at a standstill, and to start it moving he would do anything. He was the first advertiser—in a day when even to announce in the public prints the location of your store was to intimate to the public that you were in financial difficulties, were about to go to the wall and were trying the last desperate expedient to which no self-respecting merchant would stoop.

It was as easy as child's play to connect this energy with dishonesty. The Jew was not playing the game, at least so the staid English merchant thought. As a matter of fact he was playing the game to get it all in his own hands—which he has practically done.

The Jew has shown that same ability ever since. His power of analyzing the money currents amounts to an instinct. His establishment in one country represented another base from which the members of his race could operate. Whether by the natural outworking of innate gifts, or the deliberate plan of race unity and loyalty, all Jewish trading communities had relations, and as these trading communities increased in wealth, prestige and power, as they formed relations with governments and great interests in the countries where they operated, they simply put more power into the central community wherever it might be located, now in Spain, now in Holland, now in England. Whether by intention or not, they became more closely allied than the branches of one business could be, because the cement of racial unity, the bond of racial brotherhood cannot in the very nature of things exist among the Gentiles as it exists among the Jews. Gentiles never think of themselves as Gentiles, and never feel that they owe anything to another Gentile as such. Thus they have been convenient agents of Jewish schemes at times and in places when it was not expedient that the Jewish controllers should be publicly known; but they have never been successful competitors of the Jew in the field of world-control.

From these separated Jewish communities went power to the central community where the master bankers and the master analysts of conditions lived. And back from the central community flowed information of an invaluable character and assistance wherever needed. It is not difficult to understand how, under such a condition, the nation that did not deal kindly with the Jews was made to suffer, and the nation that yielded to them their fullest desire was favored by them. And it is credibly stated that they have made certain nations feel the power of their displeasure.

This system, if it ever existed, exists in greater power today. It is today, however, threatened as it has never been. Fifty years ago, international banking, which was mostly in control of the Jews as the money brokers of the world, was on top of business. It exercised the supercontrol of governments and finance everywhere. Then came that new thing, Industry, which expanded to a degree unguessed by the shrewdest prophets and analysts. As Industry gathered strength and power it became a powerful money magnet, drawing the wealth of the world in its train, not, however, merely for the sake of possessing the money, but of making it work. Production and profit on production, instead of loans and interest on loans, became the master method for a time. The war came, in which the former broker-masters of the world had undoubtedly their large part. And now the two forces, Industry and Finance, are in a struggle to see whether Finance is again to become the master, or creative Industry. This is one of the elements which is bringing the Jewish Question to the bar of public opinion.

To state this and to prove it may be nothing more than to establish the superiority of Jewish ability. Certainly it is not a tenable position to say that the Jew is extraordinarily successful and therefore must be curbed. It would be equally aside from the truth to say that the co-ordination of Jewish activity has been, on the whole, a harmful thing for the world. It may be possible to show that up to this point it has been useful. Success cannot be attacked nor condemned. If any moral question arises at all, it must concern the use made of the success which has been attained. The whole matter centers there, after the previous fact is established. May the Jew go on as he has gone, or does his duty to the world require another use of his success?

This inquiry obviously leads to further discussion, as well as a gathering up of the remaining threads of the present discussion, which future articles will attempt to do.

---

Issue of June 12, 1920.

*"To this end we must organize. Organize, in the first place, so that the world may have proof of the extent and the intensity of our desire for liberty. Organize, in the second place, so that our resources may become known and be made available . . . .*

*"Organize, organize, organize, until every Jew must stand up and be counted—counted with us, or prove himself, wittingly or unwittingly, of the few who are against their own people."*

*—Louis D. Brandeis, Justice of the United States Supreme Court, "Zionism," pp. 113, 114.*

V.

# Anti-Semitism—Will It Appear in the U. S.?

ANYONE who essays to discuss the Jewish Question in the United States or anywhere else must be fully prepared to be regarded as an Anti-Semite, in high-brow language, or in low-brow language, a Jew-baiter. Nor need encouragement be looked for from people or from press. The people who are awake to the subject at all prefer to wait and see how it all turns out; while there is probably not a newspaper in America, and certainly none of the advertising mediums which are called magazines, which would have the temerity even to breathe seriously the fact that such a Question exists. The press in general is open at this time to fulsome editorials in favor of everything Jewish (specimens of the same being obtainable almost anywhere), while the Jewish press, which is fairly numerous in the United States, takes care of the vituperative end.

Of course, the only acceptable explanation of any public discussion at present of the Jewish Question is that some one—writer, or publisher, or a related interest—is a Jew-hater. That idea seems to be fixed; it is fixed in the Jew by inheritance; it is sought to be fixed in the Gentile by propaganda, that any writing which does not simply cloy and drip in sirupy sweetness toward things Jewish is born of prejudice and hatred. It is, therefore, full of lies, insult, insinuation, and constitutes an instigation to massacre. These terms are culled at random from Jewish editorial utterances at hand.

It would seem to be necessary for our Jewish citizens to enlarge their classification of Gentiles to include the class which recognizes the existence of a Jewish Question and still is not anti-Semitic.

There are four distinct parties traceable among the Jews themselves. First, those whose passionate purpose is to keep Jewish faith and life alive at the cost of any sacrifice of popularity or success; second, those who are willing to make whatever sacrifice may be needed to preserve Jewish religion, but are not so particular about the traditional customs of Jewish life; third, those who have no very strong convictions either way, but are opportunists, and will always swerve in the direction of success; and, fourth, those who believe and preach that the only solution of the differences between the Jew and other men is the complete absorption of the Jewish race by the other races. The fourth is the weakest, most unpopular and least to be considered of all the parties.

With Gentiles there are only two classes, as far as this special question is concerned: those who dislike Jews, they cannot tell why; and those who are disposed to fairness, in spite of the accident of congeniality or uncongeniality, and who recognize the Jewish Question as, at least, a problem. Both these attitudes, whenever they become apparent, are subject to the charge of "anti-Semitism."

Anti-Semitism is a term which is bandied about too loosely. It ought to be reserved to denote the real anti-Jewish temper of violent prejudice. If used indiscriminately about all who attempt to discuss Jewish characteristics and Jewish world-power, it may in time arrive at the estate of respectability and honor.

Anti-Semitism in almost every form is bound to come to the United States; indeed, it may be said that it is here now, and has been here for a long time. If it be mislabeled now, the United States will not be able to work within it the transformation which has been effected upon so many other ideas that have arrived here in their journey round the globe.

## I.

It may be a serviceable clearing of the ground to define what anti-Semitism is not:

1. It is not recognition of the Jewish Question. If it were, then it could be set down that the bulk of the American people are destined to become anti-Semites, for they are beginning to recognize the existence of a Jewish Question and will steadily do so in increasing numbers as the Question is forced upon them from the various practical angles of their lives.

The Question is here. We may be honestly blind to it. We may be timidly silent about it. We may even make dishonest denial of it. But it is here. In time all will have to recognize it. In time the polite "hush, hush" of over-sensitive or intimidated circles will not be powerful enough to suppress it. But to recognize it will not mean that we have gone over to a campaign of hatred and enmity against the Jews. It will only mean that a stream of tendency which has been flowing through our civilization has at last accumulated bulk and power enough to challenge attention, to call for some decision with regard to it, to call for the adoption of a policy which will not repeat the mistakes of the past and yet will forestall any possible social menace of the future.

2. Again, the public discussion of the Jewish Question is not anti-Semitism. Publicity is sanitary. The publicity given the Jewish Question, or certain aspects of it, in this country has been very misleading. It has been discussed more fully in the Jewish press than elsewhere, but not with candor or breadth of vision. The two dominant notes—they are sounded over and over again with monotonous regularity in the Jewish press—are Gentile unfairness and Christian prejudice. These apparently are the two chief aspects of life which impress Jewish publicists when they look over the line of their own race. It is said in all soberness that it is fortunate for Jews generally that the Jewish press does not circulate very widely among Gentiles, for it is probably the one established agency in the United States which, without altering its program in the least, could stir up anti-Jewish sentiment by the simple expedient of a general reading among non-Jews. Jewish writers writing for Jewish readers present unusual material for the study of race consciousness and its accompaniment of contempt for other races. It is true that in the publications referred to, America is constantly praised, but not America as the land of the American people; America, rather, as the land of the Jews' opportunity.

On the side of the daily press, there has been no serious discussion at all. This is neither surprising nor reprehensible. The daily press deals with matters that have reached the overheated stage. When it mentions the Jews at all, it has stock phrases for the purpose; the effort includes a list of the famous Jews of history, and usually closes with complimentary references to certain local Jews of commendable qualities, whose advertisements are not infrequently found in another part of the paper. Summing up, it may be said that the publicity given the question in this country consists in misrepresentative criticism of the Gentiles by the Jewish press and misrepresentative praise of the Jews by the non-Jewish press. An independent effort to give a constructive publicity cannot, therefore, be laid to anti-Semitism, even when some of the statements which are made in the course of it arouse the resentment of Jewish readers.

3. Nor is it anti-Semitism to say that the suspicion is abroad in every capital of civilization and the certainty is held by a number of important men that there is active in the world a plan to control the world, not by territorial acquisition, not by military aggression, nor by governmental subjection, not even by economic control in the scientific sense, but by control of the machinery of commerce and exchange. It is not anti-Semitism to say that, nor to present the evidence which supports that, nor to bring the proof of that. Those who could best disprove it if it were not true are the international Jews themselves, but they have not disproved it. Those who could best prove it would be those Jews whose ideals include the good of the whole of humanity on an equality and not the good of one race only, but they have not proved it. Some day a prophetic Jew may arise who will see that the promises bestowed upon the Ancient People are not to be fulfilled by Rothschild methods, and that the promise that all the nations were to be blessed through Israel is not to be fulfilled by making the nations the economic vassals of Israel; and when that time comes we may hope for a re-direction of Jewish energy into channels that will drain the present sources of the Jewish Question. In the meantime, it is not anti-Semitism, it may even be found to be a world service to the Jew, to throw light on what purpose motivates certain higher circles.

If the above propositions are true, then the term "anti-Semitic," so freely bestowed on this series of articles, betrays a worse spirit in the critics than in the author. But enough of that. There is much yet to do, and what is done must stand on what merit remains after friend and foe alike are through with praise and blame.

## II.

Anti-Semitism has unquestionably swayed large sections of humanity at various times, warping the vision, twisting the characters and staining the hands of its victims, but the most amazing statement that can be made of it is that it has never accomplished anything in behalf of those who used it, and it has never taught anything to the Jews against whom it was used.

The grades of anti-Semitism are fairly numerous, and a few of them may be cited here:

1. There is first that degree of anti-Semitism, if it may be so described, which consists in a plain dislike of the Jew as a person, no matter whom he may be. This is often found in people of all grades. It is found mostly, however, in those whose contact with Jews has been very limited. It begins sometimes in childhood with an instinctive dislike for the word "Jew." It is encouraged by the misuse of the word "Jew" as an epithet, or as an adjective generally descriptive of unpopular practices. The feeling is not different from that which exists toward Gentiles, concerning whom the same notions are held, but it differs in that it is extended to the race of unknown individual Jews instead of being restricted to known individuals who may justify such a feeling.

Congeniality is not within our choice, but control of the sentiment of uncongeniality is. Every fair-minded person is compelled at times to reflect that it is not impossible that the person for whom he feels a dislike may be as good and possibly a better person than he. Our dislike merely registers the result of attraction and repulsion as they operate between another person and oneself; it does not indicate that the disliked person is unworthy. Of course, wherever intelligence is joined with this instinctive withdrawal from social contact with members of the Jewish race, prejudice is forestalled, except, of course, in those persons who hold that there are no individuals among the Jews worthy of respect. This is an extreme attitude and is composed of other elements beside natural dislike. It is possible for people to dislike Jews and not be anti-Semitic. Indeed, it is not at all uncommon, it grows more and more common, that intelligent and refined Jews themselves do not relish the society of their own people except in cases of exceptional refinement.

This really calls for some comment on the manners and characteristics of the ordinary member of the Jewish race, the accidents of behavior which stand out most obnoxiously and of which Jews themselves are often the most unsparing critics, but these comments must fall into place later.

2. A second stage of the spirit of anti-Semitism may be designated as hatred and enmity. It should be noted that the antipathy referred to immediately above was not hatred. Dislike is not hatred, nor is it necessarily enmity. One may dislike sugar in his tea without troubling to hate sugar. But undoubtedly there are people who because they have let their dislikes deepen into prejudice, and perhaps also because of unpleasant experiences with members of the Jewish race (probably a million Americans have been brought to the verge of becoming Jew-haters this winter because of contact with Jewish merchants and landlords) may be classified as, at least, incipient anti-Semites. This is most of all unfortunate for the persons who harbor these emotions. It is unfortunate in that it unfits the mind to consider intelligently the facts which constitute the Jewish Question, and also unfits it to deal with them in a fair and constructive way. For one's own sake, whatever the provocation otherwise, it is better not to let passion deflect the needle of one's mind. Hatred at the wheel means hazard on the course. Enmity lives in the vicinity of the Jews more than of any other race, and the reason for this is one of the puzzles of the ages. The Jewish nature itself, as shown in ancient and modern history, is not without its own share of enmity, and it either evokes or provokes enmity where it comes in contact with those Aryan races which follow their natural impulses unchecked by cultural and ethical influences. This age-long conflict of the Jew has puzzled the minds of students for generations. Some explain it Biblically as the curse of Jehovah upon His Chosen People for

their disobedience to the discipline by which He would have made them the Prophet Nation of the world. If this offense must come, if it is part of the Jew's heritage, an old saying—Christian and Scriptural, by the way—would still remain true: "It must needs be that offenses come, but woe to that man by whom the offense cometh."

3. In some parts of the world at various times this feeling of hatred has broken into murderous violence, which has roused, as wholesale physical outrage always does, the horror and resentment of humanity. This is the extreme form in which anti-Semitism has exhibited itself, and it is the charge of intending to stimulate it here and elsewhere which every public discussion of the Jewish Question has to bear. There is, of course, no excuse for these outbreaks, but there is sufficient explanation of them. The Jews usually explain them as expressions of religious prejudice, and the Gentiles as rebellion against an economic yoke which the Jews have woven for the people. It is an astonishing fact that, to take one country, the parts of Russia where anti-Semitic violence has been most marked are the most prosperous parts, so prosperous indeed and with a prosperity so unquestionably due to Jewish enterprise that the Jews have openly declared that they have the power to throw those parts of Russia back into commercial lethargy again by simply withdrawing. It is utterly idle to throw denials at this statement. It is confirmed time and time again by men who have gone to Russia full of resentment against the attitude of the Russians toward the Jews, as that attitude is represented in the Anglo-Saxon press, and who have come home with a new light on the cause of these outbreaks, though not excusing their character. Impartial observers have also found that some of the outbreaks have been precipitated by the Jews themselves. A correspondent, known the world over for his trenchant defense of the Jews under Russian persecution, was always bitterly attacked by the Jews themselves whenever he stated the truth about this, notwithstanding his protest to them that if he did not tell the truth when they were in the wrong the world would not be ready to believe him when he said they were blameless. To this day, in every country, the Jews are slow to admit blameworthiness for any-

thing. They must be excused, whoever else may be accused. It is a trait which will have to be disciplined before they can be brought to assist, if ever they can, the removal of those characteristics which arouse the antagonism of other peoples. Elsewhere in the world, it may be said that out-and-out enmity to the Jews has an economic basis. This, of course, leads to the question whether the Jew shall have to become a deliberate failure, or deny his genius, and forego his just meed of prosperity before he can win the approval of the other races—a question which will arise for discussion later.

As to the *religious prejudice* which the Jews are, as a rule, readiest to affirm, it is safe to say that it does not exist in the United States. Yet it is charged up to Americans by Jewish writers just as freely as it is charged up to Russians. Each non-Jew reader is competent to settle this for himself. He can easily do so by asking himself whether in all his life he has ever felt a moment's resentment against the Jew on account of his religion. In an address recently delivered in a Jewish lodge and reported in the Jewish press, the speaker, a Jew, stated that if 100 non-Jews on the street were approached at random and casually asked what a Jew is, the reply of the majority would be, "He is a Christ-killer." One of the best known and most highly respected rabbis in the United States said recently in a sermon that children in Christian Sunday schools were taught to regard the Jew as a Christ-killer. He repeated it in a conversation several weeks later.

It would probably be the testimony of Christians generally that they never heard this term until they heard it in a Jewish complaint, and certainly themselves never used it. The charge is absurd. Let the 20,000,000 now in the Christian Sunday schools of Canada and the United States testify as to the instruction given. There is no hesitation in stating that there is no prejudice whatever in the Christian churches against the Jew on account of his religion. On the contrary, there is not only a deep sense of indebtedness, but a feeling of sharing with the Jew in his religion. The Sunday schools of the Christian churches of the world are spending six months of this year studying the International Lessons which are appointed for the Books of the Judges, Ruth, First and Second Samuel and the Books of the Kings, and every year is devoted in part to the Old Testament.

Here, however, is something for Jewish religious leaders to consider: there is more downright bitterness of religious prejudice on the part of the Jews against Christianity than could ever be possible in the Christian churches of America. Simply take the church press of America and compare it with the Jewish press in this regard, and there is no answer. No Christian editor would think it either Christian or intelligent to attack the Jewish religion, yet any six months' survey of the Jewish press would yield a mass of attack and prejudice on the other side. Moreover, no religious bitterness in America attains within infinite distances to that bitterness visited upon the Jew who becomes a Christian in his faith. It amounts almost to a holy vendetta. A Christian may become a Jewish proselyte and his motives be respected; it is never so when a Jew becomes a Christian. These statements are true of both the orthodox and liberal wings of Judaism. It is not his religion that gives prominence to the Jew today; it is something else. And yet, with undeviating monotony, it is repeated wherever the Jew takes cognizance of the feeling toward him that it is on account of three things, first and most prominent of which is his religion. It may be comforting to him to think that he is suffering for his faith, but it is not true. Every intelligent Jew must know it.

Every Jew ought to know also that in every Christian church where the ancient prophecies are received and studied, there is a great revival of interest in the future of the Ancient People. It is not forgotten that certain Promises were made to them regarding their position in the world, and it is held that these prophecies will be fulfilled. The future of the Jew, as prophetically outlined, is intimately bound up with the future of this planet, and the Christian church in large part—at least by the evangelical wing, which the Jews most condemn—sees a Restoration of the Chosen People yet to come. If the mass of the Jews knew how understandingly and sympathetically all the prophecies concerning them are being studied in the Church, and the faith that exists that these prophecies will find fulfillment and that they will result in great Jewish service to society at large, they would probably regard the Church with another mind. They would at least know that the Church does *not* believe that it will be the instrument in the conversion of the Jews—a point on which Jewish leaders are tragically misled and which evokes more bitterness than anything else—but that it depends on quite other instruments and conditions, which it is not the function of this article to point out except to say that it will be the Jews' very own Messiah which will accomplish it and not the "wild olive," or the Gentile.

Curiously enough, there is a phase of anti-Semitism having to do with religion, but not in the way here discussed. There are those, very few in number and of atheistical tendencies, who assert that all religion is a sham, being the invention of Jews for the purpose of enslaving the minds of the people of the world to an enervating superstition. This position, however, has had no effect on the main issue. It is a far extreme.

## III.

Now, which of these exhibitions of anti-Semitism will show itself in America? If certain tendencies continue, as they are certain to do, what form will the feeling toward the Jew take? Not that of mass violence, we may be sure. The only mass action visible now is that of Jewish agencies themselves against any person or institution that dares to bring the Jewish Question to public attention.

1. Anti-Semitism will come to America because of the habit which emotions and ideas apparently have of making their way westward around the world. North of Palestine, where the Jews have been longest settled and where they are now in great numbers, anti-Semitism is acute and well-defined. Westward, in Germany, it is clearly defined but, until the seizure of German revolutionary agencies, was devoid of violence. Still farther westward, in Great Britain, it is defined, but because of the comparatively small number of Jews in the British Isles and their coalition with the ruling class, it is more a feeling than a movement. In the United States it is not so definite, but shows itself in a restlessness, a questioning, a sensible friction between the traditional tendency of the American to fair-mindedness and his respect for the cold facts.

Because the Question will assume more and more pressure in America it behooves everyone of foresight to disregard the shortsighted protests of the Jews themselves and see to it that the Question shall not present itself among us as it has done among other people, in its most distressing and confusing forms. It is a public duty to seize this problem at its beginning and train it up, so to speak; that is, so prepare for it that it may be handled here in a manner which will form a model for all other countries, which will indeed supply all other countries with the essential materials for a permanent solution. And this can be done only by exposing and recognizing and treating with the serum of publicity the conditions before which, heretofore, the nations have helplessly floundered because they lacked either the desire or the means to get at the great root of the difficulty.

2. Another cause of the Question appearing here will be the great influx of the Jews which is planned for America. There will probably be a million Jews enter the country this year, increasing our Jewish population to nearly 4,500,000. This does not mean merely an immigration of persons, but an immigration of ideas. No Jewish writer has ever told us, in systematic fashion, just what is the Jews' idea of non-Jews, how they regard the Gentiles in their private minds. But there are indications of it, although one would not attempt to reconstruct the Jewish attitude toward Gentiles. A Jew ought to do this for us, but he would probably be cast out by his own people if he discharged his task with rigorous jealousy for the exact fact.

These people are coming here regarding the Gentile as an hereditary enemy, as perhaps they have good ground for doing, and so believing they are going to model their behavior in a manner that will show it. Nor will these Jews be so helpless as they appear. In stricken Poland, where the Jews are represented as having been stripped of everything during the war, there are hundreds daily appearing before the consulate to arrange their passage here. The fact is significant. In spite of their reputed suffering and poverty, they are able to travel a great distance and to insist on coming. No other people are financially able to travel in such numbers. But the Jews are. It will readily be seen that they are not objects of charity. They have been able to keep afloat in a storm that has wrecked the other people. They know it and they joy in it, as is natural. And they will bring here the same thoughts toward the majority which they have harbored in their present lands of domicile. They may hail America; they will have their own thoughts about the majority of the American people. They may be in the lists as Russians or Poles or what not, but they will be Jews with the full Jewish consciousness, and they will make themselves felt.

All this is bound to have its effect. And it is not race prejudice to prepare for it, and to invite American Jews themselves to consider the fact and contribute to the solution of the problem which it presents.

3. Every idea which has ruled Europe has met with transformation when it was transplanted in America. It was so with the idea of Liberty, the idea of Government, the idea of War. It will be so with the idea of anti-Semitism. The whole problem will center here and if we are wise and do not shirk it, it will find its solution here. A recent Jewish writer has said: "Jewry today largely means American Jewry ......... all former Jewish centers were demolished during the war and were shifted to America." The problem will be ours, whether we choose it or not.

And what course will it take? Much depends on what can be accomplished before it becomes very strong. It may be said, however, that the first element to appear will be a show of resentment against certain Jewish commercial successes, more particularly against the united action by which they are attained. Our people see the spectacle of a people in the midst of a people, in a sense which the Mormons never were, and they will not like it. The Mormons made an Exodus; Israel is going back into Egypt to subjugate it.

The second element which will undoubtedly appear is prejudice and its incitement. The majority may always be right, but they are not always initially reasonable. That prejudice which exists now, and which is freely admitted by both Jew and Gentile, may become more marked, to the distress of both parties, for neither the subject nor the object of prejudice can attain that freedom of mind which is happiness.

Then we may most confidently look for a reaction of Justice. It is here that the whole matter will begin to bend to the genius of Americanism. The innate justice of the American mind has come to the aid of every object that ever roused American resentment. The natural reaction with us is of very brief duration; the intellectual and ethical reaction swiftly follows. The American mind will never rest with merely resenting certain individuals. It will probe deeper. Already this deeper probe has been begun in Great Britain and America. We characteristically do not stop with persons when principles are in sight.

And upon this there will be an investigation of materials, part of which may yet be presented in this series and which may possibly be disregarded for a time, but which at a future date will be found to be the clue to the maze. Upon this, the root of all the trouble will be bared to the light, to die as all roots do when deprived of their concealment of darkness, and then the Jewish people themselves may be expected to begin an adjustment to the new order of things, not to lose their identity or to curtail their energy or to dim their brilliance, but to turn all into more worthy channels for the benefit of all races, which alone can justify their claim to superiority. A race that can achieve in the material realm what the Jews have achieved while asserting themselves to be spiritually superior, can achieve in a less sordid, a less society-defying realm also.

The Jews will not be destroyed; neither will they be permitted to maintain the yoke which they have been so skillful in fastening upon society. They are the beneficiaries of a system which itself will change and force them to other and higher devices to justify their proper place in the world.

---

Issue of June 19, 1920.

*"We must force the Gentile governments to adopt measures which will promote our broadly conceived plan already approaching its triumphal goal by bringing to bear the pressure of stimulated public opinion which has in reality been organized by us with the help of the so-called 'great power' of the Press. With few exceptions, not worth considering, it has already fallen into our hands."*

*—The Seventh Protocol.*

VI.

# Jewish Question Breaks Into the Magazines

ONCE upon a time an American faculty member of an American university went to Russia on business. He was expert in a very important department of applied science and a keen observer. He entered Russia with the average American's feeling about the treatment which the government of that people accorded the Jew. He lived there three years, came home for a year, and went back again for a similar period, and upon his second return to America he thought it was time to give the American public accurate information about the Jewish Question in Russia. He prepared a most careful article and sent it to the editor of a magazine of the first class in the Eastern United States. The editor sent for him, spent most of two days with him, and was deeply impressed with all he learned—but he said he could not print the article. The same interest and examination occurred with several other magazine editors of the first rank.

It was not because the professor could not write—these editors gladly bought anything he would write on other subjects. But it was impossible for him to get his article on the Jews accepted or printed in New York.

The Jewish Question, however, has at last broken into a New York magazine. Rather it is a fragment of a shell hurled from the Jewish camp at the Jewish Question to demolish, if possible, the Question and thus make good the assertion that there is no such thing.

Incidentally it is the only kind of article on the Jewish Question that the big magazines, whose mazes of financial controllers make most interesting rummaging, would care to print.

Yet, the general public may learn much about the Question even from the type of article whose purpose is to prove that the Question doesn't exist.

Mr. William Hard, in the *Metropolitan* for June,

has done as well as could be expected, considering the use he was supposed to make of such material as he had at hand. And doubtless the telegraph and letter brigades, which keep watch over all printed references to the Jews, have duly congratulated the good editors of the *Metropolitan* for their assistance in soothing the public to further sleep.

It is to be hoped, for the sake of the Question, that Mr. Hard's effort will have a wide reading, for there is very much to be learned from it—much more than it was anybody's intention should be learned from it.

It may be learned, first, that the Jewish Question exists. Mr. Hard says it is discussed in the drawing-rooms of London and Paris. Whether the mention of drawing-rooms was a writer's device to intimate that the matter was unimportant and frivolous, or merely represented the extent of Mr. Hard's contact with the Question is not clear. He adds, however, that a document relating to the Question has "traveled a good bit in certain official circles in Washington." He also mentions a cable dispatch to the New York *World*, concerning the same Question, which that paper published. His article was probably published too early to note the review which the London *Times* made of the first document referred to. But he has told the reader who is looking for the objective facts in the article that there is a Jewish Question, and that it does not exist among the riff-raff either but principally in those circles where the evidence of Jewish power and control is most abundant. Moreover, the Question is being discussed. Mr. Hard tells us that much. If he does not go further and tell us that it is being discussed with great seriousness in high places and among men of national and international importance, it is probably because of one of two things, either he does not know, or he does not consider it consonant with the purpose of the article to tell.

However, Mr. Hard has already made it clear that there is a Jewish Question, that it is being discussed, that it is being discussed by people who are best situated to observe the matter they are talking about.

The reading of Mr. Hard's article makes it clear also that the Question always comes to the fore on the note of conspiracy. Of course, Mr. Hard says he does not believe in conspiracies which involve a large number of people, and it is with the utmost ease that his avowal of unbelief is accepted, for there is nothing more ridiculous to the Gentile mind than a mass conspiracy, because there is nothing more impossible to the Gentile himself. Mr. Hard, we take it, is of non-Jewish extraction, and he knows how impossible it would be to band Gentiles together in any considerable number for any length of time in even the noblest conspiracy. Gentiles are not built for it. Their conspiracy, whatever it might be, would fall like a rope of sand. Gentiles have not the basis either in blood or interest that the Jews have to stand together. The Gentile does not naturally suspect conspiracy; he will indeed hardly bring himself to the verge of believing it without the fullest proof.

It is therefore quite easy to understand Mr. Hard's difficulty with conspiracy; the point is that to write his article at all, he is forced to recognize at almost every step that whenever the Jewish Question is discussed, the idea of conspiracy occupies a large part in it. As a matter of fact, it is the central idea in Mr. Hard's article, and it completely monopolizes the heading—"Great Jewish Conspiracy."

The search for basic facts in Mr. Hard's article will disclose the additional information that there are certain documents in existence which purport to contain the details of the conspiracy, or—to drop a word that is unpleasant and may be misleading and which has not been used in this series—the tendency of Jewish power to achieve complete control. That is about all that the reader learns from Mr. Hard about the documents, except that he describes one as "strange and horrible." Here is indeed a regrettable gap in the story, for it is to discredit a certain document that Mr. Hard writes, and yet he tells next to nothing about it. Discreditable documents usually discredit themselves. But this document is not permitted to do that. The reader of the article is left to take Mr. Hard's word for it. The serious student or critic will feel, of course, that the documents themselves would have formed a better basis for an intelligent judgment. But laying that matter aside, Mr. Hard has made public the fact that there are documents.

And then Mr. Hard does another thing, as well as he can with the materials at hand, the purpose of the article being what it was, and that is to show how little the Jews have to do with the control of affairs by showing who are the Jews that do control certain selected groups of affairs. The names are all brought forward by Mr. Hard and he alone is responsible for them, our purpose in referring to them being merely to show what can be learned from him.

Mr. Hard leans heavily on Russian affairs. Sometimes it would almost seem as if the Jewish Question were conceived as the Soviet Question, which it is not, as Mr. Hard very well knows, and although the two have their plain connections, it is nothing less than well-defined propaganda to set up Bolshevist fiction and knock it down by Jewish fact for the purpose of the latter. However, what Mr. Hard offers as fact is very instructive, quite apart from the conclusion which he draws from it.

Now, take his Russian line-up first. He says that in the cabinet of Soviet Russia there is only one Jew. But he is Trotsky. There are others in the government, of course, but Mr. Hard is speaking about the cabinet now. He is not speaking about the commissars, who are the real rulers of Russia, nor about the executive troops, who are the real strength of the Trotsky-Lenin régime. No, just the cabinet. Of course, there was only one Jew prominent in Hungary, too, but he was Bela Kun. Mr. Hard does not ask us to believe, however, that it is simply because of Trotsky and Kun that all Europe believes that Bolshevism has a strong Jewish element. Else the stupid credibility of the Gentiles would be more impossible of conception than the idea of a Jewish conspiracy is to Mr. Hard's mind. Why should it be easier to believe that Gentiles are dunces than that Jews are clever?

However, it is not too much to say that Trotsky is way up at the top, sharing the utmost summit of Bolshevism with Lenin, and Trotsky is a Jew—nobody ever denied that, not even Mr. Braunstein himself (the latter being Trotsky's St. Louis, U. S. A., name).

But then, says Mr. Hard, the Mensheviks are led by Jews, too! That is a fact worth putting down beside the others. Trotsky at the head of the Bolsheviks; at the head of the Mensheviks *during their opposition* of the Bolsheviks were Lieber, Martov and Dan—"all Jews," says Mr. Hard.

There is, however, a middle party between these extremes, the Cadets, which, Mr. Hard says, are or were the strongest bourgeois political party in Russia. "They now have their headquarters in Paris. Their chairman is Vinaver—a Jew."

There are the facts as stated by Mr. Hard. He says that Jews, whose names he gives, head the three great divisions of political opinion in Russia.

And then he cries, look how the Jews are divided! How can there be conspiracy among people who thus fight themselves?

But another, looking at the same situation may say, look how the Jews control every phase of political opinion in Russia! Doesn't there seem to be some ground for the feeling that they are desirous of ruling everywhere?

The facts are there. What significance does it bring to the average mind that the three great parties of Russia are led by Jews?

But that does not exhaust the information which the matter-of-fact reader may find in Mr. Hard's article. He turns to the United States and makes several interesting statements.

"There is Otto Kahn," he says. Well, sometimes Otto Kahn is *there*, and sometimes he is in Paris on important international matters, and sometimes he is in London advocating certain alliances between British and American capital which have to do in a large way with European political conditions. Mr. Kahn is rated as a conservative, and that may mean anything. A man is conservative or not according to the angle from which he is viewed. The most conservative men in America are really the most radical; their motives and methods go to the very roots of certain matters; they are radicals in their own field. The men who controlled the last Republican Convention—if not the last, the most recent—are styled conservatives by those whose vision is circumscribed by certain limited economic interests; but they are the most radical of radicals, they have passed the red stage and are white with it. If it were known what is in the back of Mr.

Kahn's mind, if he should display a chart of what he is doing and aiming to do, the term which would then most aptly describe him might be quite different. Anyway, we have it from Mr. Hard, "There is Mr. Kahn."

"On the other hand," says Mr. Hard, "there is Rose Pastor Stokes." He adds the name of Morris Hillquit. They are, in Mr. Hard's classification, radicals. And to offset these names he adds the names of two Gentiles, Eugene V. Debs and Bill Haywood,and intimates that they are much more powerful leaders than the first two. Students of modern influences, of which Mr. Hard has long appeared as one, do not think so. Neither Debs nor Haywood ever generated in all their lives a fraction of the intellectual power which Mrs. Stokes and Mr. Hillquit have generated. Both Debs and Haywood live by the others. To every informed person, as to Mr. Hard in this article, come the Jewish names to mind when the social tendencies of the United States are passed under reflection.

This is most instructive indeed, that in naming the leaders of so-called conservatism and radicalism, Mr. Hard is driven to use Jewish names. On his showing the reader is entitled to say that Jews lead both divisions here in the United States.

But Mr. Hard is not through. "The man who does more than any other man—the man who does more than any regiment of other men—to keep American labor anti-radical is a Jew—Samuel Gompers." That is a fact which the reader will place in his list—American labor is led by a Jew.

Well, then, "the strongest anti-Gompers trade union in the country—The Amalgamated Clothing Workers—and very strong indeed, and very large—is led by a Jew—Sidney Hillman."

It is the Russian situation over again. Both ends of the movements, and the movement which operate within the movement, are under the leadership of Jews. This, whatever the construction put upon it, is a fact which Mr. Hard is compelled by the very nature of his task to acknowledge.

And the middle movement, "the Liberal Middle" as Mr. Hard calls it, which catches all between, produces in this article the names of Mr. Justice Brandeis, Judge Mack and Felix Frankfurter, gentlemen whose activities since Armistice Day would make a very interesting story.

For good measure, Mr. Hard produces two other names, "Baron Gunzberg—a Jew" who is "a faithful official" of the Russian Embassy of Ambassador Bakhmetev, a representative of the modified old regime, while the Russian Information Bureau, whose literary output appears in many of our newspapers is conducted by another Jew, so Mr. Hard calls him, whose name is familiar to newspaper readers, Mr. A. J. Sack.

It is not a complete list by any means, but it is quite impressive. It seems to reflect importance on the documents which Mr. Hard endeavors to minimize to a position of ridiculous unimportance. And it leads to the thought that perhaps the documents are scrutinized as carefully as they are because the readers of them have observed not only the facts which Mr. Hard admits but other and more astonishing ones, and have discovered that the documents confirm and explain the observations. Other readers who have not had the privilege of learning all that the documents contain are entitled to have satisfaction given to the interest thus aroused.

The documents did not create the Jewish Question. If there were nothing but the documents, Mr. Hard would not have written nor would the *Metropolitan* Magazine have printed the article here discussed.

What Mr. Hard has done is to bring confirmation in a most unexpected place that the Question exists and is pressing for discussion. Someone felt the pressure when "The Great Jewish Conspiracy" was ordered and written.

---

Issue of June 26, 1920.

*"What are you prating about? As long as we do not have the Press of the whole world in our hands, everything you may do is vain. We must control or influcnce the papers of the whole world in order to blind and deceive the people."*

*—Baron Montefiore.*

VII.

# Arthur Brisbane Leaps to the Help of Jewry

ONCE more the current of this series on the Modern Jewish Question is interrupted to give notice of the appearance of the Question in another quarter, the appearance this time consisting of a more than two-column "Today" editorial in the Hearst papers of Sunday, June 20, from the pen of Arthur Brisbane. It would be too much to say that Mr. Brisbane is the most influential writer in the country, but perhaps he is among the dozen most widely read. It is, therefore, a confirmation of the statement that the Question is assuming importance in this country, that a writer of Mr. Brisbane's prominence should openly discuss it.

Of course, Mr. Brisbane has not studied the Question. He would probably admit in private conversation—though such an admission would hardly be in harmony with the tone of certainty he publicly adopts—that he really knows nothing about it. He knows, however, as a good newspaper man, how to handle it when the exigencies of the newspaper day throw it up to him for offhand treatment. Every editorial writer knows how to do that. There is something good in every race, or there have been some notable individuals in it, or it has played a picturesque part in history—that is enough for a very readable editorial upon any class of people who may happen to be represented in the community. The Question, whatever it may be, need not be studied at all; a certain group of people may be salved for a few paragraphs, and the job need never be tackled again. Every newspaper man knows that.

And yet, having lived in New York for a long time, having had financial dealings of a large and obligating nature with certain interests in this country, having seen no doubt more or less of the inner workings of the great trust and banking groups, and being constantly surrounded by assistants and advisors who are members of the Jewish race, Mr. Brisbane must have had his thoughts. It is, however, no part of a newspaper man's business to expose his thoughts about the racial groups of his community, any more than it is a showman's business to express his opinion of the patrons of his show. The kinds of offense a newspaper will give, and the occasions on which it will feel justified in giving it, are very limited.

So, assuming that Mr. Brisbane had to write at all, it could have been told beforehand what he would write. The only wonder is that he felt he had to write. Did he really feel that the Jews are being "persecuted" when an attempt is made to uncover the extent and causes of their control in the United States and elsewhere? Did he feel, with good editorial shrewdness, that here was an opportunity to win the attention and regard of the most influential group in New York and the nation? Or—and this seems within the probabilities—was he inclined simply to pass it over, until secretarial suggestions reached him for a Sunday editorial, or until some of the bondholders made their wishes known? This is not at all to impugn Mr. Brisbane's motives, but merely to indicate on what slender strings such an editorial may depend.

But what is more important—does Mr. Brisbane consider that, having disposed of the Sunday editorial, he is through with the Question, or that the Question itself is solved? That is the worst of daily editorializing; having come safely and inoffensively through with one editorial, the matter is at an end as far as that particular writer is concerned—that is, as a usual thing.

It is to be hoped that Mr. Brisbane is not through. He ought not to leave a big question without contributing something to it, and in his Sunday editorial he did not contribute anything. He even made mistakes which he ought to correct by further study. "What about the Phoenicians?" he asks. He should have looked that up while his mind was opened receptively toward the subject, and he would not have made so miserable a blunder as to connect them so closely with the Jews. He would never find a Jew doing that. It is permissible, however, in Jewish propaganda intended for Gentile consumption. The Phoenicians themselves certainly never thought they were connected in any way with the Jews, and the Jews were equally without light on the subject. If in nothing else, they differed in their attitude toward the sea. The Phoenicians not only built boats but manned them; the Jew would rather risk his investment in a boat than himself. In everything else the differences between the two peoples were deep and distinct. Mr. Brisbane should have turned up the Jewish Encyclopedia at that point in his dictation. It is to be hoped he will resume his study and when he has found something that is not printed in "simply written" Jewish books will give the world the benefit of it. It is hardly like the question of the rotundity of the earth; this Question is not settled and it will be discussed.

Mr. Brisbane is in a position to pursue some investigations of his own on this subject. He has a large staff, and it is presumed that some of its members are Gentiles of unbiased minds; he has a world-wide organization; since his own modification of speech and views following upon his adventure in the money-making world, he has a "look-in" upon certain groups of men and certain tendencies of power—why does he not take this Question as a world problem and go after the facts and the solution?

It is a task worthy of any newspaper organization. It will assist America to make the contribution which she must make if this Question is ever to be turned from the bugbear it has been through all the centuries. All the talk on earth about "loving our fellow men" will not serve in lieu of an investigation, because it is asking men to love those who are rapidly and insidiously gaining the mastery of them. "What's wrong with the Jew?" is the first question, and then, "What's wrong with the Gentile to make it possible?"

As in the case of every Gentile writer who appears as the Jew's good-natured defender, Mr. Brisbane is compelled to state a number of facts which comprise a part of the very Question whose existence is denied.

"Every other successful name you see in a great city is a Jewish name," says Mr. Brisbane. In his own city the ratio is even higher than that.

"Jews numbering less than one per cent of the earth's population possess by conquest, enterprise, industry and intelligence 50 per cent of the world's commercial success," says Mr. Brisbane.

Does it mean anything to Mr. Brisbane? Has he ever thought how it will all turn out? Is he willing to absolve that "success" from every quality which humanity has a right to challenge? Is he entirely satisfied with the way that "success" is used where it is supreme? Would he be willing to undertake to prove that it is due to those commendable qualities he has named and nothing less commendable? Speaking of the Jew-financed Harriman railroad campaign, is Mr. Brisbane ready to write his endorsement upon that? Did he ever hear of Jewish money backing railroads that were built for railroad purposes and nothing else?

It would be very easy to suggest to Mr. Brisbane, as editor, a series of articles which would be most enlightening, both to himself and his readers, if he would only put unbiased men at work gathering the facts for them.

One of the articles might be entitled "The Jews at the Peace Conference." His men should be instructed to learn who were the most prominent figures at the Peace Conference; who came and went most constantly and most busily; who were given freest access to the most important persons and chambers; which race provided the bulk of the private secretaries to the important personages there; which race provided most of the sentinels through whom engagements had to be made with men of note; which race went furthest in the endeavor to turn the whole proceeding into a festival rout by dances and lavish entertainment; which civilians of prominence oftenest dined the leading conferees in private session.

If Mr. Brisbane, with the genius for reporting which his organization deservedly has, will turn his men loose on that assignment, and then print what they bring him, he will have a story that will make a mark even in his remarkable career as an editor.

He might even run a second story on the Peace Conference, entitled, "Which Program Won at the Peace Conference?" He might instruct his men to inquire as to the business which brought the Jews in such quality and quantity to Paris, and how it was put through. Particularly should they inquire whether any jot or tittle of the Jews' world program was refused or modified by the Peace Conference. It should also be carefully inquired whether, after getting what they went after, they did not then ask for still more and get that, too, even though it constituted a discrimination against the rest of the world. Mr. Brisbane would doubtless be surprised to learn that of all the programs submitted to that Conference, not excepting the great program on which humanity hung so many pathetic hopes, the only program to go through was the Jews' program. And yet he could learn just that if he inquired. The question is, having obtained that information, what would Mr. Brisbane do with it?

There are any number of lines of investigation Mr. Brisbane might enter, and in any one of them his knowledge of his country and of its relation to this particular Question would be greatly enlarged.

Does Mr. Brisbane know who owns Alaska? He may have been under the impression, in common with the rest of us until we learned better, that it was owned by the United States. No, it is owned by the same people who are coming rapidly to own the United States.

Is Mr. Brisbane, from the vantage point afforded by his position in national journalism, even dimly aware that there are elements in our industrial unrest which neither "capital" nor "labor" accurately define? Has he ever caught a glimpse of another power which is neither "labor" nor "capital" in the productive sense, whose purpose and interest it is to keep labor and capital as far apart as possible, now by provoking labor, now by provoking capital? In his study of the industrial situation and its perfectly baffling mystery, Mr. Brisbane must have caught a flash of something behind the backmost scene. It would be good journalistic enterprise to find out what it is.

Has Mr. Brisbane ever printed the names of the men who control the sugar supply of the United States—does he know them—would he like to know them?

Has he ever looked into the woolen situation in this country, from the change of ownership in cotton lands, and the deliberate sabotage of cotton production by banking threats, right on through to the change in the price of cloth and clothing? And has he ever noted the names of the men he found on that piece of investigation? Would he like to know how it is done, and who does it? Mr. Brisbane could find all these things and give them to the public by using his efficient staff of investigators and writers on this Question.

Whether Mr. Brisbane would feel free to do this, he himself best knows. There may be reasons why he would not, private reasons, prudential reasons.

However that may be, there are no reasons why he should not make a complete study of the Question—a real study, not a superficial glance at it with an eye to its "news value"—and arrive at his own considered conclusion. There would be no intolerance about that. As it is now, Mr. Brisbane is not qualified to take a stand on either side of the Question; he simply brushes it aside as troublesome, as the old planters used to brush aside the anti-slavery moralists; and for that reason the recent defense of the Jew is not a defense at all. It is more like a bid for favor.

Mr. Brisbane's chief aversion, apparently, is toward what he calls race prejudice and race hatred. Of course, if any man should fear that the study of an economic situation would plunge him into these serious aberrations of mind, he should be advised to avoid that line of study. There is something wrong either with the investigation or with the investigator when prejudice and hatred are the result. It is a mighty poor excuse, however, for an intelligent man to put forward either on his own behalf or on behalf of those whose minds he has had the privilege of molding over a course of years.

Prejudice and hatred are the very conditions which a scientific study of the Jewish Question will forestall and prevent. We prejudge what we do not know, and we hate what we do not understand; the study of the Jewish Question will bring knowledge and insight, and not to the Gentile only, but also to the Jew. The Jew needs this as much, even more than the Gentile. For if the Jew can be made to see, understand and deal with certain matters, then a large part of the Question vanishes in the solution of ideal common sense. Awaking the Gentile to the facts about the Jew is only part of the work; awaking the Jew to the facts about the Question is an indispensable part. The big initial victory to be achieved is to transform Gentiles from being mere attackers and to transform Jews from being mere defenders, both of them special pleaders for partisan views, and to turn them both into investigators. The investigation will show both Gentile and Jew at fault, and the road will then be clear for wisdom to work out a result, if there should perchance be that much wisdom left in the race.

There is a serious snare in all this plea for tolerance. Tolerance is first a tolerance of the truth. Tolerance is urged today for the sake of suppression. There can be no tolerance until there is first a full understanding of what is tolerated. Ignorance, suppression, silence, collusion—these are not tolerance. The Jew never has been really tolerated in the higher sense because he has never been understood. Mr. Brisbane does not assist the understanding of this people by reading a "simply written" book and flinging a few Jewish names about in a sea of type. He owes it to his own mind to get into the Question, whether he makes newspaper use of his discoveries or not.

As to the newspaper angle, it is impossible to report the world even superficially without coming everywhere against the fact of the Jews, and the Press gets around that fact by referring to them as Russians, Letts, Germans and Englishmen. This mask of names is one of the most confusing elements in the whole problem. Names that actually name, statements that actually define are needed for the clarification of the world's mind.

Mr. Brisbane should study this question for the light such a study would throw on other matters with which he is concerned. It would be a help to that study if from time to time he would publish some of his findings, because such publication would put him in touch with a phase of Judaism which mere complimentary editorials could not. No doubt Mr. Brisbane has been deluged by communications which praise him for what he has written; the real eye-opener would come if he could get several bushels of the other kind. Nothing that has ever come to him could compare with what would come to him if he should publish even one of the facts he could discover by an independent investigation.

Having written about the Jews, Mr. Brisbane will probably have a readier eye henceforth for other men's pronouncements on the same subject. In his casual reading he will find more references to the Jew than he has ever noticed before. Some of them will probably appear in isolated sentences and paragraphs of his own papers. Sooner or later, every competent investigator and every honest writer strikes a trail that leads toward Jewish power in the world. THE DEARBORN INDEPENDENT is only doing with system and detail what other publications have done or are doing piecemeal.

There is a real fear of the Jew upon the publicity sources of the United States—a fear which is felt and which ought to be analyzed. Unless it is a very great mistake, Mr. Brisbane himself has felt this fear, though it is quite possible he has not scrutinized it. It is not the fear of doing injustice to a race of people—all of us ought to have that honorable fear—it is the fear of doing anything at all with reference to them except unstintedly praising them. An independent investigation would convince Mr. Brisbane that a considerable modification of praise in favor of discriminate criticism is a course that is pressing upon American journalism.

Issue of July 3, 1920.

# Does a Definite Jewish World Program Exist?

IN all the explanations of anti-Jewish feeling which modern Jewish spokesmen make, these three alleged causes are commonly given—these three and no more: religious prejudice, economic jealousy, social antipathy. Whether the Jew knows it or not, every Gentile knows that on his side of the Jewish Question no religious prejudice exists. Economic jealousy may exist, at least to this extent, that his uniform success has exposed the Jew to much scrutiny. A few Jewish spokesmen seek to turn this scrutiny by denying that the Jew is preeminent in finance, but this is loyalty in extremity. The finances of the world are in control of Jews; their decisions and their devices are themselves our economic law. But because a people excels us in finance is no sufficient reason for calling them to the bar of public judgment. If they are more intellectually able, more persistently industrious than we are, if they are endowed with faculties which have been denied us as an inferior or slower race, that is no reason for our requiring them to give an account of themselves. Economic jealousy may explain some of the anti-Jewish feeling; it cannot account for the presence of the Jewish Question except as the hidden causes of Jewish financial success may become a minor element of the larger problem. And as for social antipathy—there are many more undesirable Gentiles in the world than there are undesirable Jews, for the simple reason that there are more Gentiles.

None of the Jewish spokesmen today mention the political cause, or if they come within suggestive distance of it, they limit and localize it. It is not a question of the patriotism of the Jew, though this too is very widely questioned in all the countries. You hear it in England, in France, in Germany, in Poland, in Russia, in Rumania—and, with a shock, you hear it in the United States. Books have been written, reports published and scattered abroad, statistics skillfully set forth for the purpose of showing that the Jew does his par for the country in which he resides; and yet the fact remains that in spite of these most zealous and highly sponsored campaigns, the opposite assertion is stronger and lives longer. The Jews who did their duty in the armies of Liberty, and did it doubtless from true-hearted love and allegiance, have not been able to overcome the impression made upon officers and men and civilians by those who did not.

But that is not what is here meant as the political element in the Jewish Question. To understand why the Jew should think less of the nationalities of the world than do those who comprise them is not difficult. The Jew's history is one of wandering among them all. Considering living individuals only, there is no race of people now upon the planet who have lived in so many places, among so many peoples as have the Jewish masses. They have a clearer world-sense than any other people, because the world has been their path. And they think in world terms more than any nationally cloistered people could. The Jew can be absolved if he does not enter into national loyalties and prejudices with the same intensity as the natives; the Jew has been for centuries a cosmopolitan. While under a flag he may be correct in the conduct required of him as a citizen or resident, inevitably he has a view of flags which can hardly be shared by the man who has known but one flag.

The political element inheres in the fact that the Jews form a nation in the midst of the nations. Some of their spokesmen, particularly in America, deny that, but the genius of the Jew himself has always put these spokesmen's zeal to shame. And why this fact of nationhood should be so strenuously denied is not always clear. It may be that when Israel is brought to see that her mission in the world is not to be achieved by means of the Golden Calf, her very cosmopolitanism with regard to the world and her inescapable nationalistic integrity with regard to herself will together prove a great and serviceable factor in bringing about human unity, which the total Jewish tendency at the present time is doing much to prevent. It is not the fact that the Jews remain a nation in the midst of the nations; it is the use made of that inescapable status, which the world has found reprehensible. The nations have tried to reduce the Jew to unity with themselves; attempts toward the same end have been made by the Jews themselves; but destiny seems to have marked them out to continuous nationhood. Both the Jews and the World will have to accept that fact, find the good prophecy in it, and seek the channels for its fulfillment.

Theodor Herzl, one of the greatest of the Jews, was perhaps the farthest-seeing public exponent of the philosophy of Jewish existence that modern generations have known. And he was never in doubt of the existence of the Jewish nation. Indeed, he proclaimed its existence on every occasion. He said, "*We are a people—One people.*"

He clearly saw that what he called the Jewish Question was political. In his introduction to "The Jewish State" he says, "I believe that I understand anti-Semitism, which is really a highly complex movement. I consider it from a Jewish standpoint, yet without fear or hatred. I believe that I can see what elements there are in it of vulgar sport, of common trade jealousy, of inherited prejudice, of religious intolerance and also of pretended self-defense. I think the Jewish Question is no more a social than a religious one, notwithstanding that it sometimes takes these and other forms. *It is a national question, which can only be solved by making it a political world-question* to be discussed and controlled by the civilized nations of the world in council."

Not only did Herzl declare that the Jews formed a nation, but when questioned by Major Evans Gordon before the British Royal Commission on Alien Immigration in August, 1902, Dr. Herzl said: "I will give you my definition of a nation, and you can add the adjective 'Jewish.' A nation is, in my mind, an historical group of men of a recognizable cohesion held together by a common enemy. That is in my view a nation. *Then if you add to that the word 'Jewish' you have what I understand to be the Jewish nation.*"

Also, in relating the action of this Jewish nation to the world, Dr. Herzl wrote—"When we sink, we become a revolutionary proletariat, the subordinate officers of the revolutionary party; when we rise, there rises also our terrible power of the purse."

This view, which appears to be the true view in that it is the view which has been longest sustained in Jewish thought, is brought out also by Lord Eustace Percy, and re-published, apparently with approval, by the Canadian *Jewish Chronicle*. It will repay a careful reading:

"Liberalism and Nationalism, with a flourish of trumpets, threw open the doors of the ghetto and offered equal citizenship to the Jew. The Jew passed out into the Western World, saw the power and the glory of it, used it and enjoyed it, laid his hand indeed upon the nerve centers of its civilization, guided, directed and exploited it, and then—refused the offer * * *Moreover—and this is a remarkable thing—the Europe of nationalism and liberalism, of scientific government and democratic equality is more intolerable to him than the old oppressions and persecutions of despotism * * * In the increasing consolidation of the western nations, it is no longer possible to reckon on complete toleration * * *

"In a world of completely organized territorial sovereignties he (the Jew) has only two possible cities of refuge: he must either pull down the pillars of the whole national state system or he must create a territorial sovereignty of his own. In this perhaps lies the explanation both of Jewish Bolshevism and of Zionism, for at this moment Eastern Jewry seems to hover uncertainly between the two.

"In Eastern Europe Bolshevism and Zionism often seem to grow side by side, just as Jewish influence molded Republican and Socialist thought throughout the nineteenth century, down to the Young Turk revolution in Constantinople hardly more than a decade ago —*not because the Jew cares for the positive side of radical philosophy, not because he desires to be a partaker in Gentile nationalism or Gentile democracy, but because no existing Gentile system of government is ever anything but distasteful to him.*"

All that is true, and Jewish thinkers of the more fearless type always recognize it as true. *The Jew is against the Gentile scheme of things.* He is, when he gives his tendencies full sway, a Republican as against the monarchy, a Socialist as against the republic, and a Bolshevist as against Socialism.

What are the causes of this disruptive activity? First, his essential lack of democracy. Jewish nature is autocratic. Democracy is all right for the rest of the world, but the Jew wherever he is found forms an aristocracy of one sort or another. Democracy is merely a tool of a word which Jewish agitators use to raise themselves to the ordinary level in places where they are oppressed below it; but having reached the common level they immediately make efforts for special privileges, as being entitled to them—a process of which the late Peace Conference will remain the most startling example. The Jews today are the only people whose special and extraordinary privileges are written into the world's Treaty of Peace. But more of that at another time.

No one now pretends to deny, except a few spokesmen who really do not rule the thought of the Jews but are set forth for the sole benefit of influencing Gentile thought, that the socially and economically disruptive elements abroad in the world today are not only manned but also moneyed by Jewish interests. For a long time this fact was held in suspense owing to the vigorous denial of the Jews and the lack of information on the part of those agencies of publicity to which the public had looked for its information. But now the facts are coming forth. Herzl's words are being proved to be true—"when we sink, we become a revolutionary proletariat, *the subordinate officers of the revolutionary party*" —and these words were first published in English in 1896, or 24 years ago.

Just now these tendencies are working in two directions, one for the tearing down of the Gentile states all over the world, the other for the establishment of a Jewish state in Palestine. The latter project has the best wishes of the whole world, but it is far from having the best wishes of the whole, or even the larger part of Jewry. The Zionist party makes a great deal of noise, but it is really an unrepresentative minority. It can scarcely be designated as more than an unusually ambitious colonization scheme.* It is doubtless serving, however, as a very useful public screen for the carrying on of secret activities. International Jews, the controllers of the world's governmental and financial power, may meet anywhere, at any time, in war time or peace time, and by giving out that they are only considering the ways and means of opening up Palestine to the Jews, they easily escape the suspicion of being together on any

* See note on page 95.

other business. The Allies and enemies of the Gentile nations at war thus met and were not molested. It was at a Zionist conference—the sixth, held in 1903—that the recent war was exactly predicted, its progress and outcome indicated, and the relation of the Jews to the Peace Treaty outlined.

That is to say, though Jewish nationalism exists, its enshrinement in a state to be set up in Palestine is not the project that is engaging the whole Jewish nation now. The Jews will not move to Palestine just yet; it may be said that they will not move at all merely because of the Zionist movement. Quite another motive will be the cause of the exodus out of the Gentile nations, when the time for that exodus fully comes.

As Donald A. Cameron, late British Consul-General at Alexandra, a man fully in sympathy with Zionism and much quoted in the Jewish press, says: "The Jewish immigrants (into Palestine) will tire of taking in one another's washing at three per cent, of winning one another's money in the family, and their sons will hasten by train and steamer to win 10 per cent in Egypt * * * The Jew by himself in Palestine will eat his head off; he will kick his stable to pieces." Undoubtedly the time for the exodus—at least the motive for the exodus—is not yet here.

The political aspect of the Jewish Question which is now engaging at least three of the great nations—France, Great Britain and the United States—has to do with matters of the present organization of the Jewish nation. Must it wait until it reaches Palestine to have a State, or is it an organized State now? Does Jewry know what it is doing? Has it a "foreign policy" with regard to the Gentiles? Has it a department which is executing that foreign policy? Has this Jewish State, visible or invisible, if it exists, a head? Has it a Council of State? And if any of these things is so, who is aware of it?

The first impulsive answer of the Gentile mind would be "No" to all these questions—it is a Gentile habit to answer impulsively. Never having been trained in secrets or invisible unity, the Gentile immediately concludes that such things cannot be, if for no other reason than that they have not crossed his path and advertised themselves.

The questions, however, answered thus, require some explanation of the circumstances which are visible to all men. If there is no deliberate combination of Jews in the world, then the control which they have achieved and the uniformity of the policies which they follow must be the simple result, not of deliberate decisions, but of a similar nature in all of them working out the same way. Thus, we might say that as a love for adventure on the water drove the Britisher forth, so it made him the world's great colonist. Not that he deliberately sat down with himself and in formal manner resolved that he would become a colonizer, but the natural outworking of his genius resulted that way. But would this be a sufficient account of the British Empire?

Doubtless the Jews have the genius to do, wherever they go, the things in which we see them excel. But does this account for the relations which exist between the Jews of every country, for their world councils, for their amazing foreknowledge of stupendous events which break with shattering surprise on the rest of the world, for the smoothness and preparedness with which they appear, at a given time in Paris, with a world program on which they all agree?

The world has long suspected—at first only a few, then the secret departments of the governments, next the intellectuals among the people, now more and more the common people themselves—that not only are the Jews a nation distinct from all the other nations and mysteriously unable to sink their nationality by any means they or the world may adopt to this end, but that they also constitute a state; that they are nationally conscious, not only, but consciously united for a common defense and for a common purpose. Revert to Theodor Herzl's definition of the Jewish nation, as held to gether by a common enemy, and then reflect that this common enemy is the Gentile world. Does this people which knows itself to be a nation remain loosely unorganized in the face of that fact? It would hardly be like Jewish astuteness in other fields. When you see how closely the Jews are united by various organizations in the United States, and when you see how with practiced hand they bring those organizations to bear as if with tried confidence in their pressure, it is at least not inconceivable that what can be done within a country can be done, or has been done, between all the countries where the Jews live.

At any rate, in the *American Hebrew* of June 25, 1920, Herman Bernstein writes thus: "About a year ago a representative of the Department of Justice submitted to me a copy of the manuscript of 'The Jewish Peril' by Professor Nilus, and asked for my opinion of the work. He said that the manuscript was a translation of a Russian book published in 1905 which was later suppressed. The manuscript was supposed to contain 'protocols' of the Wise Men of Zion and was supposed to have been read by Dr. Herzl at a secret conference of the Zionist Congress at Basle. He expressed the opinion that the work was probably that of Dr. Theodor Herzl. . . . . He said that some American Senators who had seen the manuscript were amazed to find that so many years ago a scheme had been elaborated by the Jews which is now being carried out, and that Bolshevism had been planned years ago by Jews who sought to destroy the world."

This quotation is made merely to put on record the fact that it was a representative of the Department of Justice of the United States Government, who introduced this document to Mr. Bernstein, and expressed a certain opinion upon it, namely, "that the work was probably that of Dr. Theodor Herzl." Also that "some American Senators" were amazed to note the comparison between what a publication of the year 1905 proposed and what the year 1920 revealed.

The incident is all the more preoccupying because it occurred by action of the representative of a government who today is very largely in the hands of, or under the influence of, Jewish interests. It is more than probable that as soon as the activity became known, the investigator was stopped. But it is equally probable that whatever orders may have been given and apparently obeyed, the investigation may not have stopped.

The United States Government was a little late in the matter, however. At least four other world powers had preceded it, some by many years. A copy of the Protocols was deposited in the British Museum and bears on it the stamp of that institution, "August 10, 1906." The notes themselves probably date from 1896, or the year of the utterances previously quoted from Dr. Herzl. The first Zionist Congress convened in 1897.

The document was published in England recently under auspices that challenged attention for it, in spite of the unfortunate title under which it appeared. Eyre and Spottiswoode are the appointed printers to the British Government, and it was they who brought out the pamphlet. It was as if the Government Printing Office at Washington should issue them in this country. While there was the usual outcry by the Jewish press, the London *Times* in a review pronounced all the Jewish counter-attacks as "unsatisfactory."

The *Times* noticed what will probably be the case in this country also that the Jewish defenders leave the text of the protocols alone, while they lay heavy emphasis on the fact of their anonymity. When they refer to the substance of the document at all there is one form of words which recurs very often—"it is the work of a criminal or a madman."

The protocols, without name attached, appearing for the most part in manuscripts here and there, laboriously copied out from hand to hand, being sponsored by no authority that was willing to stand behind it, assiduously studied in the secret departments of the governments and passed from one to another among higher officials, have lived on and on, increasing in power and prestige by the sheer force of their contents. A marvelous achievement for either a criminal or a madman! The only evidence it has is that which it carries within it, and that internal evidence is, as the London *Times* points out, the point on which attention is to be focused, and the very point from which Jewish effort has been expended to draw us away.

The interest of the Protocols at this time is their bearing on the questions: Have the Jews an organized world system? What is its policy? How is it being worked?

These questions all receive full attention in the Protocols. Whosoever was the mind that conceived them possessed a knowledge of human nature, of history and of statecraft which is dazzling in its brilliant completeness, and terrible in the objects to which it turns its powers. Neither a madman nor an intentional criminal, but more likely a super-mind mastered by devotion to a people and a faith could be the author, if indeed one mind alone conceived them. It is too terribly real for fiction, too well-sustained for speculation, too deep in its knowledge of the secret springs of life for forgery.

Jewish attacks upon it thus far make much of the fact that it came out of Russia. That is hardly true. It came *by way of Russia*. It was incorporated in a Russian book published about 1905 by a Professor Nilus, who attempted to interpret the Protocols by events then going forward in Russia. This publication and interpretation gave it a Russian tinge which has been useful to Jewish propagandists in this country and England, because these same propagandists have been very successful in establishing in Anglo-Saxon mentalities a certain atmosphere of thought surrounding the idea of Russia and Russians. One of the biggest humbugs ever foisted on the world has been that foisted by Jewish propagandists, principally on the American public, with regard to the temper and genius of the truly Russian people. So, to intimate that the Protocols are Russian, is partially to discredit them.

The internal evidence makes it clear that the Protocols were not written by a Russian, nor originally in the Russian language, nor under the influence of Russian conditions. But they found their way to Russia and were first published there. They have been found by diplomatic officers in manuscript in all parts of the world. Wherever Jewish power is able to do so, it has suppressed them, sometimes under the supreme penalty.

Their persistence is a fact which challenges the mind. Jewish apologists may explain that persistence on the ground that the Protocols feed the anti-Semitic temper, and therefore are preserved for that service. Certainly there was no wide nor deep anti-Semitic temper in the United States to be fed or that felt the greed for agreeable lies to keep itself alive. The progress of the Protocols in the United States can only be explained on the ground that they supply light and give meaning to certain previously observed facts, and that this light and meaning is so startling as to give a certain standing and importance to these otherwise unaccredited documents. Sheer lies do not live long, their power soon dies. These Protocols are more alive than ever. They have penetrated higher places than ever before. They have compelled a more serious attitude to them than ever before.

The Protocols would not be more worthy of study if they bore, say, the name of Theodor Herzl. Their anonymity does not decrease their power any more than the omission of a painter's signature detracts from the art value of a painting. Indeed, the Protocols are better without a known source. For if it were definitely known that in France or Switzerland in the year 1896, or thereabouts, a group of International Jews, assembled in conference, drew up a program of world conquest it would still have to be shown that such a program was more than a mere vagary, that it was confirmed at large by efforts to fulfill it. The Protocols are a World Program—there is no doubt anywhere of that. Whose program, is stated within the articles themselves. But as for outer confirmation, which would be the more valuable—a signature, or six signatures, or twenty signatures, or a 25-year unbroken line of effort fulfilling that program?

The point of interest for this and other countries is not that a "criminal or a madman" conceived such a program, but that, when conceived, this program found means of getting itself fulfilled in its most important particulars. The document is comparatively unimportant; the conditions to which it calls attention are of a very high degree of importance.

NOTE: The statements indicated are those of non-Zionist Jews. The real Jewish program is that program which is executed. It was the Zionist program that was followed by the Peace Conference. It must therefore be regarded as the official program.

Issue of July 10, 1920.

*"We are a people—One people . . . . When we sink, we become a revolutionary proletariat, the subordinate officers of a revolutionary party; when we rise, there rises also our terrible power of the purse."*

*—Theodor Herzl, "A Jewish State," pp. 5, 23.*

# The Historic Basis of Jewish Imperialism

A GREAT unloosening of speech with reference to the Jewish Question and the Jewish program for world power has occurred in this country since the beginning of this series of articles. It is now possible to pronounce the word "Jew" in a perfectly serious discussion, without timidity, or without intimidation. Heretofore that has been regarded as the special prerogative of the Jewish publicists themselves and they have used the name exclusively in well-organized and favorable propaganda. They can oust portions of Shakespeare from the public schools on the ground that the Jews are offended; they can demand the removal of one of Sargent's paintings from the Boston Library because it represents the Synagogue in a decline. But when anything emanates from the Gentile side which indicates that the Gentile is also conscious of the Jew, then the charge of prejudice is instantly and strongly made. The effect of that in this country has been a ban on speech which has had few parallels in our history. Recently at a banquet a speaker used the term "Jews" in reference to the actions of a group of Jewish bankers. A Jewish guest leaped to his feet demanding to know if the speaker considered it "American" to single out a race that way. The speaker replied, "I do, sir," and received the approval of the audience. In that particular part of the country, business men's tongues had been tied for years by the unwritten law that Jews must never be singled out as Jews.

No one would have predicted a year ago that a newspaper like the Chicago *Tribune* could have convinced itself that it was good newspaper policy to print in the first column of its first page a copyrighted article on the Jewish program for world rule, printing the word "Jew" in large letters in its headline, and abstaining from editorial retouching of the word "Jew" in the body of the article. The usual plan is to do what an eastern newspaper did when dealing with the same subject: wherever the term "international Jew" occurred in the article which it printed, it was retouched to "financiers."

The Chicago *Tribune*, however, on Saturday, June 19, 1920, printed in the first column of the first page a cable dispatch from John Clayton, its special correspondent, under the heading: "Trotsky Leads Jew-Radicals to World Rule. Bolshevism Only a Tool for His Scheme."

The first paragraph reads as follows:

> "For the last two years army intelligence officers, members of the various secret service organizations of the Entente, have been bringing in reports of a world revolutionary movement other than Bolshevism. At first these reports confused the two, but latterly the lines they have taken have begun to be more and more clear."

As previously stated in THE DEARBORN INDEPENDENT, our own secret service is one of these, though there is reason to believe that because of the influence of Jews upon the government these investigations were not pursued with the persistency that might otherwise have been given them However, we know from Jewish sources, not to mention any other, that the Department of Justice of the United States was at one time interested enough to make inquiries.

What the *Tribune* writer does in the above paragraph is to show that this interest has been sustained for two years by officials of the Entente, a fact which ought to be borne in mind by those who declare that the whole matter is of German instigation. The emergence of the Jewish Question into American thought was immediately met by the statement from Jewish sources that it was a German importation, and that the anti-Semitism which flowed over Germany and resulted in cleaning out the overwhelming Jewish revolutionary influences from the new German Government, was only a trick to throw the blame for the defeat of Germany on the Jews. American rabbis are even now unitedly preaching that history shows that every great war is followed by a new "attack" on the Jews. It is undoubtedly a fact that every war newly opens the people's eyes to the power which international Jewish financiers exert with reference to war—and it would seem that such a fact is worthy of a better explanation than that of "prejudice." However, as the *Tribune* article shows, and as all the facts confirm, the interest is not confined to the German side; indeed, it is not even strongest there. It is "the various secret service organizations of the Entente" that have been most active in the matter.

The second paragraph further distinguishes between Bolshevism and Jewish imperialism:

> "Bolshevism aims for the overthrow of existing society and the establishment of an international brotherhood of men who work with their hands as rulers of the world. The second movement aims for the establishment of a *new racial domination of the world.* So far as the British, French and our own department's inquiry have been able to trace, the moving spirits in the second scheme are Jewish radicals."

Other statements in the article are:

> "Within the ranks of communism is a group of this party, but it does not stop there. To its leaders, communism is only an incident."

(This will recall the statement of Lord Eustace Percy, quoted last week from the Canadian *Jewish Chronicle*—"Not because the Jew cares for the positive side of radical philosophy, not because he desires to be a partaker in Gentile nationalism or Gentile democracy, but because no existing Gentile system of government is anything but distasteful to him.")

> "They are ready to use the Islamic revolt, hatred by the central empires for England, Japan's designs on India, and commercial rivalry between America and Japan."

> "As any movement of world revolution must be, this is primarily anti-Anglo-Saxon."

> "The organization of the world Jewish-radical movement has been perfected in almost every land."

> "The aims of the Jewish-radical party have nothing of altruism behind them beyond liberation of their own race."

It will be conceded that these are rather startling statements. If they were found in a propagandist publication of no responsibility, the average reader might pass them by as preposterous, so little does the average reader know of the secret influences which shape his life and frame his problems. But appearing in a great newspaper, they must receive a different evaluation.

Nor did the *Tribune* stop at the news article. On June 21, 1920, an editorial appeared entitled "World Mischief." The editorial is evidently an effort to prevent possible misunderstanding of what the news article was driving at.

"The Jewish phase of the movement, he asserts, aims at *a new racial domination of the world* . . ."

The *Tribune* also says that while it is perhaps natural for the Jews of other countries to be engaged in this "world mischief," the Jews of England and the United States "are loyal nationalists and conservative upholders of the national traditions." It were well if this were true. Perhaps it is true of tens of thousands of Jews as individuals; it certainly is not true of those internationalists who pull the strings of all the governments and who during the last six tragic years have been meddling with world affairs in a way which must soon be plainly told. The unfortunate circumstance is that all the American and English Jews must for a time feel a distress which no one desires them to feel, which everyone would do much to save them from, but which seems inevitable until the whole story is told and until the mass of the Jews themselves cut off from their name and support some who now receive their deepest homage.

It is worth while observing the contrasts and similarities between the Gentile and Jewish reaction to this alleged movement to establish a Jewish imperialism over the world. Jewish publicists first deny it without qualification. It is all false, all a lie, all hatched up by enemies of the Jews in order to stir up hatred and murder. As the evidence accumulates, the Jewish tone changes: "Well, suppose it is true," the publicists say; "is it any wonder that the poor oppressed Jews, driven to madness through their sufferings, should dream dreams of overthrowing their enemies and placing themselves in the seat of authority?"

The Gentile mind, confronted with the statement, says: "Yes, but they are Russian Jews. Don't mind them. American Jews are all right. They would never be taken in by anything like that." Going a little deeper into the subject, the Gentile mind is forced to admit the existence of some kind of a subversive world movement, the power of which has shaken even this country, and that the moving spirits in it are revolutionary Jews. And then the tendency from that point forward is either to fall in with the theory that the movement is really Jewish in its origin, agitation, execution and purpose, or to set up the theory that it is a "world movement" undoubtedly, but only incidentally Jewish. The end of both Jewish and Gentile reaction is an admission that something answering to the movement charged actually exists.

For example, the *Christian Science Monitor*, whose standard as a newspaper no one will question, has this to say in a lengthy editorial on the subject:

> "In spite of this, it would be a tremendous mistake to conclude that the Jewish peril, given another name and atmosphere, does not exist. It might, indeed, be renamed, out of one of the grandest of the books of the Old Testament, 'the terror by night,' for it is, essentially, the Psalmist's concept of the forces of mental evil at which, consciously or unconsciously, Professor Nilus is aiming. In other words, that a secret international political organization exists, working unremittingly by means of its Bureau of Psychology, though the world which should be awake to it is entirely asleep to it, is, to the man who can read the signs of the times, a thing unquestionable."

The *Monitor* gives warning against prejudice and disregard of the laws of evidence which is exceedingly timely and is, indeed, the desire of anyone who has ever undertaken to deal with this subject, but too often it is a disregard of facts and not of evidence that makes the difficulty. It is safe to say that most of the prejudice today is *against* the facts, it has not been caused *by* them.

There are two preconceptions to be guarded against in making an approach to this question. One is that the Jewish imperialistic program, if such a thing exists, is of recent origin. Upon the mere mention of such a program, Gentiles are likely to think that it was formulated last week, or last year, or within recent time. That need not be the case at all, and in Jewish matters it is very likely not to be the case. It is very easy to see how, if the program were to be formulated today, it would be wholly different from the one which is to be considered. The kind of program that would be made today indeed exists too, but it is not to be compared in extent and profundity with that which has existed for a very long time. Perfect constitutions of invisible governments are not the creations of secret conventions; they are the accumulated thought and experience of centuries. Moreover, no matter how prone a modern generation may be to disregard such things, the mere fact that they may have existed as a secret racial ideal for centuries is a powerful argument for their respectable acceptance, if not active execution, by the generation that now is. There is no idea deeper in Judaism than that Jews constitute a Chosen People and that their future is to be more glorious than their past. A large part of the Christian world accepts that, too, and it may well be true, but in a moral universe it cannot come to pass by the methods which have been and are being used.

But to mention the ancient lineage of the idea of the Chosen People is merely to suggest that of all the programs that may have gathered round it to assist its full historical realization, it is not strange that there should be one very old one to which the wisest minds of Israel have contributed their best of mind and heart to insure its success. That there is such a plan has been the belief of many deep delvers in the hidden things of the world, and that such a plan has at times had its dress rehearsals, so to speak, on a limited stage, as if in preparation for its grand finale on the universal stage, is another belief held by men at whose knowledge it is impossible to cavil.

So, then, it may be that we are dealing with something for which present-day Jews, even the more important internationalists, are not originally responsible. It may have come to them as part of their ancient Jewish inheritance. Certainly, if it were a mere modern thing, hastily conceived and thrown together after the modern fashion, it could be expected to disappear in the same era which saw it born.

Another preconception to be guarded against is that every Jew one meets has secret knowledge of this program. That is not the case. With the general idea of the ultimate triumph of Israel every Jew who has retained contact with his people is familiar, but with the special plans which for centuries have existed in formulated form for the attainment of that triumph, the average Jew is no more familiar than anyone else—no more so than was the average German with the secret plans of the Pan-Germanic party whose ideas started and guided the recent war. The average Jew enters into the plans of the secret group just to this extent, except in specially selected cases: It is perfectly understood that the consummation of the Jewish triumph will not be distasteful to any Jew, and if the methods to be used toward the end are a bit violent, every Jew can be depended upon to see in that violence a very insufficient retribution visited upon the Gentile world for the sufferings which it has caused the sons of Judah throughout the centuries.

Still, with even these preconceptions guarded against, there is no escape from the conclusion that if such a program of Jewish world imperialism exists today, it must exist with the cognizance and active support of certain individuals, and that these groups of individuals must have somewhere an official head.

This is, perhaps, the one point at which more investigators stop than at any other. The idea of a Jewish autocrat is too strange for the mind which has not been much in contact with the main question. And yet there is no race which more instinctively supports autocracy than does the Jewish race, no race which more craves and respects position. It is their sense of the value of position which explains the main course their activities take. The Jew is primarily a money-maker for the reason that up to this time money is the only means he knows by which to gain position. The Jews who have gained position for any other reason are comparatively few. This is not a Gentile gibe; it is the position of a famous Anglo-Jewish physician, Dr. Barnard Von Oven, who wrote: "All other means of distinction are denied him; he must rise by wealth, or not at all. And if, as he well knows, to insure wealth will be to insure rank, respect and attention in society, does the blame rest with him who endeavors to acquire wealth for the distinction which it will purchase, or with that society which so readily bows down to the shrine of Mammon?"

The Jew is not averse to kings, only to the state of things which prevents a Jewish king. The future autocrat of the world is to be a Jewish king, sitting upon the throne of David, so ancient prophecies and the documents of the imperialistic program agree.

Is such a king in the world now? If not, the men who could choose a king are in the world. There has been no king of the Jews since before the Christian Era, but until about the eleventh century there were Princes of the Exile, those who represented the headship of the Jews who were dispersed through the nations. They were and still are called "exilarchs," or Princes of the Exile. They were attended by the wise men of Israel, they held court, they gave the law to their people. They lived abroad wherever their circumstances or convenience dictated, in Christian or Mohammedan countries. Whether the office was discontinued with the last publicly known exilarch or merely disappeared from the surface of history, whether today it is entirely abandoned or exists in another form, are questions which must wait. That there are offices of world jurisdiction held by Jews is well known. That there are world organizations of Jews—organizations, that is, within the very strong solidarity of the Jewish nation itself—is well known. That there is world unity on certain Jewish activities, defensive and offensive, is well known. There is nothing in the condition or thought of the Jews which would render the existence today of an exilarch distasteful to them; indeed, the thought would be very comfortable.

The Jewish Encyclopedia remarks: "Curiously enough, the exilarchs are still mentioned in the Sabbath services of the Ashkenazim ritual * * * The Jews of the Sephardic ritual have not preserved this anachronism, nor was it retained in most of the Reform synagogues of the nineteenth century."

Is there, then, a Jewish Sanhedrin?—a governing or counseling body of Jews who take oversight of the affairs of their people throughout the world?

The Jewish Sanhedrin was a most interesting institution. Its origin and method of constitution are obscure. It consisted of 71 members, with the president, and performed the functions of a political senate. There is nothing to show whence the Sanhedrin derived its authority. It was not an elective body. It was not democratic. It was not representative. It was not responsible to the people. In these qualities, it was typically Jewish. The Sanhedrin was chosen by the prince or priest, not with the purpose of safeguarding the people's interest, but to assist the ruler in the work of administration. It was thus assembled by call, or it was self-perpetuating, calling its own members. The arrangement seems to have been that well-known device by which an aristocracy can maintain itself in power whatever the political construction of the nation may be. The Jewish Encyclopedia says: "The Sanhedrin, which was entirely aristocratic in character, probably assumed its own authority, since it was composed of members of the most influential families of the nobility and priesthood."

This body was flanked by a similar body, which governed the religious interests of the nation, the members being drawn apparently from classes nearer the common people.

The Sanhedrin exercised authority not only over the Jews of Palestine, but wherever they were scattered throughout the world. As a senate exercising direct political authority, it ceased with the downfall of the Jewish State in the year 70, but there are indications of its continuance as an advisory body down to the fourth century.

In 1806, in order to satisfy the mind of Napoleon upon some questions which had arisen concerning the Jews, an Assembly of Notables was called, whose membership consisted of prominent Jews of France. They, in turn, to bring the sanction of all Jewry to the answers which they should give Napoleon, convoked the Sanhedrin. The Sanhedrin assembled in Paris on February 9, 1807. It followed the prescribed ancient forms; it was comprised of Jews from all parts of Europe; it was assembled to put the whole authority of Jewry behind any compact the French Jews may have been able to make with Napoleon.

In putting forth its decisions, this Sanhedrin of 1807 declared that it was in all respects like the ancient Sanhedrin, "a legal assembly vested with power of passing ordinances in order to promote the welfare of Israel."

The significance of these facts is this: Whatever the leaders of the Jews may do today in the way of maintaining the policy and constitution of Israel, would not constitute a new departure. It would not signify a new attitude. It would not be evidence of a new plan.

It would be entirely natural, Jewish solidarity being what it is, that the Sanhedrin should still be continued. The ancient Sanhedrin appears to have had a group of ten who were somewhat exalted in importance above the rest; it would be perfectly natural if the leaders of the Jews were today divided into committees, by countries or by objects.

There are always being held, year by year, world meetings of the principal Jews of all lands. They come together whenever called, to the disregard of everything else. Great judges from the high courts of the various countries, international financiers, Jewish orators of the "liberal type" who have the ear of the Gentiles, political maneuverers from all the parties represented in the world, they assemble wherever they will, and the subjects of their deliberations are made known only to the extent they will. It is not to be supposed that all of the attendants on these conventions are members of the inner circle. The list of delegates will show scores of persons with whom no one would associate Lord Reading and Judge Brandeis. If the modern Sanhedrin meets, and it would be the most natural thing in the world if it should, we may be sure it meets within the closed circle of those persons which the Jewish aristocracy of money, intellect and power approves.

The machinery of a Jewish world government exists ready-made. The Jew is convinced that he has the best religion, the best morality, the best method of education, the best social standards, the best ideal of government. He would not have to go outside the circle of that which he considers best to get anything which he may need to advance the welfare of his people, or to execute any program which may have to do with the outside world.

It is the ancient machinery that the international Jew uses in all those activities which he permits the world to see in part. There are gatherings of the financial, political and intellectual chief rulers of the Jews. These gatherings are announced for one or another thing—sometimes. Sometimes there is a gathering of Jews in a world capital, with no announced purpose. They all appear in one city, confer and depart.

Whether there is a recognized head to all of this is yet to be disclosed. There can be little doubt, however, as to the existence of what may be called a "foreign policy," that is, a definite point of view and plan of action with reference to the Gentile world. The Jew feels that he is in the midst of enemies, but he also feels that he is a member of a people—"one people." He must have some policy with regard to the outer world. He cannot help but consider present conditions, he cannot consider them without being stirred to speculate upon what the outcome must be, and he cannot speculate on the outcome without in some manner endeavoring to make it as he would like it to be.

The invisible government of the Jews, its attitude toward the Gentile world, its policy with regard to the future, are not, then, the abnormal things that some would make them appear. Given the Jewish position, they are of all things most natural. Jewish existence in this world is not such as woos the Jew into sleepy contentment; it is such as stirs him into organization against future contingencies and into programs which may shape those contingencies to the benefit of his race. That there should be a Sanhedrin of the Jews, a world body of the leading men of all countries; that there should even be an exilarch, a visible and recognized head of the Sanhedrin, mystically foreshadowing the autocrat to come: that there should even be a world program, just as every government has its foreign policy, are not strange, uncanny suppositions. They grow normally out of the situation itself.

And it is also natural that not every Jew should know this. The Sanhedrin always was the aristocracy, and would be today. When rabbis cry from their pulpits that they know nothing about this thing, they are doubtless telling the truth. What the international Jew depends upon is the likelihood of every Jew approving that which brings power and prestige to his people. At any rate, it is well enough known that however little the ordinary Jewish leader may have been told about world programs, he regards with the greatest respect and confidence the very men who must put these programs through, if these exist at all.

The twenty-fourth Protocol of the Learned Elders of Zion has this to say:

"Now I will discuss the manner in which the roots of the house of King David will penetrate to the deepest strata of the earth. This dynasty, even to this day, has given the power of controlling world affairs to our wise men, the educational directors of all human thought."

This would indicate, if reliable, that, as the Protocol goes on to recite, the Autocrat himself has not appeared, but the dynasty, or the Davidic line in which he must appear, have entrusted the work of preparing for him to the Wise Men of Zion. These wise men are represented not only as preparing those who exercise rulership over Judaism's affairs, but also as framing and influencing the world's thought toward ends which shall be propitious to these plans. Whatever may be hidden in the program, it is certain that its execution or the effects of its execution cannot be hidden. Therefore, it may be possible to find in the outer world the clues which, traced back to their source, reveal the existence of a program, whose promise for the world, good or bad, ought to be widely known.

Issue of July 17, 1920.

# X.

# An Introduction to the "Jewish Protocols"

THE documents most frequently mentioned by those who are interested in the theory of Jewish World Power rather than in the actual operation of that power in the world today, are those 24 documents known as "The Protocols of the Learned Elders of Zion."

The Protocols have attracted much attention in Europe, having become the center of an important storm of opinion in England only recently, but discussion of them in the United States has been limited. These are the documents concerning which the Department of Justice was making inquiries more than a year ago, and which were given publication in London by Eyre and Spottiswoode, the official printers to the British Government.

Who it was that first entitled these documents with the name of the "Elders of Zion" is not known. It would be possible without serious mutilation of the documents to remove all hint of Jewish authorship, and yet retain all the main points of the most comprehensive program for world subjugation that has ever come to public knowledge.

Yet it must be said that thus to eliminate all hint of Jewish authorship would be to bring out a number of contradictions which do not exist in the Protocols in their present form. The purpose of the plan revealed in the Protocols is to undermine all authority in order that a new authority in the form of autocracy may be set up. Such a plan could not emanate from a ruling class which already possessed authority, although it might emanate from anarchists. But anarchists do not avow autocracy as the ultimate condition they seek. The authors might be conceived as a company of French Subversives such as existed at the time of the French Revolution and had the infamous Duc d'Orleans as their leader, but this would involve a contradiction between the fact that those Subversives have passed away, and the fact that the program announced in these Protocols is being steadily carried out, not only in France, but throughout Europe, and very noticeably in the United States.

In their present form which bears evidence of being their original form, there is no contradiction. The allegation of Jewish authorship seems essential to the consistency of the plan.

If these documents were the forgeries which Jewish apologists claim them to be, the forgers would probably have taken pains to make Jewish authorship so clear that their anti-Semitic purpose could easily have been detected. But only twice is the term "Jew" used in them. After one has read much further than the average reader usually cares to go into such matters, one comes upon the plans for the establishment of the World Autocrat, and only then it is made clear of what lineage he is to be.

But all through the documents there is left no doubt as to the people against whom the plan is aimed. It is not aimed against aristocracy as such. It is not aimed against capital as such. It is not aimed against government as such. Very definite provisions are made for the enlistment of aristocracy, capital and government for the execution of the plan. It is aimed against the people of the world who are called "Gentiles." It is the frequent mention of "Gentiles" that really decides the purpose of the documents. Most of the destructive type of "liberal" plans aim at the enlistment of the people as helpers; this plan aims at the degeneration of the people in order that they may be reduced to confusion of mind and thus manipulated. Popular movements of a "liberal" kind are to be encouraged, all the disruptive philosophies in religion, economics, politics and domestic life are to be sown and watered, for the purpose of so disintegrating social solidarity that a definite plan, herein set forth, may be put through without notice, and the people then molded to it when the fallacy of these philosophies is shown.

The formula of speech is not, "We Jews will do this," but "The Gentiles will be made to think and do these things." With the exception of a few instances in the closing Protocols, the only distinctive racial term used is "Gentiles."

To illustrate: the first indication of this kind comes in the first Protocol in this way:

"The great qualities of the people—honesty and frankness—are essentially vices in politics, because they dethrone more surely and more certainly than does the strongest enemy. These qualities are attributes of Gentile rule; we certainly must not be guided by them."

And again:

"On the ruins of the hereditary aristocracy of the Gentiles we have set up the aristocracy of our educated class, and over all the aristocracy of money. We have established the basis of this new aristocracy on the basis of riches, which we control, and on the science guided by our wise men."

Again:

"We will force up wages, which however will be of no benefit to workers, for we at the same time will cause a rise in the prices of prime necessities, pretending that this is due to the decline of agriculture and of cattle raising. We will also artfully and deeply undermine the sources of production by instilling in the workmen ideas of anarchy and encourage them in the use of alcohol, at the same time taking measures to drive all the intellectual forces of the Gentiles from the land."

(A forger with anti-Semitic malice might have written this any time within the last five years, but these words were in print at least 14 years ago according to British evidence, a copy having been in the British Museum since 1906, and they were circulated in Russia a number of years prior.)

The above point continues: "That the true situation shall not be noticed by the Gentiles prematurely we will mask it by a pretended effort to serve the working classes and promote great economic principles, for which an active propaganda will be carried on through our economic theories."

These quotations will illustrate the style of the Protocols in making reference to the parties involved. It is "we" for the writers, and "Gentiles" for those who are being written about. This is brought out very clearly in the Fourteenth Protocol:

> "In this divergence between the Gentiles and ourselves in ability to think and reason is to be seen clearly the seal of our election as the chosen people, as higher human beings, in contrast with the Gentiles who have merely instinctive and animal minds. They observe, but they do not foresee, and they invent nothing (except perhaps material things). It is clear from this that nature herself predestined us to rule and guide the world."

This, of course, has been the Jewish method of dividing humanity from the earliest times. The world was only Jew and Gentile; all that was not Jew was Gentile.

The use of the word Jew in the Protocol may be illustrated by this passage in the eighth section:

> "For the time being, until it will be safe to give responsible government positions to our brother Jews, we shall entrust them to people whose past and whose characters are such that there is an abyss between them and the people."

This is the practice known as using "Gentile fronts" which is extensively practiced in the financial world today in order to cover up the evidences of Jewish control. How much progress has been made since these words were written is indicated by the occurrence at the San Francisco convention when the name of Judge Brandeis was proposed for President. It is reasonably to be expected that the public mind will be made more and more familiar with the idea of Jewish occupancy—which will be really a short step from the present degree of influence which the Jews exercise—of the highest office in the government. There is no function of the American Presidency in which the Jews have not already secretly assisted in a very important degree. Actual occupancy of the office is not necessary to enhance their power, but to promote certain things which parallel very closely the plans outlined in the Protocols now before us.

Another point which the reader of the Protocols will notice is that the tone of exhortation is entirely absent from these documents. They are not propaganda. They are not efforts to stimulate the ambitions or activity of those to whom they are addressed. They are as cool as a legal paper and as matter-of-fact as a table of statistics. There is none of the "Let us rise, my brothers" stuff about them. There is no "Down with the Gentiles" hysteria. These Protocols, if indeed they were made by Jews and confided to Jews, or if they do contain certain principles of a Jewish World Program, were certainly not intended for the firebrands but for the carefully prepared and tested initiates of the higher groups.

Jewish apologists have asked, "Is it conceivable that if there were such a world program on the part of the Jews, they would reduce it to writing and publish it?" But there is no evidence that these Protocols were ever uttered otherwise than in *spoken* words by those who put them forth. The Protocols as we have them are apparently the notes of lectures which were made by someone who heard them. Some of them are lengthy; some of them are brief. The assertion which has always been made in connection with the Protocols since they have become known is that they are the notes of lectures delivered to Jewish students presumably somewhere in France or Switzerland. The attempt to make them appear to be of Russian origin is absolutely forestalled by the point of view, the references to the times and certain grammatical indications.

The tone certainly fits the supposition that they were originally lectures given to students, for their purpose is clearly *not to get a program accepted* but to *give information concerning* a program which is represented as being already in process of fulfillment. There is no invitation to join forces or to offer opinions. Indeed it is specifically announced that neither discussion nor opinions are desired. ("While preaching liberalism to the Gentiles, we shall hold our own people and our own agents in unquestioning obedience." "The scheme of administration must emanate from a single brain * * * Therefore, we may *know* the plan of action, but we must not *discuss* it, lest we destroy its unique character * * * The inspired work of our leader therefore must not be thrown before a crowd to be torn to pieces, or even before a limited group.")

Moreover, taking the Protocols at their face value, it is evident that the program outlined in these lecture notes was not a new one at the time the lectures were given. There is no evidence of its being of recent arrangement. There is almost the tone of a tradition, or a religion, in it all, as if it had been handed down from generation to generation through the medium of specially trusted and initiated men. There is no note of new discovery or fresh enthusiasm in it, but the certitude and calmness of facts long known and policies long confirmed by experiment.

This point of the age of the program is touched upon at least twice in the Protocols themselves. In the First Protocol this paragraph occurs:

> "Already *in ancient times* we were the first to shout the words, 'Liberty, Equality, Fraternity,' among the people. These words have been repeated many times since by unconscious poll-parrots, flocking from all sides to this bait, with which they have ruined the prosperity of the world and true personal freedom * * * The presumably clever and intelligent Gentiles did not understand the symbolism of the uttered words; did not observe their contradiction in meaning; did not notice that in nature there is no equality * * *."

The other reference to the program's finality is found in the Thirteenth Protocol:

> "Questions of policy, however, are permitted to no one except those who have originated the policy and have directed it *for many centuries*."

Can this be a reference to a secret Jewish Sanhedrin, self-perpetuating within a certain Jewish caste from generation to generation?

Again, it must be said that the originators and directors here referred to cannot be at present any ruling caste, for all that the program contemplates is directly opposed to the interests of such a caste. It cannot refer to any national aristocratic group, like the Junkers of Germany, for the methods which are proposed are the very ones which would render powerless such a group. It cannot refer to any but a people who have no government, who have everything to gain and nothing to lose, and who can keep themselves intact amid a crumbling world. There is only one group that answers that description.

Again, a reading of the Protocols makes it clear that the speaker himself was not seeking for honor. There is a complete absence of personal ambition throughout the document. All plans and purposes and expectations are merged in the future of Israel, which future, it would seem, can only be secured by the subtle breaking down of certain world ideas held by the Gentiles. The Protocols speak of what has been done, what was being done at the time these words were given, and what remained to be done. Nothing like them in completeness of detail, in breadth of plan and in deep grasp of the hidden springs of human action has ever been known. They are verily terrible in their mastery of the secrets of life, equally terrible in their consciousness of that mastery. Truly they would merit the opinion which Jews have recently cast upon them, that they were the work of an inspired madman, were it not that what is written in the Protocols in words is also written upon the life of today in deeds and tendencies.

The criticisms which these Protocols pass upon the Gentiles for their stupidity are just. It is impossible to disagree with a single item in the Protocols' description of Gentile mentality and veniality. Even the most astute of the Gentile thinkers have been fooled into receiving as the motions of progress what has only been insinuated into the common human mind by the most insidious systems of propaganda.

It is true that here and there a thinker has arisen to say that science so-called was not science at all. It is true that here and there a thinker has arisen to say that the so-called economic laws both of conservatives and radicals were not laws at all, but artificial inventions. It is true that occasionally a keen observer has asserted that the recent debauch of luxury and extravagance was not due to the natural impulses of the people at all, but was systematically stimulated, foisted upon them by design. It is true that a few have discerned that more than half of what passes for "public opinion" is mere hired applause and booing and has never impressed the public mind.

But even with these clues here and there, for the most part disregarded, there has never been enough continuity and collaboration between those who were awake, to follow all the clues to their source. The chief explanation of the hold which the Protocols have had on many of the leading statesmen of the world for several decades is that they explain whence all these false influences come and what their purpose is. They give a clue to the modern maze. It is now time for the people to know. And whether the Protocols are judged as proving anything concerning the Jews or not, they constitute an education in the way the masses are turned about like sheep by influences which they do not understand. It is almost certain that once the principles of the Protocols are known widely and understood by the people, the criticism which they now rightly make of the Gentile mind will no longer hold good.

It is the purpose of future articles in this series to study these documents and to answer out of their contents all the questions that may arise concerning them.

Before that work is begun, one question should be answered—"Is there likelihood of the program of the Protocols being carried through to success?" The program is successful already. In many of its most important phases it is already a reality. But this need not cause alarm, for the chief weapon to be used against such a program, both in its completed and uncompleted parts, is clear publicity. Let the people *know.* Arousing the people, alarming the people, appealing to the passions of the people is the method of the plan outlined in the Protocols. The antidote is merely *enlightening* the people.

That is the only purpose of these articles. Enlightenment dispels prejudice. It is as desirable to dispel the prejudice of the Jew as of the Gentile. Jewish writers too frequently assume that the prejudice is all on one side. The Protocols themselves ought to have the widest circulation among the Jewish people, in order that they may check those things which are bringing suspicion upon their name.

---

Issue of July 24, 1920.

## XI.

# "Jewish" Estimate of Gentile Human Nature

"Upon completing *this program of our present and future actions,* I will read to you the principles of these theories."—Protocol 16.

"In all that I have discussed with you hitherto, I have endeavored *to indicate carefully the secrets of past and future events and of those momentous occurrences of the near future toward which we are rushing in a stream of great crises,* anticipating the hidden principles of future relationships with the Gentiles and of our financial operations."—Protocol 22.

THE Protocols, which profess themselves to be an outline of the Jewish World Program, are found upon analysis to contain four main divisions. These, however, are not marked in the structure of the documents, but in the thought. There is a fifth, if the object of it all is included, but this object is assumed throughout the Protocols, being only here and there defined in terms. And the four main divisions are great trunks from which there are numerous branches.

There is first what is alleged to be the Jewish conception of human nature, by which is meant Gentile nature. It is inconceivable that such a plan as that which the Protocols set forth could have been evolved by a mind that had not previously based the probability of success on a certain estimate of the ignobility and corruptibility of human nature—which all through the Protocols is referred to as Gentile nature.

Then, secondly, there is the account of what has already been accomplished in the realization of the program—things actually done.

Thirdly, there is a complete instruction in the methods to be used to get the program still further fulfilled—methods which would themselves supply the estimate of human nature upon which the whole fabric is based, if there were nothing else to indicate it.

Fourth, the Protocols contain in detail some of the achievements which, at the time these words were uttered, were yet to be made. Some of these desired things have been achieved in the meantime, for it should be borne in mind that between the year 1905 and the year 1920 there has been time to set many influences in motion and attain many ends. As the second quotation at the head of this article would indicate, the speaker knew that events were "rushing in a stream of great crises," a knowledge which is amply attested by Jewish sources outside the Protocols.

If this series of articles represented a special pleading upon the Jewish Question, the present article would seek to win the reader's confidence by presenting first the set of facts which are described under "secondly" in the above list of main divisions. To begin with the estimate of human nature here disclosed is to court alienation of the reader's interest, especially if the reader be a Gentile. We know from abundant sources what the Jewish estimate of human nature is, and it tallies in all respects with what is disclosed in the Protocols, but it has always been one of the fallacies of Gentile thought that human nature is, now, full of dignity and nobility. There is little question, when the subject is considered in all its lights, that the Jewish conception is right. And so far as these Protocols are concerned, their low estimate of mankind, though harsh to human pride and conceit, are very largely true.

Just to run through the Protocols and select the salient passages in which this view is expressed is to find a pretty complete philosophy of the motives and qualities of human beings.

Take these words from the First Protocol:

> "It should be noted that people with evil instincts are more numerous than those with good ones; therefore, the best results in governing them are attained by intimidation and violence, and not by academic argument. Every man aims for power; everyone desires to be a dictator, if possible; moreover, few would not sacrifice the good of others to attain their own ends."
>
> "People in masses and people of the masses are guided by exceptionally shallow passions, be-

liefs, customs, traditions and sentimental theories and are inclined toward party divisions, a fact which prevents any form of agreement, even when this is founded on a thoroughly logical basis. Every decision of the mob depends upon an accidental or prearranged majority, which, owing to its ignorance of the mysteries of political secrets, gives expression to absurd decisions that introduce anarchy into government."

"In working out an expedient plan of action, it is necessary to take into consideration the meanness, the vacillation, the changeability of the crowd * * * It is necessary to realize that the force of the masses is blind, unreasoning and unintelligent, prone to listen now to the right, and now to the left * * *"

"Our triumph has also been made easier because, in our relations with the people necessary to us, we have always played upon the most sensitive strings of the human mind—on calculation, greed, and the insatiable material desires of men. Each of these human weaknesses, taken separately, is capable of paralyzing initiative and placing the will of the people at the disposal of the purchaser of their activities."

In the Fifth Protocol, this shrewd observation on human nature is to be found:

"In all times, nations as well as individuals, accepted words for acts. They have been satisfied by what is shown them, rarely noticing whether the promise has been followed by fulfillment. For this reason we will organize 'show' institutions which will conspicuously display their devotion to progress."

And this from the Eleventh Protocol:

"The Gentiles are like a flock of sheep * * * They will close their eyes to everything because we will promise them to return all the liberties taken away, after the enemies of peace have been subjugated and all the parties pacified. Is it worth while to speak of how long they will have to wait? For what have we conceived all this program and instilled its measures into the minds of the Gentiles without giving them the possibility of examining its underside, if it is not for the purpose of attaining by circuitous methods that which is unattainable to our scattered race by a direct route?"

Notice also this very shrewd observation upon the "joiners" of secret societies—this estimate being made by the Protocols to indicate how easily these societies may be used to further the plan:

"Usually it is the climbers, careerists and people, generally speaking, who are not serious, who most readily join secret societies, and we shall find them easy to handle and through them operate the mechanism of our projected machine."

The remarks under this head are curtailed by the present writer, because the Protocols make reference to a very important secret order, the mention of whose name in this connection might lead to misunderstanding, and which is therefore reserved for future and fuller attention. It will, however, be of interest to the members of that order to see what the Protocols have to say of it, and then to check up the facts and see how far they correspond with the words.

To continue: "The Gentiles join lodges out of curiosity or in the hope that through them they may worm their way into social distinction * * * We therefore give them this success so that we can take advantage of the self-conceit to which it gives birth and because of which people unconsciously accept our suggestions without examination * * * You cannot imagine to what an extent the most intelligent Gentiles may be brought to a state of unconscious naivete under conditions of self-deceit, and how easy it is to discourage them by the least failure, even the stopping of applause, or to bring them into a state of servile subjection for the sake of regaining it. The Gentiles are as ready to sacrifice their plans for the sake of popular success as our people are to ignore success for the sake of carrying out our plans. This psychology of theirs facilitates the task of directing them."

These are a few of the passages in which this estimate of human or Gentile nature is made out in words. But even if it were not so baldly stated, it could be easily inferred from various items in the program which was depended upon to break up Gentile solidarity and strength.

The method is one of disintegration. Break up the people into parties and sects. Sow abroad the most promising and utopian of ideas and you will do two things: you will always find a group to cling to each idea you throw out; and you will find this partisanship dividing and estranging the various groups. The authors of the Protocols show in detail how this is to be done. Not one idea, but a mass of ideas are to be thrown out, and there is to be no unity among them. The purpose is *not* to get the people thinking one thing, but to think so diversely about so many different things that there will be no unity among them. The result of this will be vast disunity, vast unrest—and that is the result aimed for.

When once the solidarity of Gentile society is broken up—and the name "Gentile society" is perfectly correct, for human society is overwhelmingly Gentile—then this solid wedge of another idea which is not at all affected by the prevailing confusion can make its way unsuspectedly to the place of control. It is well enough known that a body of 20 trained police or soldiers can accomplish more than a disordered mob of a thousand persons. So the minority initiated into the plan can do more with a nation or a world broken into a thousand antagonistic parties, than any of the parties could do. "Divide and rule" is the motto of the Protocols.

The division of society is perfectly easy, according to the estimate of human nature made in these documents. It is human nature to take promises for acts. No one who considered the list of dreams and vagaries and theories that have swayed the people through the centuries can doubt this. The more utopian, the more butterfly-like the theory, the more it commands public adherence. Just as the Protocols say, Gentile society does not scrutinize the origin or the consequences of the theories it adopts. When a theory makes its appeal to the mind, the tendency is to believe that the mind which receives it always had it in essence, and therefore the experience has all the glow of original discovery.

In this manner, theory after theory has been exploited among the masses, theory after theory has been found to be impracticable and has been discarded, but the result is precisely that which the program of the Protocols aims for—with the discarding of each theory, society is a little more broken than it was before. It is a little more helpless before its exploiters. It is a little more confused as to where to look for leadership. As a consequence society falls an easy victim again to a theory which promises it the good it seeks, and the failure of this theory leaves it still more broken. There is no longer any such thing as public opinion. Distrust and division are everywhere. And in the midst of the confusion everyone is dimly aware that there is a higher group that is not divided at all, but is getting exactly what it wants by means of the confusion that obtains all around. It will be shown, as claimed by the Protocols, that most of the disruptive theories abroad in the world today are of Jewish origin; it will also be shown that the one solid unbroken group in the world today, the group that knows where it wants to go and is going there regardless of the condition of society, is the Jewish group.

The most dangerous theory of all is that which explains the rise of theories and the social break-up which follows them. These are all "symptoms of progress" we are told. If so, then "progress" is toward dissolution. No one can predicate the fact of "progress" on the ground that, whereas our fathers made wheels to go round with the blowing wind or the running water, we make them go round by successive small explosions of gasoline. The question of "progress" is, Where are the wheels taking us? Was windmill and water wheel society better or worse than the present society? Was it more unified in its morality? Did it more highly respect law, did it produce a higher and sturdier type of character?

The modern theory of "ferment," that out of all the unrest and change and transvaluation of values a new and better mankind is to be evolved is not borne out by any fact on the horizon. It is palpably a theory whose purpose is to make a seeming good out of that which is undeniable evil. The theories which *cause the disruption* and the theory which *explains the disruption as good*, come from the same source. The whole science of economics, conservative and radical, capitalistic and anarchistic, is of Jewish origin. This is another of the announcements of the Protocols which the facts confirm.

Now, all this is accomplished, not by acts, but by words. The *word-brokers* of the world, those who wish words to do duty for things, in their dealings with the world outside their class, are undoubtedly the Jewish group—the international Jews with which these articles deal—and their philosophy and practice are precisely set forth in the Protocols.

Take for illustration these passages: The first is from the First Protocol:

"Political freedom is an *idea, not a fact.* It is necessary to know how to apply this idea when there is need of a clever bait to gain the support of the people for one's party, if such a party has undertaken to defeat another party already in power. This task is made easier if the opponent has himself been infected by principles of freedom or so-called liberalism, and for the sake of the idea will yield some of his own power."

Or consider this from the Fifth Protocol:

> "To obtain control over public opinion, *it is first necessary to confuse it by the expression from various sides of so many conflicting opinions* that the Gentiles will lose themselves in the labyrinth and come to understand that it is best to have no opinion on political questions, which it is not given to society at large to understand but only to the ruler who directs society. This is the first secret.
>
> "The second secret consists in so increasing and intensifying the shortcomings of the people in their habits, passions and mode of living that no one will be able to collect himself in the chaos, and, consequently, people will lose all their mutual understanding. This measure will serve us also in breeding disagreement in all parties, in disintegrating all those collective forces which are still unwilling to submit to us and in discouraging all personal initiative which can in any way interfere with our undertaking."

And this from the Thirteenth Protocol:

"* * * and you may also notice that *we seek approval, not for our acts, but for our words* uttered in regard to one or another question. We always announce publicly that we are guided in all our measures by the hope and the conviction that we are serving the general good.

"To divert over-restless people from discussing political questions, we shall now bring forward new problems apparently connected with the people—problems of industry. In these, let them lose themselves as much as they like. Under such conditions we shall make them think that the new questions have also a political bearing."

(It is to be hoped that the reader, as his eye passes over these details of the Program, is also permitting his mind to pass over the trend of events, to see if he may detect for himself these very developments in the life and thought of the past few years.)

"To prevent them from really thinking out anything themselves, we shall deflect their attention to amusements, games, pastimes, excitements and people's palaces. Such interests will distract their minds completely from questions on which we might be obliged to struggle with them. Becoming less and less accustomed to independent thinking, people will express themselves in unison with us because we alone offer new lines of thought —of course through persons whom they do not consider as in any way connected with us."

In this same Protocol it is plainly stated what is the purpose of the output of "liberal" theories, of which Jewish writers, poets, rabbis, societies and influences are the most prolific sources:

"The role of the liberal Utopians will be completely played out when our government is recognized. Until that time they will perform good service. For that reason *we will continue to direct thought into all the intricacies of fantastic theories, new and supposedly progressive*. Surely we have been completely successful in turning the witless heads of the Gentiles by the word 'progress.'"

Here is the whole program of confusing, enervating and trivializing the mind of the world. And it would be a most outlandish thought to put into words, were it not possible to show that this is just what has been done, and is still being done, by agencies which are highly lauded and easy to be identified among us.

A recent writer in a prominent magazine has pointed out what he calls the impossibility of the Jewish ruling group being allied in one common World Program because, as he showed, there were Jews acting as the leading minds in all the divisions of present-day opinion. There were Jews at the head of the capitalists, Jews at the head of the labor unions, and Jews at the head of those more radical organizations which find even the labor unions too tame. There is a Jew at the head of the judiciary of England and a Jew at the head of Sovietism in Russia. How can you say, he asked, that they are united, when they represent so many points of view?

The common unity, the possible common purpose of it all, is thus expressed in the Ninth Protocol:

> "People of all opinions and of all doctrines are at our service, restorers of monarchy, demagogues, Socialists, communists and other Utopians. We have put them all to work. Every one of them from his point of view is undermining the last remnant of authority, is trying to overthrow all existing order. All the governments have been tormented by these actions. But we will not give them peace until they recognize our super-government."

The function of the *idea* is referred to in the Tenth Protocol also:

> "When we introduced *the poison of liberalism* into the government organism, its entire political complexion changed."

The whole outlook of these Protocols upon the world is that the *idea* may be made a most potent poison. The authors of these documents do not believe in liberalism, they do not believe in democracy, but they lay plans for the constant preaching of these ideas because of their power to break up society, to divide it into groups, to destroy the power of collective opinion through a variety of convictions. The poison of an idea is their most relied-on weapon.

The plan of thus using ideas extends to education:

> "We have misled, stupefied and demoralized the youth of the Gentiles by means of education in principles and theories, patently false to us, but which we have inspired."—Protocol 9.

It extends also to family life:

> "Having in this way inspired everybody with the thought of his own importance, we will break down the influence of family life among the Gentiles, and its educational importance."—Protocol 10.

And in a passage which might well provide the material for long examination and contemplation by the thoughtful reader, this is said:

> "Until the time is ripe, let them amuse themselves * * * Let *those theories of life which we have induced them to regard as the dictates of science* play the most important role for them. To this end we shall endeavor to inspire blind confidence in these theories by means of our Press * * *
>
> "Note the successes we have arranged in *Darwinism*, *Marxism*, and *Nietzscheism*. The demoralizing effect of these doctrines upon the minds of the Gentiles should be evident at least to us."—Protocol 2.

That this disintegration and division of Gentile society was proceeding at a favorable rate when the Protocols were uttered is evident from every line of them. For it must be remembered that the Protocols are not bidding for support for a proposed program, but are announcing progress on a program which has been in process of fulfillment for "centuries" and "from ancient times." They contain a series of statements regarding things accomplished, as well as a forelook at things yet to be accomplished. The split of Gentile society was very satisfactorily proceeding in 1896, or thereabouts, when these oracles were uttered.

It is to be noticed that the purpose is nowhere stated to be the extermination of the Gentiles, but their subjugation, at first under the invisible rule which is proposed in these documents, at length under the rule of one whom the invisible forces would be able to put in control of the world through political changes which would create an office of World President or Autocrat. The Gentiles are to be subdued, first intellectually, as here shown, and then economically. Nowhere is it hinted that they are to be deprived of the earth, but only of their independence of those whom the Protocols represent to be Jews.

How far the division of society had proceeded when these Protocols were given may be gathered from the Fifth Protocol:

> "A world coalition of Gentiles could cope with us temporarily, but we are assured against this by roots of dissension among them so deep that they cannot be torn out. We have created antagonism between the personal and national interests of the Gentiles by arousing religious and race hatreds which we have nourished in their hearts for twenty centuries."

As far as that concerns the dissensions of the Gentiles or Christian world, it is absolutely true. And we have seen in our own nation how "the antagonism between personal and national interests" have rested on "religious and race hatreds." But whoever suspected a common source for these? More amazing still, who would expect any man or group to avow themselves the source? Yet it is thus written in the Protocols—"*we* have created the antagonism—*we* thus assure ourselves against the possibility of a Gentile coalition against us." And whether these Protocols are of Jewish origin or not, whether they represent Jewish interests or not, this is exactly the state of the world, of the Gentile world, today.

But a still deeper division is aimed for, and there are signs of even this coming to pass. Indeed, in Russia it has already come to pass, ***the spectacle of a Gentile lower class led by Jewish leaders against a Gentile upper class!*** In the First Protocol, describing the effects of a speculative industrial system upon the people, it is said that this sort of economic folly—

> "* * * has already created and will continue to create a society which is disillusioned, cold and heartless. Such a society is completely estranged from politics and religion. Lust of gold will be the only guide of the people * * * THEN, not for the sake of good, nor even for the sake of riches, but solely on account of their hatred of the privileged classes, the lower classes of the Gentiles

will follow us in the struggle against our rivals for power, the Gentiles of the intellectual classes."

"*The lower classes of the Gentiles will follow us * * * against * * * the Gentiles of the intellectual classes.*"

If that struggle were to occur today, the leaders of the Gentile insurgents against Gentile society would be Jewish leaders. They are in the leader's place now—not only in Russia, but also in the United States.

*"There is all the difference in the world," said a young Jewish philosopher, "between an American Jew and a Jewish American. A Jewish American is a mere amateur Gentile, doomed to be a parasite forever."*

*—"The Conquering Jew," p. 91.*

Issue of July 31, 1920.

XII.

# "Jewish Protocols" Claim Partial Fulfillment

> "With the present instability of all authority, our power will be more unassailable than any other, because it will be invisible until it has gained such strength that no cunning can undermine it."—Protocol 1.
>
> "It is indispensable for our purposes that, as far as possible, wars should bring no territorial advantages. This will shift war to an economic footing . . . . Such a condition of affairs will place both sides under the control of our international agents with their million eyes, whose vision is unhampered by any frontiers. Then, our international rights will eliminate national rights in the narrow sense, and will govern the governments as they govern their subjects."—Protocol 2.

As a mere literary curiosity, these documents which are called "The Protocols of the Learned Elders of Zion," would exercise a fascination by reason of the terrible completeness of the World Plan which they disclose. But they discourage at every turn the view that they are literature; they purport to be statesmanship, and they provide within their own lines the clue by which their status may be determined. Besides the things they look forward to doing, they announce the things they have done and are doing. If, in looking about the world, it is possible to see both the established conditions and the strong tendencies to which these Protocols allude, it will not be strange if interest in a mere literary curiosity gives way to something like alertness, and it may be alarm.

A few general quotations will serve to illustrate the element of present achievement in the assertions of these documents, and in order that the point may be made clear to the reader the key words will be emphasized.

Take this from Protocol Nine:

"In reality there are no obstacles before us. Our super-government *has* such an extra-legal status that it may be called by the energetic and strong word—dictatorship. I can conscientiously say that, at the present time, *we are* the law-makers. *We create* courts and jurisprudence. *We rule* with a strong will because *we hold* in our hands the remains of a once strong party, now subjugated by us."

And this from the Eighth Protocol:

"We will surround our government with a whole world of economists. It is for this reason that *the science of economics is the chief subject of instruction taught by the Jews.* We shall be surrounded by a whole galaxy of bankers, industrialists, capitalists, and especially by millionaires because, actually, everything will be decided by an appeal to figures."

These are strong claims, but not too strong for the facts that can be marshaled to illustrate them. They are, however, but an introduction to further claims that are made and equally paralleled by the facts. All through the Protocols, as in this quotation from the Eighth, the pre-eminence of the Jews in the teaching of political economy is insisted upon, and the facts bear that out. They are the chief authors of those vagaries which lead the mob after economic impossibilities, and they are also the chief teachers of political economy in our universities, the chief authors of those popular textbooks in the subject, which hold the conservative classes to the fiction that economic *theories* are economic *laws.* The *idea,* the *theory,* as instruments of social disintegration are common to both the university Jew and the Bolshevik Jew. When all this is shown in detail, public opinion upon the importance of academic and radical economics may undergo a change.

And, as claimed in the quotation just given from the Ninth Protocol, the Jewish world power does today constitute a super-government. It is the Protocol's own word, and none is more fitting. No nation can get all that it wants, but the Jewish World Power can get all that it wants, even though its demands exceed Gentile equality. "*We are* the lawmakers," say the Protocols, and Jewish influences have been lawmakers in a greater degree than any but the specialists realize. In the past ten years Jewish international rule, or the power of the group of International Jews has quite dominated the world. More than that, it has been powerful enough to prevent the passage of salutary laws, and where one law may have slipped through to a place on the statute books, it has been powerful enough to get it interpreted in a sense that rendered it useless for its purpose. This, too, can be illustrated by a large collection of facts.

Moreover, the method by which this is done was outlined long ago in the program of which the Protocols purport to be an outline. "*We create* courts," continues the quotation, and it is followed in other Protocols by numerous references to "our judges." There is a Jewish court sitting in a public building in the city of New York every week, and other courts, for the sole advantage and use of this people whose spokesmen deny that they are a "separate people," are in formation everywhere. The Zionist plan has already been used in some of the smaller European countries to confer an extra-citizenship upon Jews who already enjoy citizenship in the lands of their residence, and in addition to that a degree of self-rule under the very governments which they demand to protect them. Wherever Jewish tendencies are permitted to work unhindered, the result is not "Americanization," nor "Anglicization" nor any other distinctive nationalism, but a strong and ruling reversion back to essential "Judaization."

The "agents" referred to in the first quotation will receive attention in another article. To resume the claims of the Protocols: This from the Seventeenth Protocol:

> "*We have* taken good care long ago to discredit the Gentile clergy and thereby to destroy their mission, which at present might hamper us considerably. Their influence over the people diminishes daily.
>
> "Freedom of conscience *has been* proclaimed everywhere. Consequently it is only a question of time when the complete crash of the Christian

religion will occur. It will be easier still to handle the other religions, but it is too early to discuss this phase of the subject."

This will be of considerable interest, perhaps, to those clergymen who are laboring with Jewish rabbis to bring about some kind of religious union. Such a union would of necessity dispose of Christ as a well-meaning but wholly mistaken Jewish prophet, and thus distinctive Christianity would cease to exist insofar as the "union" was effective. The principal religious aversion of the Protocols, however, so far as it is expressed, is against the Catholic church in general and the pontifical office in particular.

A curious paragraph in this Protocol claims for the Jewish race a particular skill in the art of insult:

> "Our contemporary press will expose governmental and religious affairs and the incapacity of the Gentiles, always using expressions so derogatory as to approach insult, the faculty of employing which is so well known to our race."

This from the Fifth Protocol:

> "Under our influence the execution of the laws of the Gentiles *is* reduced to a minimum. Respect for the law *is* undermined by the liberal interpretation we have introduced in this sphere. The courts *decide* as we dictate, even in the most important cases in which are involved fundamental principles or political issues, *viewing* them in the light in which *we present* them to the Gentile administration through agents with whom we have apparently nothing in common, through newspaper opinion and other avenues.
>
> "In Gentile society where *we have* planted discord and protestantism * * * *"

The word "protestantism" is evidently not used in the religious or sectarian sense, but to denote a temper of querulous fault-finding destructive of harmonious collective opinion.

This from the Fourteenth Protocol:

> "In countries called advanced, *we have created* a senseless, filthy and disgusting literature. For a short time after our entrance into power we shall encourage its existence so that it may show in greater relief the contrast between it and the

written and spoken announcements which will emanate from us."

Discussing in the Twelfth Protocol the control of the Press—a subject which must be treated more extensively in another article—the claim is made:

"*We have attained this at the present time* to the extent that all news is received through several agencies in which it is centralized from all parts of the world. These agencies will then be to all intents and purposes our own institutions and will publish only that which we permit."

This from the Seventh Protocol bears on the same subject:

"We must force the Gentile governments to adopt measures which will promote our broadly conceived plan, already approaching its triumphant goal, by bringing to bear the pressure of stimulated public opinion, *which has been organized by us* with the help of the so-called 'great power' of the press. With a few exceptions not worth considering, *it is already* in our hands."

To resume the Twelfth Protocol:

"If *we have already managed* to dominate the mind of Gentile society to such a point that almost all see world affairs through the colored lenses of the spectacles which *we place* before their eyes, and *if now there is not one government with barriers erected against our access to* that which by Gentile stupidity is called *state secrets*, what then will it be when we are the recognized masters of the world in the person of our universal ruler?"

The Jewish nation is the only nation that possesses the secrets of all the rest. No nation long protects a secret which directly concerns another nation, but even so, no nation has all the secrets of all the other nations. Yet it is not too much to say that the International Jews have this knowledge. Much of it, of course, amounts to nothing and their possession of it does not materially add to their power, but the fact that they have the *access*, that they can get whatever they want when they want it is the important point—as many a secret paper could testify if it could talk, and many a custodian of secret papers could tell if he would The real secret diplomacy of the world is that which hands over the world's so-called secrets to a few men who are members of one race. The surface of diplomacy, those activities which get written down in the memoirs of comfortably aging statesmen, those coups and treaties which are given high-sounding fame as if they really were important—that is incomparable with the diplomacy of Judah, and its matchless enginery for worming out the hidden knowledge of every ruling group. The United States is included in all these statements. Perhaps there is no government in the world so completely at their service as is our own at present, their control having been gained during the past five or six years.

The Protocols do not regard the dispersal of the Jews abroad upon the face of the earth as a calamity, but as a providential arrangement by which the World Plan can be the more certainly executed, as see these words of the Eleventh Protocol:

> "God gave to us, His Chosen People, as a blessing, the dispersal, and *this which has appeared to all to be our weakness* has been our *whole strength*. *It has now brought us* to the threshold of universal rule."

The claims to accomplishment which are put forth in the Ninth Protocol would be too massive for words were they too massive for concrete realization, but there is a point where the word and the actuality meet and tally.

> "In order not to destroy prematurely the Gentile institutions, *we have* laid our efficient hands on them, and rasped the springs of their mechanism. They were formerly in strict and just order, but *we have* replaced them with a liberal disorganized and arbitrary administration. *We have* tampered with jurisprudence, the franchise, the press, freedom of the person, and, most important of all, education and culture, the corner stone of free existence.
>
> "*We have* misled, stupefied and demoralized the youth of the Gentiles by means of education in principles and theories patently false to us, but which *we have* inspired.
>
> "Above existing laws, without actual change

but by distorting them through contradictory interpretations, *we have* created something stupendous in the way of results."

Everyone knows that, in spite of the fact that the air was never so full of theories of liberty and wild declarations of "rights," there has been a steady curtailment of "personal freedom." Instead of being socialized, the people, under a cover of socialistic phrases, are being brought under an unaccustomed bondage to the state. The Public Health is one plea. Various forms of Public Safety are other pleas. Children are hardly free to play nowadays except under play-masters appointed by the State, among whom, curiously enough, an astonishing proportion of Jews manage to find a place. The streets are no longer as free as they were; laws of every kind are hedging upon the harmless liberties of the people. A steady tendency toward systematization, every phase of the tendency based upon some very learnedly stated "principle," has set in, and curiously enough, when the investigator pursues his way to the authoritative center of these movements for the regulation of the people's life, he finds Jews in power. Children are being lured away from the "social center" of the home for other "centers"; they are being led away (and we are speaking of Gentile children—no Gentiles are ever allowed to regulate the lives of Jewish children) from their natural leaders in home, church and school, to institutionalized "centers" and scientific "play spots," under "trained leaders" whose whole effect, consciously or unconsciously, is to lead the modern child to look to the State, instead of its natural environment, for leadership. All this focuses up to the World Plan for the subjugation of the Gentiles, and if it is not the Jewish World Plan it would be interesting to know why the material for it is so largely Gentile children and the leaders of it so often of the Jewish race.

Jewish liberties are the best safeguarded in the United States. Gentiles take their chance with public matters, but every Jewish community is surrounded by special protectors who gain special recognition by various devices—political and business threats not the least of them. No public spirited Gentiles are welcomed to the task of regulating the lives of Jewish children. The Jewish community in every city is all-sufficient in itself as far as such activities go. The most secret of all parochial schools are the Jewish schools, whose very locations are not all known to the officials of large cities. The Jew is almost anxious in his efforts to mold the Gentile mind; he insists on being permitted to tell the Gentile what to think, especially about the Jew; he is not averse to influencing general Gentile thought in a manner which, though it come about by wide circles, works ultimately into the Jewish scheme of things. The anxiety and the insistence, so well known to all who have observed them, are only reflections of the Jew's conviction that his is the superior race and is capable of directing the inferior race—of which there is but one, including the whole non-Jewish world.

Every influence that leads to lightness and looseness in Gentile youth today heads up in a Jewish source. Did the young people of the world devise the "sport clothes" which have had so deleterious an effect on the youth of the times that every publicist has thought it worthy of mention? Those styles come out of Jewish clothing concerns, where certainly art is not the rule nor moral influence the main consideration. The moving picture is an interesting development of photography allied with the show business, but whose is the responsibility for its development along such lines as make it a menace to the minds of millions—so serious a menace that it has not escaped observation and condemnation everywhere? Who are the masters of musical jazz in the world? Who direct all the cheap jewelry houses, the bridge-head show parks, the "coney islands," the centers of nervous thrills and looseness? It is possible to take the showy young man and woman of trivial outlook and loose sense of responsibility, and tag them outwardly and inwardly, from their clothing and ornaments to their hectic ideas and hopes, with the same tag, "Made, introduced and exploited by a Jew."

There is, therefore, something most sinister in the light which events cast upon that paragraph:

> "*We have* misled, stupefied, and demoralized the youth of the Gentiles by means of education

in principles and theories, patently false to us, but which we have inspired."

"Principles and theories" do not necessarily imply lofty or even modest intellectual qualities. The youngster who spends his noon hours and evenings at the movies is getting his "principles and theories" just as the more intellectual youngster from a higher grade of society who listens to a Jewish "liberal" expound "sex liberty" and the "control of population" is getting his. The looseness which inheres in these "principles and theories" does not emanate from the Gentile home, or the Gentile church, or from any line of money-making which is filled principally with Gentiles, but from theories, movements and lines of money-making mostly fancied by Jews. This line of accusation could be run much deeper, but it is preferred to restrict it to what is observable by decent eyes everywhere.

And that "the youth of the Gentiles" are the principal victims, and not the youth of the Jews, is also observable. While a certain percentage of Jewish youth itself is overcome by this social poison, the percentage is almost nothing compared with the results among the youth of the Gentiles. It is a significant fact that Jews who link this process of enervation of Gentiles with large profits are not themselves, nor are their sons and daughters, the victims of this enervation. Jewish youth comes through more proudly and more cleanly than the mass of Gentile youth.

Many a father and mother, many a sound-minded, uncorrupted young person, and thousands of teachers and publicists have cried out against *luxury*. Many a financier, observing the manner in which the people earned and flung away their money, has warned against *luxury*. Many an economist, knowing that the nonessential industries were consuming men and materials that were necessary to the stabilizing of essential industries; knowing that men are making knick-knacks who should be making steel; knowing that men are engaged in making gew-gaws who should be working on the farm; that materials are going into articles that are made only to *sell* and never to *use*, and that materials are thus diverted from the industries that support the people's life—every observer knowing th crazy insistence on luxurious nonessentials has lifted up a strong voice against it.

But, according to these Protocols, we have been starting at the wrong end. The people, it is true, buy these senseless *nonessentials* which are called *luxuries*. But the people do not devise them. And the people grow tired of them one by one. But the stream of varieties continues—always something else being thrust at the people, dangled before their eyes, set bobbing down the avenue on enough manikins to give the impression that it is "style"; newspaper print and newspaper pictures; movie pictures; stage costumes enough to force the new thing into "fashion" with a kind of force and compulsion which no really worthy essential thing can command.

Where does it come from? What power exists whose long experience and deliberate intent enable it to frivolize the people's minds and tastes and compel them to pay most of their money for it too? Why this spasm of luxury and extravagance through which we have just passed? How did it occur that before luxury and extravagance were apparent, all the material to provoke and inflame them had been prepared beforehand and shipped beforehand, ready for the stampede which also had been prepared?

If the people of the United States would stop to consider, when the useless and expensive thing is offered them—if they would trace its origin, trace the course of the enormous profits made out of it, trace the whole movement to flood the market with uselessness and extravagance and thus demoralize the Gentile public financially, intellectually and socially—if, in short, it could be made clear to them that Jewish financial interests are not only pandering to the loosest elements in human nature, but actually engaged in a calculated effort to render them loose in the first place and keep them loose—it would do more than anything else to stop this sixfold waste—the waste of material, the waste of labor, the waste of Gentile money, the waste of Gentile mind, the waste of Jewish talent, and the worse than waste of Israel's real usefulness to the world.

We say the *Gentile public* is the victim of this stimulated trade in useless luxuries. Did you ever see

Jewish people so victimized? They might wear very noticeable clothing, but its price and its quality agree. They might wear rather large diamonds, but they are diamonds. The Jew is not the victim of the Jew, the craze for luxuries is just like the "coney island" crowd to him; he knows what attracts them and the worthlessness of it.

And it is not so much the financial loss that is to be mourned, nor yet the atrocities committed upon good taste, but the fact that the silly Gentile crowds walk into the net willingly, even gaily, supposing the change of the fashion to be as inevitable as the coming of spring, supposing the new demand on their earnings to be as necessary and as natural as taxes. The crowds think that somehow they have part in it, when their only part is to pay, and then pay again for the new extravagance when the present one palls. There are men in this country who know two years ahead what the frivolities and extravagances of the people will be, because they decree what they shall be. These things are all strictly business, demoralizing to the Gentile majority, enriching to the Jewish minority.

Look at the Sixth Protocol for a sidelight on all this:

This is an excerpt from a longer passage dealing with the plans by which the people's interest could be swung from political to industrial questions, how industry could be made insecure and unfair by the introduction of speculation into its management, and finally how against this condition the people could be rendered restless and helpless. Luxury was to be the instrument:

> "To destroy Gentile industry, we shall, as an incentive to this speculation, *encourage among the Gentiles a strong demand for luxuries—all enticing luxuries.*"

And in the First Protocol:

> "Surely we cannot allow our own people to come to this. The people of the Gentiles are stupefied with spirituous liquors * * *"

—incidentally, the profits of spirituous liquors flow in large amounts to Jewish pockets. The history of the whisky ring in this country will show this. Historically, *the whole prohibition movement may be described as a contest between Gentile and Jewish capital*, and in this instance, thanks to the Gentile majority, the Gentiles won.

The amusement, gambling, jazz song, scarlet fiction, side show, cheap-dear fashions, flashy jewelry, and every other activity that lived by reason of an invisible pressure upon the people, and that exchanged the most useless of commodities for the prices that would just exhaust the people's money surplus and no more—every such activity has been under the mastery of Jews.

They may not be conscious of their participation in any wholesale demoralization of the people. They may only be conscious of "easy money." They may sometimes yield to surprise as they contrast the silly Gentiles with their own money-wise and fabric-wise and metal-wise Jews. But however this may be, there is the conception of a program by which a people may be deliberately devastated materially and spiritually, and yet kept pleasant all the time—and there also is the same program translated into terms of daily transactions and for the most part, perhaps altogether under control of the members of one race.

---

Issue of August 7, 1920.

XIII.

# "Jewish" Plan to Split Society by "Ideas"

THE method by which the Protocols work for the breakdown of society should now be fairly evident to readers of these articles. An understanding of the *method* is necessary if one is to find the meaning of the currents and cross-currents which make so hopeless a hodge-podge of the present times. People who are confused and discouraged by the various voices and discordant theories of today, each seeming to be plausible and promising, may find a clear clue to the value of the voices and the meaning of the theories if they understand that their *confusion* and *discouragement* comprise the very objective which is sought. The uncertainty, hesitation, hopelessness, fear; the eagerness with which every promising plan and offered solution is grasped—these are the very reactions which the program outlined in the Protocols aims to produce. The condition is proof of the efficacy of the program.

It is a method that takes time, and the Protocols declare that it *has* taken time, indeed, centuries. Students of the matter find the identical program of the Protocols, announced and operated by the Jewish race, from the first century onward.

It has taken 1900 years to bring Europe to its present degree of subjugation—violent subjugation in some countries, political subjugation in some, economic subjugation in all—but in America the same program, with almost the same degree of success, has required about 50 years. Certain mistaken *ideas* of liberalism, certain flabby *ideas* of tolerance, all of them originating at European sources which the Protocolists had completely polluted, were transported to America, and here under cover of the blindness and innocence of a false liberalism and tolerance, together with modern appliances for the swift acceleration of opinion, ther has been worked a subjugation of our institutions ar public thought which is the amazement of Europe observers. It is a fact that some of the important students of the Jewish Question, whom Jewish publicists are pleased to damn with the term "Anti-Semites," have been awakened to the existence of the Question not by what they have observed in Europe, but by what they have seen in the swift and distinct "close-up" which has been afforded in American affairs.

The center of Jewish power, the principal sponsors of the Jewish program, are resident in America, and the leverage which was used at the Peace Conference to fasten Jewish power more securely upon Europe, was American leverage exercised at the behest of the strong Jewish pressure which was brought from the United States for that purpose. And these activities did not end with the Peace Conference.

The whole *method* of the Protocols may be described in one word, *Disintegration*. The undoing of what has been done, the creation of a long and hopeless interim in which attempts at reconstruction shall be baffled, and the gradual wearing down of public opinion and public confidence, until those who stand outside the created chaos shall insert their strong calm hand to seize control—that is the whole method of procedure.

Putting together the estimate of human nature which obtains in these Protocols, and their claims to a rather definite though as yet incomplete fulfillment of the World Program (these two comprising the themes of the previous two articles), some of the aspects of this propaganda of disintegration have become clear. But not all of them. There are yet other aspects of these methods, which will be dealt with in the present article, and there are yet future reaches of the program which will be considered later.

The first point of attack is Collective Opinion, that body of ideas which through men's agreement with them, holds large groups together in political, racial, religious or social unity. Sometimes we call them "standards," sometimes we call them "ideals"; whatever they may be called, they are the invisible bonds of unity, they are the common faith, they are the great overarching reason for group unity and loyalty.

The Protocols assert that here the first attack has

been made. The history of Jewish propaganda in the world shows that also.

The first wave of attack is to *corrupt* Collective Opinion. Now, to "corrupt" in the real sense does not mean anything unsavory or unclean. The whole power of every heresy is its attractiveness to the good mind. The whole explanation of the strong hold which untruth has gained upon the world of our day, is that the untruth is reasonable, inspiring and apparently good. It is only after a long discipline in false ideals—which are reasonable, inspiring and good—that the evil fruits appear in acts and conditions which are unreasonable, destructive and wholly evil. If you will trace the idea of Liberty as it has appeared in Russian history, from its philosophic beginning (a Jewish beginning, by the way) to its present ending (a Jewish ending also), you will see the process.

The Protocols claim that the Gentiles are not thinkers, that attractive ideas have been thrown at them so strategically and persistently that the power of thought is almost destroyed out of them. Fortunately this is a matter on which any Gentile may apply his own test. If he will segregate his ruling ideas, especially those that center round the thought of "democracy," he will discover that he is being ruled in his mind by a whole company of ideas into whose authority over him he has not inquired at all. He is ruled by "say so" whose origin he has not traced. And when, pursuing those ideas, he finds that they are not practicable, he is received by the explanation that "we are not yet sufficiently advanced." Yet when he does see men who are sufficiently "advanced" to put these very ideas into operation, he recoils from what he sees them do, because he knows that "advancement" such as that is deterioration—a form of disintegration. Yet every one of the ideas were "good," "reasonable," "inspiring," "humane," to begin with. And, if this Gentile will observe a little further, he will see that they are the most persistently preached ideas in the world; he will also see who the preachers are.

The Protocols distinctly declare that it is by means of the set of ideas which cluster around "democracy," that their first victory over public opinion was obtained. The *idea* is the weapon. And to be a weapon it must be an *idea* at variance with the natural trend of life. It must indeed be a theory opposed to the facts of life. And no theory so opposed can be expected to take root and become the ruling factor, unless it appeals to the mind as reasonable, inspiring and good. The Truth frequently seems unreasonable; the Truth frequently is depressing; the Truth sometimes seems to be evil; but it has this eternal advantage, it is the Truth, and what is built thereon neither brings nor yields to *confusion.*

This first step does not give the control of public opinion, but leads up to it. It is worthy of note that it is this sowing of "the poison of liberalism," as the Protocols name it, which comes first in order in those documents. Then, following upon that, the Protocols say:

> "To obtain control over public opinion it is first necessary to *confuse* it."

Truth is one and cannot be confused, but this false, appealing liberalism which has been sown broadcast, and which is ripening faster under Jewish nurture in America than ever it did in Europe, is easily confused because it is not truth. It is error, and error has a thousand forms. Take a nation, a party, a city, an association in which "the poison of liberalism" has been sown, and you can split that up into as many factions as there are individuals simply by throwing among them certain modifications of the original idea. This is a piece of strategy well known to the forces that invisibly control mass-thought. Theodor Herzl, the arch-Jew, a man whose vision was wider than any statesman's and whose program paralleled the Protocols, knew this many years ago when he said that the Zionist (cryptic for "Jewish") state would come before the Socialist state could come; he knew with what endless divisions the "liberalism" which he and his predecessors had planted would be shackled and crippled.

The process of which all Gentiles have been the victims, but never the Jews—never the Jews!—is just this—

First, to create an ideal of "broad-mindedness." That is the phrase which appears in every Jewish remonstrance against public mention of the Jew and his alleged World Program: "We thought you were too broad-minded a man to express such thoughts;" "we thought Mr. So-and-So was too broad-minded a man to suspect the Jews of this;" "we thought the daily or weekly or monthly such-and-such a paper was too broad-minded editorially to consider such material." It is a sort of keyword, indicative of the state of mind in which it is desired that the Gentiles be kept. It is a state of flabby tolerance. A state of mind which mouths meaningless phrases about Liberty, phrases which act as an opiate on the mind and conscience and which allow all sorts of things to be done under cover. The phrase, the slogan, is a very dependable Jewish weapon. ("In all times people have accepted words for acts."—Protocol 5.) The reality behind the phrase the Protocols frankly admit to be non-existent.

Nothing has served to create "broad-mindedness," a state of mind whose breadth indicates its lack of depth, so much as the ideas of liberalism which the Jews are constantly teaching to Gentiles and on which they never themselves act. We need a new sort of allegiance to the reality of life, to the facts as they are, which will enable us to stand up under all cajoling to "broad-mindedness" and assert a new intolerance of everything but truth. The terms "narrow" and "broad" as they are used today represent lies. The liberal man ought to believe more, he ought to be deep and wide in his beliefs in order to merit that name; but as a usual thing he believes nothing. He is not liberal at all. When you seek belief, belief with a foundation, belief with vitality, you must seek it among men who are sneered at, under this false Jewish-promoted notion of liberality, as "narrow men." Jewish propaganda, in common with the Protocols, is against men who have dug down to the rock; they want "broad-minded men" who can easily be shifted about the surface, and thus serve the invisible scheme in any manner desired. This type of men, on their part, never imagine but that their "broad-mindedness" is a mark of their superiority and independence.

Now, see what follows. Men are born believers. For a time they may believe in "broad-mindedness" and under the terrific social pressure that has been set up in its favor they will openly espouse it. But it is too shallow to satisfy any growing roots of life. They must believe, deeply, something. For proof of this, notice the undeniable strength of the negative beliefs which are held by men who fancy that they believe nothing. Therefore, some who are highly endowed with independence of spirit, root down into those prohibited matters which at some point touch Jewish concerns—these are the "narrow" men. But others find it more convenient to cultivate those departments which promise a highway whereon there shall be no clashes of vital opinion, no chance of the charge of "intolerance"; in short they transfer all their contemplative powers to the active life, even as it is written in the Protocols—

> "*To divert Gentile thought and observation, interest must be deflected to industry and commerce.*"

It is amazing to look around and see the number of men who have been actually browbeaten into committing their whole lives to these secondary or even tertiary things, while they look with great timidity and aversion at the vital things which really rule the world and upon the issue of which the world really depends.

But it is just this deflection to the materialistic base that offers the Protocolists, and similarly Jewish propagandists, their best hold. "Broad-mindedness" today consists in leaving vital matters severely alone. It descends quickly to material-mindedness. Within this lower sphere all the discord which distresses the world today is to be found.

First, there is the ruin of the upper circles of industry and commerce:

> "*To make it possible for liberty definitely to disintegrate and ruin Gentile society, industry must be placed on a speculative basis.*"

No one needs to be told what this means. It means, as everything about us shouts, the prostitution of service to profits and the eventual disappearance of the profits. It means that the high art of management degenerates into exploitation. It means reckless confusion among the managers and dangerous unrest among the workmen.

But it means something worse: it means the split-up of Gentile society. Not a division between "Capital" and "Labor," but the division between the Gentiles at both ends of the working scheme. Gentile managers and manufacturers are not the "capitalists" of the United States. Most of them have to go to the "capitalists" for the funds with which they work—and the "capitalists" are Jewish, International Jews.

But with Jewish capital at one end of the Gentile working scheme putting the screws on the manufacturers, and with Jewish agitators and disruptionists and subversives at the other end of the Gentile working scheme putting the screws on the workmen, we have a condition at which the world-managers of the Protocol program must be immensely satisfied.

> "We might fear the combined strength of the Gentiles of vision with the blind strength of the masses, *but we have taken all measures* against such a possible contingency *by raising a wall of mutual antagonism between these two forces.* Thus, the blind force of the masses remains our support. We, and we alone, shall serve as their leaders. Naturally, we will direct their energy to achieve our end."—Protocol 9.

The indication that they are highly satisfied is that they are not only not doing anything to relieve the situation, but are apparently willing to have it made worse, and if it be at all possible for them to do so they would like to see this coming winter, and the privations which are scheduled for it (unless Gentile flabbiness before the Jewish power, high and low, receives a new backbone), bring the United States to the verge of, if not across the very line of Bolshevism. They know the whole method of artificial scarcity and high prices. It was practiced in the French Revolution and in Russia. All the signs of it are in this country too.

Industrial problems for their mental food and light amusement for their leisure hours, these are the Protocols' method with regard to the Gentile mind, and under cover of these the work is to be done—the work which is best expressed by the motto, "Divide and Rule."

Read this:

"To divert over-restless people from discussing political questions, *we shall now bring forward* new problems apparently connected with them—problems of industry."—Protocol 13.

Has not everyone been struck by the divorcement which exists in this country between the mass-thought which is almost exclusively devoted to industrial questions, and the party-thought which is endeavoring to keep the field of pure politics? And is it not a fact that our friends, the Jews, are strongly entrenched in both fields—in politics to keep it reactionary, and in industrial circles to keep it radical—and so widen the split? And what is this split but a split of the Gentiles?—for society is Gentile, and the disruptive influences are Jewish.

Read this:

"*We have included* in the constitution rights for the people that are fictitious and not actual rights. All those so-called 'rights of the people' can only exist in the abstract and can never be realized in practice * * * The proletarian gains no more from the constitution than the miserable crumbs *thrown from our table* in return for his votes to elect *our* agents and pass *our* measures. Republican rights are a bitter irony to the poor man, for the pressure of daily labor prevents him from using them, and at the same time, deprives him of the guaranty of a permanent and certain livelihood by making him dependent upon *strikes*, organized either by his *employers* or his *comrades*."—Protocol 3.

This remark about strikes is not at all puzzling to anyone who has studied the different types of strikes in this country. The number fomented from above the working class is astoundingly large.

Read this also:

"*We will force up wages* which, however, will be of no benefit to the workers, for *we will at the same time cause a rise in the prices of necessities*, pretending that this is due to the decline of agriculture and of cattle raising. *We will also artfully and deeply undermine the sources of production by instilling in the workmen ideas of anarchy.*"—Protocol 6.

And this:

"We will represent ourselves as the saviors of the working class who have come to liberate them from this oppression by suggesting that they join our army of socialists, anarchists, communists, to whom we always extend our help under the guise of the fraternal principles of universal human solidarity."—Protocol 3.

"Broad-mindedness" again! In this connection it is always well to remember the words of Sir Eustace Percy, heretofore quoted, words which are sponsored by Jews themselves—"Not because the Jew cares for the positive side of radical philosophy, not because he desires to be a partaker in Gentile nationalism or Gentile democracy, but because no existing Gentile system of government is ever anything but distasteful to him."

Or, as the author of "The Conquering Jew" says: "He is democratic in his sentiments, but not in his nature. When he proclaims the common brotherhood of man, he is asking that the social gate now closed against him in so many quarters shall be open to him; not because he wants equality, but because he desires to be master in the social world, as he is showing himself in so many other spheres. Many an honorable Jew will, I doubt not, dispute the accuracy of this distinction; but if he does it will be because he has lived so long in the atmosphere of the West that he is unconscious of what is bred in the bone of his Eastern race."

It is not difficult, therefore, to see the genealogy of the Jewish ideas of liberalism from their origin to their latest effects upon Gentile life. The *confusion* aimed for is here. There is not a reader of these lines who has not felt in his own life the burden of it. Bewilderment characterizes the whole mental climate of the people today. They do not know what to believe. First one set of facts is given to them, then another. First one explanation of conditions is given to them, and then another. The fact-shortage is acute. There is a whole market-full of explanations that explain nothing, but only deepen the *confusion*. The government itself seems to be hampered, and whenever it starts on a line of investigation finds itself mysteriously tangled up so that procedure is difficult. This governmental aspect is also set forth in the Protocols.

Add to this the onslaught on the human tendency toward religion, which is usually the last barrier to fall before violence and robbery unashamed stalk forth. In order to bring the condition about at which this World Program aims, the Fourth Protocol says:

> "It is for this reason that we must undermine faith, eradicate from the minds of the Gentiles the very principles of God and Soul, and replace these conceptions by mathematical calculations and material desires."

> "When *we deprived* the masses of their belief in God, ruling authority was thrown into the gutter, where it became public property, and *we seized* it."—Protocol 5.

> "*We have taken good care long ago* to discredit the Gentile clergy."—Protocol 17.

> "When we become rulers we shall regard as undesirable the existence of any religion except our own, proclaiming One God with Whom our fate is tied as The Chosen People, and by Whom our fate has been made one with the fate of the world. For this reason we must destroy all other religions. If thereby should emerge contemporary atheists, then, *as a transition step*, this will not interfere with our aims."—Protocol 14.

This will probably offer matter for reflection by the "broad-minded."

It is curious to note how this religious program has worked out in Russia where Trotsky (as loudly heralded in the American Jewish press) is said to have no religion, and where Jewish commissars tell dying Russians who ask for priests, "We have abolished the Almighty." Miss Katherine Dokoochief is reported, under a Philadelphia date, to have told the Near East Relief that Russian Christian churches have been subjected to the vilest indignities by the Bolsheviki, details of which she gives; but "the synagogues remain untouched, meeting with no damage."

All these lines of attack, whose object is the destruction of the natural rallying points of Gentile thought, and the substitution of other rallying points of an unwholesome and destructive nature, are assisted, as we saw in the last article, by the propaganda for luxury. Luxury is recognizedly one of the most enervating influences. Its course runs from ease, through softness, to flabbiness, to degeneracy, mental, physical and moral. Its beginnings are attractive, its end is lasciviousness in some form, testifying to the complete breakdown of all the strong fiber of the life. It may make a theme for a more complete study some day, this lure to lasciviousness through luxury, and the identity of the forces that set the lure.

But now, to conclude this general view of the method, rather this part of the method, the confusion itself, which all these influences converge to produce, is expected to produce another more deeply helpless state. And that state is, *Exhaustion.*

It needs no imagination to see what this means. Exhaustion is today one of the conditions that menace the people. The recent political conventions and their effect upon the public fully illustrate it. Nobody seemed to care. Parties might make their declarations and candidates their promises—nobody cared. The war and its strain began the exhaustion; the "peace" and its confusion have about completed it. The people believe little and expect less. Confidence is gone. Initiative is nearly gone. The failure of movements falsely heralded as "people's movements" has gone far to make the people think that no people's movement is possible.

So say the Protocols:

> "To *wear everyone out* by dissensions, animosities, feuds, famine, inoculation of diseases, want, until the Gentiles see no other way of escape except an appeal to our money and power."
> —Protocol 10.
>
> "We will *so wear out and exhaust the Gentiles* by all this that they will be compelled to offer us an international authority, which by its position will enable us to absorb without disturbance all the governmental forces of the world and thus form a super-government.
>
> "We must so direct the education of Gentile society that its hands will drop in the weakness

of discouragement in the face of any undertaking where initiative is needed."—Protocol 5.

The Jews have never been worn out or exhausted. They have never been nonplused. This is the true psychic characteristic of those who have a clue to the maze. It is the unknown that exhausts the mind, the constant wandering around among tendencies and influences whose source is not known and whose purpose is not understood. Walking in the dark is wearing work. The Gentiles have been doing it for centuries. The others, having a pretty accurate idea what it was all about, have not succumbed. Even persecution is endurable if it is understandable, and the Jews of the world have always known just where it fitted in the scheme of things. Gentiles have suffered more from Jewish persecutions than have the Jews, for after the persecutions were over, the Gentile was as much in the dark as ever; whereas Judaism simply took up again its century-long march toward a goal in which it implicitly believes, and which, some say who have deep knowledge of Jewish roots in the world and who too may be touched with exhaustion, they will achieve. However this may be, the revolution which would be necessary to unfasten the International Jewish system from its grip on the world, would probably have to be just as radical as any attempts the Jews have made to attain that grip. There are those who express serious doubts that the Gentiles are competent to do it at all. Maybe not. Let them at least know who their conquerors are.

---

Issue of August 14, 1920.

# Did the Jews Foresee the World War?

BEFORE proceeding to a more detailed study of the connection between the *written* program of the documents which are called "The Protocols of the Learned Elders of Zion," and the *actual* program as it can be traced in real life, we shall now view those plans which were future when the Protocols were uttered. It must be borne in mind, however, that what was *future* in 1896 and 1905, may be *past* today, that what was *plan* then may be *fulfillment* now. To bear this in mind will be in exact accord with the expression of Protocol 22—"I have endeavored to indicate carefully the secrets of past and future events, *and of those momentous occurrences of the near future toward which we are rushing in a stream of great crises.*" Some of those "momentous occurrences" have come to pass, and with them a brighter light on the Question which we are studying.

An illustration of this which is fresh in the minds of all was furnished by the Great War. Jewish comment on this series of articles has made much of the fact that one of the articles was devoted to the then prominence of the Jewish Question in Germany, and it was sought to mislead the people to think that this series was really a part of subtle German after-the-war propaganda. The fact is that articles on the Question in a number of countries were set aside in order to bring the Question itself prominently before the minds of Americans with the least delay. The postponed articles will appear in due season, though out of their order. Germany is today, with perhaps the possible exception of the United States, the most Jew-controlled country in the world—controlled within and from without—and a much stronger set of facts could be presented now than was presented in the original article (the facts of which were at first denied and later admitted by the Jewish spokesmen in the United States). For, since that article was written, public sentiment in Germany has swept the Jews largely out of public office. German public opinion exerted itself to the utmost to put German political administration back into German hands. But did that liberate Germany from the Jews? Not at all. For their entrenchments stretched further and deeper than mere display of official power. Their hold on the basic industries, the finances, the future of Germany has not been loosened in the least. It is there, unmovable. In what that hold consists, the reader will be told at some convenient time.

Germany is mentioned now, in connection with the Jews, for this purpose: It will be remembered that it was from Germany that the first cry of "annexations" came, and it came at a time when all German war activities and war sentiment were admittedly in Jewish control. "Annexations" was the cry that flashed across the world one day. And back across the world, from the United States, a nation that was not even a party to the war at that time, the word flashed back, "No Annexations." Thus by a dramatic play the whole question was thrust before the world.

Soon the people of all countries had forgotten the blood of battle, the war profiteers and every other vital point, and were discussing a matter which belonged to the end of the war and not the beginning, the question of "annexations." Now, when it is known who were controlling the formulation of war-aims in Germany and who were the chief counselors of the foreign policy of the United States at the same time, the projection of this question of "annexations" into the world's mind becomes interesting; interesting but not wholly intelligible.

Not until you read the Protocols do you get a full light on this—and this report of the Protocols which is now given the world probably dates from 1896: There is absolutely ironclad proof of the date 1905.

The Second Protocol begins on the note of war, and its opening words are these:

> "*It is indispensable for our purpose* that, *as far as possible*, wars should bring *no territorial advantages*. This will *shift war to an economic footing*, and nations will perceive the strength of our superiority in *the aid we render*."

Who was thinking, between 1896 and 1905, of the new "no annexations" rule to be applied to war? Were you? Do you know of any statesman who was? We know that military men were concerned about the appliances and operations of any future war that might occur. We know that statesmen, of the more responsible sort, were working to consolidate a balance of interests that would make war extremely improbable. Who had outdistanced them all in foresight and planning sufficiently to lay down a definite program of "no annexations?"

Fortunately the clue to the answer is supplied to us by unquestionable Jewish sources. The *American Jewish News*, of September 19, 1919, had an advertisement on its front page which read thus:

"WHEN PROPHETS SPEAK
By Litman Rosenthal
Many years ago Nordau prophesied the Balfour Declaration. Litman Rosenthal, his intimate friend, relates this incident in a fascinating memoir."

The article, on page 464, begins: "It was on Saturday, the day after the closing of the Sixth Congress, when I received a telephone message from Dr. Herzl asking me to call on him."

This fixes the time. The Sixth Zionist Congress was held at Basle in August, 1903.

The memoir continues: "On entering the lobby of the hotel I met Herzl's mother who welcomed me with her usual gracious friendliness, and asked me whether the feelings of the Russian Zionists were now calmer.

" 'Why just the Russian Zionists, Frau Herzl?' I asked. 'Why do you only inquire about these?'

" 'Because my son,' she explained, 'is mostly interested in the Russian Zionists. He considers them the quintessence, the most vital part of the Jewish people.' "

At this Sixth Congress the British Government ("Herzl and his agents had kept in contact with the English Government"—Jewish Encyclopedia, Vol. 12, page 678) had offered the Jews a colony in Uganda, East Africa. Herzl was in favor of taking it, not as a substitute for Palestine, but as a step toward it.

It was this which formed the chief topic of conversation between Herzl and Litman Rosenthal in that Basle hotel. Herzl said to Rosenthal, as reported in this article: "There is a difference between the final aim and the ways we have to go to achieve this aim."

Suddenly Max Nordau, who seems at the conference held last month in London to have become Herzl's successor, entered the room, and the Rosenthal interview was ended.

Let the reader now follow attentively the important part of this Rosenthal story:—(the italics are ours)

"About a month later I went on a business trip to France. On my way to Lyons I stopped in Paris and there I visited, as usual, our Zionist friends. One of them told me that this very same evening Dr. Nordau was scheduled to speak about the Sixth Congress, and I, naturally, interrupted my journey to be present at this meeting and to hear Dr. Nordau's report. When we reached the hall in the evening we found it filled to overflowing and all were waiting impatiently for *the great master*, Nordau, who, on entering, received a tremendous ovation. But Nordau, without paying heed to the applause showered upon him, began his speech immediately, and said:

" 'You all came here with a question burning in your hearts and trembling on your lips, and the question is, indeed, a great one, and of vital importance. I am willing to answer it. What you want to ask is: How could I—I who was one of those who formulated the Basle program—how could I dare to speak in favor of the English proposition concerning Uganda, how could Herzl as well as I betray our ideal of Palestine, because you surely think that we have betrayed it and forgotten it. Yet listen to what I have to say to you. I spoke in favor of Uganda after long and careful consideration; deliberately I advised the Congress to consider and to accept the proposal of the English Government, a proposal made to the Jewish nation through the Zionist Congress, and my reasons—but instead of my reasons let me tell you a political story as a kind of allegory.

" 'I want to speak of a time which is now almost forgotten, a time when the European powers had decided to send a fleet against the fortress of Sebastopol. At this time Italy, the United Kingdom of Italy, did not exist. Italy was in reality only a little principality of Sardinia, and the great, free and united Italy was but a dream, a fervent wish, a far ideal of all Italian patriots. The leaders of Sardinia, who were fighting for and planning this free and united Italy, were the three great popular heroes: Garibaldi, Mazzini, and Cavour.

" 'The European powers invited Sardinia to join in the demonstration at Sebastopol and to send also a fleet to help in the siege of this fortress, and this proposal gave rise to a dissension among the leaders of Sardinia. Garibaldi and Mazzini did not want to send a fleet to the help of England and France and they said: "Our program, the work to which we are pledged, is a free and united Italy. What have we to do with Sebastopol? Sebastopol is nothing to us, and we should concentrate all our energies on our original program so that we may realize our ideal as soon as possible."

" 'But Cavour, who even at this time was the most prominent, the most able, and the most far-sighted statesman of Sardinia, insisted that his country should send a fleet and beleaguer with the other powers Sebastopol, and, at last, he carried his point. *Perhaps it will interest you to know that the right hand of Cavour, his friend and adviser, was his secretary, Hartum, a Jew,* and in those circles, which were in opposition to the government, one spoke fulminantly of Jewish treason. And once at an assembly of Italian patriots one called wildly for Cavour's secretary, Hartum, and demanded of him to defend his dangerous and treasonable political actions. And this is what he said: "Our dream, our fight, our ideal, an ideal for which we have paid already in blood and tears, in sorrow and despair, with the life of our sons and the anguish of our mothers, our one wish and one aim is a free and united Italy. *All means are sacred if they lead to this great and glorious goal.* Cavour knows full well that after the fight before Sebastopol *sooner or later a peace conference will have to be held,* and at this peace conference *those powers will participate who have joined in the fight.* True, Sardinia has no immediate concern, no direct interest at Sebastopol, but if we will help now with our fleet, *we will sit at the future peace conference, enjoying equal rights with the other powers.*

and at this peace conference Cavour, as the representative of Sardinia, will proclaim the free and independent, united Italy. Thus our dream for which we have suffered and died, will become, at last, a wonderful and happy reality. And if you now ask me again, what has Sardinia to do at Sebastopol, then let me tell you the following words, *like the steps of a ladder*: Cavour, Sardinia, the siege of Sebastopol, the future European peace conference, the proclamation of a free and united Italy."'

"The whole assembly was under the spell of Nordau's beautiful, truly poetic and exalted diction, and his exquisite, musical French delighted the hearers with an almost sensual pleasure. For a few seconds the speaker paused, and the public, absolutely intoxicated by his splendid oratory, applauded frantically. But soon Nordau asked for silence and continued:

"'Now this great progressive world power, England, has after the pogroms of Kishineff, in token of her sympathy with our poor people, offered through the Zionist Congress the autonomous colony of Uganda to the Jewish nation. Of course, Uganda is in Africa, and Africa is not Zion and never will be Zion, to quote Herzl's own words. But Herzl knows full well that *nothing is so valuable to the cause of Zionism as amicable political relations* with such a power as England is, and so much more valuable as England's main interest is concentrated in the Orient. Nowhere else is precedent as powerful as in England, and so it is most important to accept a colony out of the hands of England and create thus a precedent in our favor. Sooner or later the Oriental question will have to be solved, and the Oriental question means, naturally, also the question of Palestine. England, who had addressed a formal, political note to the Zionist Congress—the Zionist Congress which is pledged to the Basle program, England will have the deciding voice in the final solution of the Oriental question, and Herzl has considered it his duty to maintain valuable relations with this great and progressive power. *Herzl knows that we stand before a tremendous upheaval of the whole world. Soon, perhaps, some kind of a world-congress will have to be called*, and England, the great, free and powerful England, will then continue the work it has begun with its generous offer to the Sixth Congress. And if you ask me now what has Israel to do in Uganda, then let me tell you as the answer the words of the statesmen of Sardinia, only applied to our case and given in our version; let me tell you the following words as if I were showing you *the rungs of a ladder leading upward and upward: Herzl, the Zionistic Congress*, the English Uganda proposition, *the future world war, the peace conference* where with the help of England a free and Jewish Palestine will be created.'

"Like a mighty thunder these last words came to us, and we all were trembling and awestruck as if we had seen a vision of old. And in my ears were sounding the words of our great brother Achad Haam, who said of Nordau's address at the First Congress:

" 'I felt that one of the great old prophets was speaking to us, that his voice came down from the free hills of Judea, and our hearts were burning in us when we heard his words, filled with wonder, wisdom and vision.' "

The amazing thing is that this article by Litman Rosenthal should ever have been permitted to see print. But it did not see print until the Balfour Declaration about Palestine, and it never would have seen print had not the Jews believed that one part of their program had been accomplished.

The Jew never betrays himself until he believes that what he seeks has been won, then he lets himself go. It was only to Jews that the 1903 "program of the Ladder"—*the future world war—the peace conference—the Jewish program*—was communicated. When the ascent of that ladder seemed to be complete, then came the public talk.

A similar illustration of this is to be found in the fall of the Czar. When that event transpired it was an occasion of great rejoicing in New York, and a Gentile of world-wide fame made a speech in which he lauded an American Jew of national reputation for having begun the downfall of the Czar by providing the money with which propaganda had been made among Russian prisoners in Japan during the Russo-Japanese war. The story came out only after the success of the plot. It is not at all out of keeping that the last men to see the last act of the plot carried out, the actual murder of Nicholas Romanovitch, his wife, his young daughters and his invalid boy, were "five Soviet deputies, the latter five all Jews." What began with the assistance of an American financier, finished with Soviet deputies.

Did International Jews in 1903 foresee the war? This Rosenthal confession is but one bit of evidence that they did. And did they do nothing but foresee it? It were well if the facts stopped at foresight and did not run on to provocation.

For the present the reader is invited to retain in his mind two points in this Rosenthal article: "Perhaps it will interest you to know that the right hand of Cavour, his friend and adviser, was his secretary, Hartum, a Jew." This is the way the Jewish press speaks of its own. If this paper, or a Chicago paper, or a New York paper should go through the list of the secretaries of the men of power in the world today and make the note after the names—"His secretary, a Jew," the Jewish Anti-Defamation Society would send letters of protest. There is one rule for the Gentile and one for the Jew, in the Jewish mind. Writing in the public prints about Hartum, he would be described as an "Italian."

Were the Jewish secretaries who abounded before the war, during the war and throughout the Peace Conference of less brilliance than Hartum? Were there not Hartums in England, France, Germany, yes and in Russia too (in the United States there were many) who saw the "program of the Ladder"? Did Max Nordau who saw it so clearly in 1903 forget it in 1914 and 1918?

We know this: the Jews in their Congress at Basle in 1903 foresaw "the future world war." How did they know it was to be a "*world war*"?

We know this also: the Protocols, perhaps as early as 1896, certainly not later than 1905, foresaw the policy of "no annexations."

The World War came to pass.

"No annexations" came to pass. What was then future in the Jewish world program, is now past.

In the Protocols there are two forms of declaration. One is, "we have." The other is, "we shall." If somewhere in the world this summer the high secret spokesman of the World Program is addressing his class of International Initiates, he will have to say "we have" in many places where the spokesman of 1896 said "we shall." Things have been accomplished.

"We will represent ourselves as the saviors of the laboring classes." That has been and is being done. "We will deflect the thoughts of the Gentiles to industry and commerce." That has been done. "We will create a strongly centralized administration so as to grasp all the social forces strongly in our hands." That has been done. "We will adopt for ourselves the liberal side of all parties and all movements and provide orators." That has been done. "We will force up wages." That has been done. "We will at the same time cause a rise in the price of prime necessities." That has been done. "We will also undermine the sources of production by instilling in the workmen ideas of anarchy." That has been done.

> "*To demonstrate our enslavement of the Gentile governments of Europe, we shall show our power to one by crimes of violence, that is, by a reign of terror.*"—Protocol 7.

Who that sees Russia and beholds the attitude of the premiers of England, France and Italy toward the Soviets, the "enslavement" of statesmanship by a condition that tangles more gnarledly the more it is dealt with—who that sees the prostration of Europe before a wound that is deliberately kept from healing, can forbear to say: That too has been done!

"Our plans will not upset contemporary institutions immediately. Their management will only be altered and consequently the whole procedure of their activity will thus be directed according to plans laid down by us." That has been done.

"We shall saddle the press and keep a tight rein upon it." That has been done. The rein is being strongly pulled in the United States at this moment, as many an editor can testify.

"Even if there should be those who desire to write against us, no one will print their writings." In large part, that has been done. It has been done completely with the profit-making press.

"We shall, as an incentive to speculation, encourage among the Gentiles a strong demand for luxuries—all-enticing luxuries." That has been done.

"To each act of opposition we must be in a position to respond by bringing on war through the neighbors of any country that dares to oppose us, and if these neighbors should plan to stand collectively against us, we must let loose a world war." (Protocol 7). The term "world war" is the same as that used by Rosenthal and Nordau. "Herzl knows," said Nordau in 1903, "that we stand before *a tremendous upheaval of the whole world.*"

"We must create unrest, dissension and mutual animosities throughout Europe and, with the help of her relationships, on other continents." This has been done. This passage continues: "There is a double advantage in this. First, we shall command the respect of all countries by this method, for they will realize that we have the power to create disorder or establish order at will." This too has been done.

Truly did the spokesman of 1896 speak of "those momentous occurrences of the near future toward which we are rushing in a stream of great crises."

Not only was "no annexations" achieved "as far as possible," just as the Protocols outlined it, but a host of other plans have matured in achievement along with it. "No annexations" as a matter of political morality is one thing; and "no annexations" for the reason that "this will shift war to an economic footing and nations will perceive the strength of our superiority in the aid we render" is quite another thing. The world was with the "no annexations" program as a matter of political morality; the other program, which used this morality as its vehicle, was hidden.

There are still other matters in this group which must receive attention, but another article will be necessary to do it. In the meantime, it is natural to wonder whether, with the program as outlined in this report of the Protocols having received fulfillment in so many particulars, a new Protocol, or a further unfolding of the Ladder has been made by the Wise Men to their Initiates; and whether any additional unveiling will ever come to the knowledge of the world. It would seem that a proper estimate of the knowledge now available would lead to such an awakening as to nullify the present program and make all future ones impossible. But Gentiles like their ease, and Judah is beckoned on by a bright star.

Issue of August 21, 1920.

XV.

# Is the Jewish "Kahal" the Modern "Soviet"?

THE Soviet is not a Russian but a Jewish institution. Nor is it the invention of Russian Jews of the present time, a new political device which has been set up as a vehicle of the ideas of Lenin and Trotsky; it is of ancient Jewish origin, a device which the Jews themselves invented to maintain their distinctive racial and national life after the conquest of Palestine by the Romans.

Modern Bolshevism, which is now known to be merely the outer cloak of a long-planned *coup* to establish the domination of a race, immediately set up the Soviet form of government because the Jews of all countries who contributed to Russian Bolshevism had long been schooled in the nature and structure of the Soviet.

The Soviet appears in the "Protocols of the Learned Elders of Zion" under the ancient name of KAHAL. In the Seventeenth Protocol this passage occurs:

> "Even now our brothers are under obligation to denounce apostates of their own family or any person known to be opposed to the *Kahal*. When *our kingdom comes*, it will be necessary for all subjects to serve the state in a similar manner."

Anyone who is acquainted with contemporary Jewish life knows what this denunciation of apostates means. The bitterness of the persecution, which falls upon a convert to Christianity, or upon the Jewish son or daughter of an orthodox family who chooses to marry a Gentile, is without parallel among men. Very recently in a western state a fine Jewish girl chose to marry a Gentile, who was a newspaperman. From the time of her announcement of intention, the girl was treated as an apostate. Had she died a most wretched death, had she descended to a status of most ignominious shame, the feelings which her fate would have aroused could not have been more terrible. A darkly solemn funeral service was held for her, and on her bridal day she was declared to be dead to her people.

The case is very far from being unusual. Perhaps one of the most moving descriptions of it is to be found in the life of Spinoza, the great philosopher whom modern Jews are fond of holding up for exhibition as a great ornament of their people. Spinoza's studies led him to question many of the dogmas the rabbis taught, those "commandments of men" of which the New Testament speaks, and as Spinoza was already a person of influence the very common Jewish tactic of bribery was tried upon him.

There would be some hesitation in using the words just set down—"the very common Jewish tactic of bribery"—if they were not known to be true. There is no desire to cast aspersions which grow out of malice. But Jewish history as written by Jews provides mountains of proof that bribery was, while present knowledge amply testifies that it still is, the favorite and most dependable weapon of the Jews. A Jewish writer, Jacob Israel De Haan, a Dutch lawyer resident in Jerusalem, has recently stated that one hope of a settlement of the Arab agitation in Palestine is the ease with which the Arab press can be bribed. His words are: "There is a strong agitation here among the Arabs against what they call the Zionist peril. But the Arabs, especially the Arabian papers, are open to bribe. This weakness will cause them, in the long run, to lose out against us."

So, young Spinoza was offered an annual stipend of 1,000 florins if he would be silent upon his convictions and from time to time show himself at the synagogue. This he refused with high-minded scorn. He made ready to earn his bread by polishing lenses for optical instruments. Upon this, he was excommunicated, a proceeding which is thus described:

"The day of excommunication at length arrived, and a vast concourse assembled to witness the awful ceremony. It began by the silent and solemn lighting of a quantity of black wax candles, and by opening the tabernacle wherein were deposited the books of the Law of Moses. Thus were the imaginations of the faithful prepared for all the horror of the scene.

The chief rabbi, the ancient friend and master, now the fiercest enemy, of the condemned, was to order the execution. He stood there pained, but implacable; the people fixed their eager eyes upon him. High above, the chanter rose and chanted forth in loud lugubrious tones the words of execration; while from the opposite side another mingled with these curses the thrilling sounds of the trumpet. And now the black candles were reversed, and were made to melt drop by drop into a huge tub filled with blood." (Lewes: Biographical History of Philosophy.)

Then came the final anathema. " 'With the judgment of the angels and of the saints, we excommunicate, cut off, curse and anathematize Baruch de Espinoza, with the consent of the elders and all this holy congregation, in the presence of the holy books: by the 613 precepts which are written therein, with the anathema wherewith Joshua cursed Jericho, with the curse which Elisha laid upon the children, and with all the curses which are written in the law. Cursed be he by day, and cursed be he by night. Cursed be he in sleeping, and cursed be he in waking, cursed in going out, and cursed in coming in. The Lord shall not pardon him, the wrath and the fury of the Lord shall henceforth be kindled against this man, and shall lay upon him all the curses written in the Book of the Law. The Lord shall destroy his name under the sun, and cut him off for his undoing from all the tribes of Israel, with all the curses of the firmament which are written in the Law * * * And we warn you that none may speak with him by word of mouth nor by writing, nor show any favor unto him, nor be under one roof with him, nor come within four cubits of him, nor read any paper composed by him.' " (Pollock: Life of Spinoza.)

"As the blasting words were uttered, the lights were all suddenly immersed in the blood, a cry of religious horror and execration burst from all; and in that solemn darkness, and to those solemn curses, they shouted Amen, Amen!" (Professor J. K. Hosmer: The Jews.)

That is a commentary on the decree of denunciation. It also throws a very strong light on the pressure which is brought against many Jews who would cry out against the anti-social ideas of their people, but who dare not because of the penalties it would bring.

This denunciation, as Protocol Seventeen orders, is to be made against anyone who is "known to be opposed to the Kahal" or ancient Soviet system of the Jews.

After the destruction of the Jewish state by the Romans, the Jews maintained a center in the Patriarch; and after the dispersion of the Jews out of Palestine this center of nationality was preserved in the Prince of the Exile, or Exilarch, an office which is believed to persist to the present time, and which some believe to be held now by an American Jew. In spite of all assertions to the contrary, the Jews have never ceased to be "a people"; that is, a consciously united racial group, different from all others, and with purposes and ideals which are strictly of the Jews, by the Jews and for the Jews in distinction from the rest of the world. That they constitute a nation within the nations, the most responsible Jewish thinkers not only declare but insist upon. And this is wholly in accord with the facts as observed. The Jew not only desires to live apart from other people, but he works with his own people as against others, and he desires as much as possible to live under his own laws. In the city of New York today, the Jews have succeeded in establishing their own court for the settlement of their own questions according to their own laws. And that is precisely the principle of the Soviet-Kahal.

From the first century forward, as any reader can see by consulting the Jewish Encyclopedia, the "community," "assembly" or "Kahal" has been the center of Jewish life. It was so earlier, in the time of the Babylonian captivity. And the last official appearance of it was at the Peace Conference, where the Jews, in accordance with their World Program, *the only program that passed successfully and unchanged through the Peace Conference*, secured for themselves the *right* to the Kahal for administrative and cultural purposes in addition to many other privileges in countries where their activities had been a matter of protest. The Polish question is purely a Jewish question, and Paderewski's failure as a statesman was entirely due to his domination by Jewish influences. The Rumanian question is likewise a Jewish question, and all Rumanians speak of the United States as "The Jews' Country" because they know through their statesmen the terrific pressure which was exerted by American Jews against their country, a pressure extending to the very necessities of life, and which compelled Rumania to sign agreements which are as humiliating as those that Austria asked of Serbia, out of which the World War grew. The Jewish Question is written all over the forces that provoked the war, and over all the hindrances to peace which the world has since seen.

Under the Kahal or ancient Soviet, the Jews lived by themselves and governed themselves, doing business with the government solely through their representatives. It was communism in a more drastic form than has been seen anywhere in the world outside Russia. Education, health, taxes, domestic affairs, all were under the absolute control of a few men who constituted the ruling board. This board, as the present-day Jewish hierarchy is supposed to be, was self-perpetuating, the office often passing in an unbroken line of hereditary succession through many generations. All property was in common, which however did not prevent the leaders becoming rich. These Kahals or Soviets existed in Rome, France, Holland, Germany, Austria, Russia, Denmark, Italy, Rumania, Turkey and England. In the United States the idea has developed around the synagogue and around national and international secret societies of Jews, of which more will be said in succeeding articles.

The Kahal is the traditional Jewish political institution during the dispersal of the race among the nations. Its international aspect is to be seen in the higher councils. These councils enlarged as the Jews spread over the world. The Jewish Encyclopedia cites the Council of Three Lands, the Council of Four Lands, and the Council of Five Lands, showing an international relationship in earlier years. But like all such records, public view of them is not easily accessible so far as they relate to modern times. The recent Zionist Congress in London, where doubtless much business was done that pertained to the Jewish people throughout the world, though not in public halls by any means, may be called the Council of Thirty-Seven Lands, for the delegates to that congress came from all parts of the world, from points remote as Lapland and South Africa, Persia and New Zealand. The purpose of these World Councils was the unification of the Jews, and the records of their assemblages run back through the centuries.

It is therefore no new thing that has arisen in Russia. It is the imposition by the Jewish revolutionists upon Gentile Russia of a form of control in which Judaism has been schooled from the earliest times of its contact with the world. Soviet Russia could not have been possible had not 90 per cent of the commissars been Jewish. Soviet Hungary could not have been possible had not Bela Kun, the chief Red, been a Jew, and had not 18 of his 24 commissars been Jews. The Jews are the only group schooled in the erection and administration of the Kahal.

An Associated Press dispatch under date of August 12 throws a light on the congeniality of the Soviet system and the Jewish mind. Speaking of the Polish towns and villages occupied by Bolshevik forces in their recent drive, the dispatch says:

> "The local Jewish parish populations already are said to be setting up Soviet and Communist governments."

Of course. Yet this is in strange contrast with what we are constantly told through the press of the sufferings of the Jews under the Soviet form and of their abhorrence of the Reds. However, most of what we read concerning this in the public press is Jewish propaganda, pure and simple, and the reports of men on the spot contradict it all. One relief worker testifies that relief work in Poland is frequently "hung up because some Jew landlord asks an exorbitant rent for his premises," while another testifies that though railroad fares in the supposedly famine-stricken districts have gone up 1,000 per cent, the best and highest-fare trains are "exclusively occupied by Jews." He adds, of his trip through Hungary, "The Hungarians have no money any more, but the Jews have."

"But American Jews abhor Trotsky and Sovietism," is the plea sometimes made.

Do they?

On page 9 of the American *Jewish World*, of July 30, a letter signed "Mrs. Samuel Rush" appears. It is headed: "Are We Really Ashamed of Trotsky?" Read a few excerpts from it:

"I have read of late several laments from editors of Jewish publications that the Jew is now libeled as a radical.

"It is true that many Jews are radicals. It is also true that some of the radical leaders are Jews.

"But before weeping over the downfall of the race, let's think a bit.

"Trotsky himself has never been represented as anything but a cultured man, a student of world economics, a powerful and efficient leader and thinker who will surely go down in history as one of the great men our race has given to the world.

"* * * Very few of us doubt any longer that behind the absurdities written about Russia is the great truth that Russia is in that unsettled state which always attends reconstruction. There is a plan behind this seeming disorder, and out of the upheaval will come order. It will not be utopia, but as good a government as the undoubtedly high-minded practical idealists who are building for Russia can build with the necessarily imperfect materials—human beings—with which they must work.

"And one of the leaders is Leon Trotsky!

"Are we really ashamed of Trotsky?"

The lady is evidently not ashamed of Trotsky, or Mr. Braunstein, as his real name is.

Or take Judge Harry Fisher, of Chicago. While drawing a salary for work in the court, Judge Fisher went abroad on Jewish relief work. His plans were changed somewhat after his departure and he landed in Russia. He asserts in several interviews that he was permitted to arrive in Russia on condition that he leave political matters alone. There has been no such restriction placed upon him since his return to the United States, for he appears as an open advocate of full trade relations with the Soviet Government of Russia.

The Chicago *Tribune* thus quotes him:

> " 'We must leave Russia alone' he said in summarizing his views. 'We should resume trade with the Soviet. The Bolshevist Government is permanent. * * * While there are only 700,000 members of the Communist party, the peasants, who represent almost 100,000,000 people, are solidly back of the Lenin regime.' "

Among the Soviet devices which the 100,000,000 peasants of Russia are said to be "solidly back of," is the following (it is particularly interesting in view of the fact that Judge Fisher is judge of the Morals Court of Chicago):

> " 'Some time ago it was published that the women of Russia had become national property,' he said. 'That is untrue, but the ease with which marriage and divorce may be effected makes for rapid changes. Everyone wanting to marry goes to what we would call the city hall and registers.
>
> " 'Inducements to marry are great. When people are hard pressed for clothes and food they sometimes make a pact to wed for a day.
>
> " 'The next day they go down to the city hall and register again. This time their names are put side by side in the divorce book. That is all that is necessary to be divorced, and they have had a good feed in the bargain.' "

Judge Harry Fisher, of Chicago, who has returned from Jewish relief work abroad, evidently is one with the others in not being ashamed of Trotsky.

Also Max Pine, for many years secretary of the United Hebrew Trades of New York, has been abroad in Soviet Russia as "a labor delegate." He too had many good things to say of the Soviets, among other things the strange contradiction that the Jews are doing very well in Russia but are not pro-Bolshevik!

Here are three persons from widely different spheres of life, yet each one of them indicates a natural liking for the Kahal or Soviet, an admiration of its methods, and a distinct good feeling toward its rulers. For Sovietism is the rankest form of autocracy, and the marriage laws of Soviet Russia are in full harmony with the program stated in the Protocols—

> "We will break down the influence of family life among the Gentiles."

Whether the Soviet-Kahals of Russia will succeed in completely undermining Russian family life is extremely doubtful. The weakness of Soviet rule is the same as that of the Protocols—a moral weakness which must eat like a cancer until it destroys the institutions which it infests.

Russia today, viewed in the light of the Protocols, does not represent the Judaic state, but it represents the Gentile state seized by Jewish forces. There are three degrees of action set forth in the Protocols. There is first the secret process of breaking up the integrity of society by the admixture of alluring but disruptive ideas. This is a work in which Gentile agitators are used. When the ideas have worked sufficiently to break up society and explode in a crisis, then as in Germany, the forces that have worked in secret come swiftly to the front to take the reins and guide the riot. In Germany this immediately occurred upon the collapse which followed the armistice, but the Germans were wise enough to know the meaning of the influx of Jews into all the official positions of the former empire, and it was not long before they were politically ousted. In Russia, however, the Jews sprang immediately into official positions and have succeeded in remaining there. It began with Kerensky compelling the Czar to lay aside his crown; it continues with Trotsky and his armies at the throat of Europe.

But this seizure of a country, as was attempted in Germany, and as was not only attempted but succeeded in Russia, is not the end of the Program. It is only the beginning of its open or public phase. The Soviet-Kahal makes for the complete breaking up of society, the entire cutting off of co-operation and communication, the ruling of each little section in the way desired, until the whole country lies helpless in isolated bits. The process includes, of course, the disintegration of industry also, the massing of Gentiles into an army, and a general destruction of morality and order. It is the Protocol program in its last stage before the reconstruction begins which shall make the conquered country a Jewish state.

The world has not seen that last stage yet. It has not come, even in Russia. If the Russian people waken from the daze into which they have been thrust, it will not come. Jewish voices loudly proclaim that Soviet Russia has come to stay. The only authoritative voice on that subject is the voice of Russia, and Russia has not yet spoken. Today the world is trembling on the very verge of Real Russia's awakening, and with it a retribution most terrible upon the Sovietists.

The program of the Protocols once came near succeeding in the French Revolution, but its essential immorality overreached itself. It has come a step nearer success in Russia, but there too its defiance of the moral law will be its undoing. The Jewish Question of today is being fought out in Russia and Poland, and the strength of the Jewish forces is largely and mostly supplied from the United States of America. No wonder those small East European independencies which are fighting for their lives refer to our country as "The Land of the Jews."

> "We will show our power to one," say the Protocols. "In order to demonstrate our enslavement of the Gentile governments of Europe, we shall show our power to one of them by crimes of violence, that is, by a reign of terror." (Protocol Seven.)

One by one the Gentile nations of Europe have been compelled to withdraw their troops from Russia. One by one the premiers of Europe have submitted to heavy shackling of their official hands with regard to the Russian question. And today the world looks on while little Poland, apparently the second country on the list of Soviet victims, is made to feel heavy vengeance for her daring to be independent of Jewish power. Russia has been made to pay for her attempted independence of the Jew; Poland is now being made to pay. It is a flame, the Jews of Eastern Europe hope, and many Jews of America also, which will sweep round the world.

If the ruling Jews of the world wished the Russian people freed, if they wished the flames of Bolshevism to be quenched, if they wished Jewish participation in revolutionary movements to be withdrawn, they could accomplish it in a week. What is going on today is going on by permission of the Jewish world powers.

There is apparently no desire to curtail a movement which largely originated in American Jewry. This is the program of "showing our power to one," and the program will be followed out. The "showing," however, is twofold; it is a showing of *power*, but it is also a showing of the *people* who wield the power, and in the end it might have been just as well had the power never been coveted, attained, or used.

Anyone who desires to test the exactitude of the Protocols' estimate of human nature may do so by observing his own reactions to the Russian Bolshevist situation. It is undeniable that there exists among all classes of Gentiles in America a kind of admiration for the *coup* which Lenin and Trotsky have managed on such a massive scale. The audacity of it, the ability to stay afloat thus long in defiance of so many laws, have conspired to draw out unwilling applause.

Consider then this passage from the Tenth Protocol:

> "The people feel an especial love and respect toward the genius who wields political power, and they say of all his high-handed actions: 'It is base, but clever! It is a trick, but how he played it! So majestic! So impudent!'
>
> "We count on attracting all nations to the constructive work of laying the foundations for the structure planned by us. It is necessary for us first of all to acquire the services of bold and fearless agents, who will overcome all obstacles in our pathway.
>
> "When we accomplish our governmental *coup d'etat*, we will say to the people: 'Everything has gone badly, all have suffered. We will eliminate the causes of your sufferings—nationality, frontiers and diversity of coinage. Of course you are free to pronounce sentence upon us, but that can scarcely be just if you do so before giving a trial to that which we offer you.' "

This is very well conceived, and this is the way in which, up to this time, it has worked out. But there will be a strong reaction set in. False promises li-

chickens come home to roost. The real originators, the real purpose of the movement hidden behind Bolshevism will become evident. And then the world will crush out again the World Program which at times has seemed so near success.

There will probably be more light upon this World Program as a result of the Russian Kahal-Soviet system than from any other attempt to realize it. For five generations the world has lived in a false light supposed to be shed by the French Revolution. It is now known that that revolution was not the Revolution of the French People, but the disorders of a minority who sought to impose upon the French People the very Plan which is now being considered. It was the French People who ultimately put down the so-called French Revolution. And France, as a result of that upheaval of a well-organized minority, has been bound by Jewish control ever since.

The Russian Revolution will go down in history with no such false halo of romance around it. The world now knows it for what it is. The world will soon know whose was the money and whose were the brains that fostered it, and from what part of the world the principal impetus came. The Russian upheaval is racial, not political nor economic. It conceals beneath all its false socialism and its empty mouthings of "human brotherhood" a clear-cut plan of racial imperialism, which is not Russian, and which the common sense and interest of the world will speedily stamp out.

---

Issue of August 28, 1920.

XVI.

# How the "Jewish Question" Touches the Farm

THE real estate speculations of the Jews are familiar to all, but unfortunately do not constitute their entire land program. Many American cities have changed their characters entirely during the past 15 years by reason of Jewish speculation in residence property, and it is a fact established in the larger eastern cities that the recent exorbitant and extortionate rise in rents was largely a matter of the Jewish landlord. The governor of one of the most important of our commonwealths was loath to sign a bill regulating rents. His hesitancy was encouraged by very heavy pressure brought to bear upon him by the weightiest Jewish financial interests in his own and neighboring states. He finally decided that he would sign the bill and give the law effect, and the fact that decided him was his personal investigation and the investigation of his personal agents into hundreds of cases of abuse where he discovered that it was a common practice among Jewish landlords to transfer the same piece of property round and round to every member of the family in turn, each "transfer" being the excuse for a new increase in the rent. Men have their eyes opened to the Jewish Question in various ways: this was the way a governor had his eyes opened.

That, however, is not the peculiarity of Jewish landlords alone; Gentile landlords have played the same trick. But landlordism is peculiarly a Jewish ambition and distinction; the Jew is the Landlord of America. Any group of tenants almost anywhere in America, except the West, could testify to this.

Nor is landlordism itself reprehensible, things being what they are, unless it is anti-social and anti-American. And just here is where it gets point. Some of the oldest and most sacred shrines of Americanism in the East have entirely lost their character as such by the invasion—not of "foreigners"—but of Jews.

The more one sees of this invasion, the more one utterly distrusts the statistics given out by Jews as to the Jewish population of the United States.

Do you know that the one nationality on which the Government of the United States is estopped from asking questions, either for immigration or census statistics, is the Jewish?

Do you know that when the Government of the United States wants to know anything about the Jews, it must go to statisticians which the Jews themselves support?

If a nation claims that it is no nation with respect to the United States Government, as the Jews claim, and has no national statistics which it will permit the government to collect in the official way, why should it treat itself as a nation and keep its own records?

The Jews of the United States, like the Jews of every European country, are a nation among themselves, with their own government, their own policy, their own records; and the United States Government does business with the Jewish Government in America through chosen Jews—no doubt of that.

It is, however, a digression. The matter of Jewish statistics will come up again. In the meantime a glance at the rapid changing of so many American cities in all parts of the land leads to the belief that the Jewish statistics furnished by the Jews for Gentile consumption entirely misstate the facts, and this belief is strengthened by the knowledge that the statistics given by the Jews for Jewish consumption are very different from those supplied for the outside world.

Landlordism may be explained by the inclination of the Jew toward speculation, and we know that real estate has been made one of the most speculative of occupations, disgracefully, almost disastrously so. The Jew cannot be condemned for becoming a landlord, for becoming the most conspicuous landlord in America; he cannot be condemned apart from his Gentile co-offenders for the abuse he has made of his advantage as landlord. But it is a matter for American concern that the cities to which, in the schoolbooks, our children are taught to look as the birthplaces of liberty and as still the spokesmen of Americanism, should become Semite cities, financially and politically, and the recruiting grounds of the world's Bolshevism.

Until recently, however, the Jew in America has not cared for the land. It is a characteristic. The Jew is not an agriculturist. Lavish fortunes have been expended to make him so, but the productive work of farming has not had, and does not now have, any appeal to him. His choice in land is this: land that produces gold from the mine, and land that produces rents. Land that produces mere potatoes and wheat has not directly interested him.

It is true, of course, that the land question has been distinctly Jewish in countries like Poland and Rumania. No law against Jews owning land in those countries has ever been effective in preventing their control of whole provinces. Not that the Jews demanded the right to farm the land, their choice was to farm the farmers. By devious methods and the use of "Gentile fronts" they could always secure control of the land, and thus dominating the peasants they could create almost any condition they wished. That is what they actually did. That is the Jewish Question in those parts of the world. Not for farming purposes, it must be understood, but for the purpose of controlling the main source of wealth in agricultural countries and for taking the control of the people away from their natural Gentile leaders.

These two things always go together in countries where there is intellectual or landed aristocracy to which the people look for leadership: the Jewish program is to destroy that leadership by gaining control of the land. It is profitable, of course, but when you survey the outworking of the plan you always see something other than profits involved. The consummate perfection of the Jewish plan for World Control is that it does not involve *sacrifice* as have other plans, it is immensely profitable at every stage, and the greater the profitableness the more surely the purpose is being achieved.

In America there was no aristocracy to be cut under by the gaining of land control. Jewish activity in the United States until recently has confined itself to the control of land products after they have been produced: that is, so to say, Jewish interests do not engage in trapping, but they control the fur trade.

Speaking of furs, it is very funny to see how some affairs turn out. During the war there was a great to-do made about the German control of the American fur trade. It was true that the fur trade was controlled from Germany, but not by Germans—by Jews! And then a great to-do was made about seizing, confiscating and absolutely selling out that "German" fur business to Americans, and the "Americans" who bought it were —Jews! The actual control has never changed; the profits still find their way to the "International" purse.

But furs is just an example. Jewish interests do not engage in raising grain, but control the grain that others produce. The need of the United States is a "Who's Who of Jewish Financiers" that the people may identify the men about whom they read as having made this "corner" or sprung that "coup." These interests, which have simply grabbed American-produced wealth and made American consumers pay and pay and pay, have been able to operate almost openly because of the sheer blindness of the American people as they read their newspapers. And, of course, while the American newspaper will gladly inform you that this man is an Italian and that man a Pole and the other man a Briton, it will never tell you that the fourth man is a Jew. There is a Jewish organization in every city, large and small, to prevent it—and they prevent it by methods that are violent and wholly subversive of the American ideal of liberty.

So, until recently, the plan in the United States has been to seize the commodity at just that point in its passage from producer to consumer where the heaviest weight of profit can be extracted from it—at the neck of the bottle, so to speak—and control it there. It is not service that the people pay for; they pay for seizure.

But a new movement has begun in the United States. Jewish millions are now being used to secure immense tracts of American lands. Formerly it was enough to control the cotton, as the bread was controlled, but now the movement is toward controlling the cotton lands. The operations are carefully guarded; "Gentile fronts" are used almost exclusively; but follow the trail through all the "blinds" and "false scents," and you come at last to the International Jew, whose throne is set up in London.

Many Jews have written THE DEARBORN INDEPENDENT saying that they do not know about these racial plans for world control. It may well be believed that they do not. One purpose of these articles is to tell them about it. But this every Jew rejoices in —the movement of his people toward power. And it is this sentiment that the International Jew implicitly trusts, and because this sentiment exists The International Program secures a maximum of success at a minimum risk of exposure. Jewry is not a democracy but an autocracy. Of course the ordinary Jew does not know! The question is, Why should he revile the Gentile who tries to tell him? If a Jew will not seal his mind against the statements made in these articles, he will find in his own knowledge sufficient corroboration of their principal features, and he will be in a better position to assist in the solution of the Jewish Question.

It is with amazement at certain men's conception of editorial honesty that THE DEARBORN INDEPENDENT has read some of the reports made of these articles. Under cover, principally of the Yiddish, alleged translations of these articles have been flung broadcast among non-English speaking Jews, translations which not only bear no resemblance to the original, but actually insert whole paragraphs of matter which never appeared in the original at all. Is there a fear of permitting the average Jew to read this series? Nothing is more desired by those whose purpose is to lay foundations for the solution of the Jewish Question in America than that every Jew in the United States should know exactly what is being printed here week by week. The Jew has been deceived by his leaders long enough.

The fact is, then, that there is a definite and already well forwarded movement toward the control of the cotton lands of the United States. The first step was to depreciate the market value of these lands as much as possible. Pressure was brought through certain banks to limit the cotton farmers' efforts. They were told that if they planted more acreage to cotton than they were told to, they would not be financed.

Cotton production was to go down while cotton prices were to go up, and the profits were not the farmers' but those who controlled the course of cotton from the first market to the wearer. Cotton farming was to be made less profitable, while cotton speculation was to become more profitable. The public was being compelled to supply the money by which the Jewish controllers were to buy the land. In brief, it was to be made more profitable to sell *cotton lands* than to sell cotton.

These statements are being deliberately restricted to the traffic in cotton lands. Jewish financiers in New York and London know these things, even if Jewish editors and rabbis do not.

This movement has been within the knowledge of certain classes of business men for a long time, indeed some have been forced by what used to be called "the pressure of circumstances," to serve the movement. But they were not able to interpret its meaning. It is only recently that the more important Gentile business men of the United States have been able to interpret certain things. The war was a potent eye-opener.

Those wonderful documents known as the "Protocols," with their strong grasp of every element of life, have not overlooked *Land*. The Land Program is found in the Sixth Protocol, which is one of the briefest of these documents and may be quoted in full to show now the relation it bears to certain excerpts made in previous articles:

*Protocol VI.*

"We shall soon begin to establish huge monopolies, colossal reservoirs of wealth, upon which even the big Gentile properties will be dependent to such an extent that they will all fall together with the government credit on the day following the political catastrophe. *The economists here present* must carefully weigh the significance of this combination. We must develop by every means the importance of *our super-government*, representing it as the protector and benefactor of all who voluntarily submit to us.

"The aristocracy of the Gentiles as a political

force has passed away. We need not take them into consideration. But, *as owners of the land,* they are harmful to us *in that they are independent in their sources of livelihood.* Therefore, at all costs, *we must deprive them of their land.*

"The best means to attain this is to *increase the taxes and mortgage indebtedness.* These measures will *keep land ownership in a state of unconditional subordination.* Unable to satisfy their needs by small inheritances, the aristocrats among the Gentiles will burn themselves out rapidly.

"At the same time it is necessary to encourage trade and industry vigorously and especially speculation, the function of which is to act as a counterpoise to industry. Without speculation, industry *will cause private capital to increase and tend to improve the condition of Agriculture BY FREEING THE LAND FROM INDEBTEDNESS FOR LOANS* by the land banks. *It is necessary for industry to deplete the land both of laborers and capital,* and, through speculations, *transfer all the money of the world into our hands,* thereby *throwing the Gentiles into the ranks of the proletariat.* The Gentiles will then bow before us to obtain the right to existence.

"*To destroy Gentile industry, we shall,* as an incentive to this speculation, *encourage among the Gentiles a strong demand for luxuries, all-enticing luxuries.*

"We will *force up wages,* which however will be of *no benefit to workers,* for *we will at the same time cause a rise in the prices of prime necessities, pretending that this is due to the decline of agriculture and of cattle raising.* We will also artfully and deeply undermine the sources of production by *instilling in the workmen ideas of anarchy,* and encourage them in the use of alcohol, at the same time taking measures to drive all the intellectual forces of the Gentiles from the land.

"That the true situation shall not be noticed by the Gentiles prematurely, we will mask it by a pretended effort to serve the working classes and promote great economic principles, for which an active propaganda will be carried on *through our economic theories.*"

The local and passing element in this is "the aristocracy of the Gentiles." That is to say, the program is not entirely fulfilled by the passing of aristocrats. Jewry goes on just the same. Its program stretches far. Jewry will retain such kings as it desires as long as it desires them. Probably the last throne to be vacated will be the British throne because what to the British mind is the honor of being Jewry's protector and therefore the inheritor of the blessing which that attitude brings, is to the Jewish mind the good fortune of being able to use a world-wide empire for the furtherance of Jewry's purpose. Each has served the other and the partnership will probably last until Jewry gets ready to throw Britain over, which Jewry can do at almost any time. There are indications that it has already started on this last task.

But the permanent elements in this Protocol are the *Land*, the *Jews*, and the *Gentiles*. A word of explanation may be necessary on this inclusion of the Gentiles as permanent: the Protocols do not contemplate the extermination of the Gentiles, nor the making of this world a completely Jewish populated world. The Protocols contemplate a Gentile world ruled by the Jews—the Jews as masters, the Gentiles as hewers of wood and drawers of water, a policy which every Old Testament reader knows to be typically Jewish and the source of divine judgment upon Israel time and again.

Now, look at this whole Program as it concerns the Land.

"*Owners of the land * * * are harmful to us in that they are independent in their sources of livelihood.*"

That is a foundation principle of the Protocols. It matters not whether the owners are the "Gentile aristocracy," the peasants of Poland, or the farmers of the United States—land ownership makes the owners "*independent in their sources of livelihood.*" And *any* form of independence is fatal to the success of the World Program which is written so comprehensively in the Protocols and which is advancing so comprehensively under Jewish guidance in the world of actual affairs today.

Not "tillers" of the land, not "dwellers" on the land, not "tenants," not an "agricultural peasantry," but "*owners* of the land"—this is the class singled out for attention in this Sixth Protocol, ***BECAUSE*** they are "***independent in their sources of livelihood.***"

Now, there has been no time in the history of the United States when apparently it was more easy for the farmer to own his land than now. Mortgages should be a thing of the past. Everywhere the propaganda of the question tells us that the farmers are growing "rich." And yet there were never so many abandoned farms!

"***Therefore, at all costs we must deprive them of their land.***"

How? "***The best means to attain this is to increase land taxes and mortgage indebtedness.***" High taxes to keep the land at all, borrowed money to finance the tilling of it.

"***These measures will keep land ownership in a state of unconditional subordination.***"

We will leave it to the farmers of the United States to say whether this is working out or not.

And in a future reference to this subject we will show that whenever an attempt is made to enable farmers to borrow money at decent rates, whenever it is proposed to lighten the burden of "mortgage indebtedness" on the farm, Jewish financial influence in the United States steps in to prevent it, or failing to prevent it, mess it all up in the operation.

By increasing the farmer's financial disability on the one hand, and by increasing industrial allurements on the other, a very great deal is accomplished. The Protocol says: "***It is necessary for industry to deplete the Land both of laborers and capital.***"

Has that been done? Have the farms of the United States been depleted both of laborers and capital? Certainly. Money is harder for the farmer to get than it is for any other man; and as for labor, he cannot get it on any terms.

What is the result of these two influences, the one working on the farm, and the other in the cities? It is precisely what the Protocol says it will be: Increased wages that buy less of the materials of life—"we will at the same time cause a rise in the prices of prime necessities, pretending that this is *due to the decline of agriculture and cattle raising.*"

The Jew who set these Protocols in order was a financier, economist and philosopher of the first order. He knew what he was talking about. His operations in the ordinary world of business always indicated that he knew exactly what he was doing. How well this Sixth Protocol has worked and is still working out in human affairs is before the eyes of everyone to see.

Here in the United States one of the most important movements toward real independence of the financial powers has been begun by the farmers. The farmers' strong advantage is that, owning the land, he is independent in his sources of livelihood. The land will feed him whether he pleases International Jewish Financiers or not. His position is impregnable as long as the sun shines and the seasons roll. It was therefore necessary to do something to hinder this budding independence. He was placed under a greater disadvantage than any other business man in borrowing capital. He was placed more ruthlessly than any other producer between the upper and nether stones of a thievish distribution system. Labor was drawn away from the farm. The Jew-controlled melodrama made the farmer a "rube," and Jew-made fiction presented him as a "hick," causing his sons to be ashamed of farm life. The grain syndicates which operate against the farmer are Jew-controlled. There is no longer any possibility of doubting, when the facts of actual affairs are put alongside the written Program, that the farmer of the United States has an interest in this Question.

What would this World Program gain if the wageworkers were enslaved and the farmers were allowed to go scot-free? Therefore the program of agricultural interference which has been only partially outlined here.

But this is not all.

Any writer who attempts fully to inform the Gentile mind on the Jewish Question must often feel that the extent of the Protocols' Conspiracy is so great as to stagger the Gentile mind. Gentiles are not conspirators. They cannot follow a clue through long and devious and darkened channels. The elaborate completeness of the Jewish Program, the perfect co-ordination of its mass of details wearies the Gentile mind. This, really more than the daring of the Program itself, constitutes the principal danger of Program being fulfilled. Gentile mental laziness is the most powerful ally the World Program has.

For example: after citing the perfectly obvious coincidence and most probable connection between the Protocols and the observable facts with reference to the farm situation, the writer is compelled to say, as above, "But this is not all." And it is a peculiarity of Gentile psychology that the Gentile reader will feel that it ought to be all because it is so complete. This is where the Jewish mind out-maneuvers the Gentile mind.

Gentiles may do a thing for one reason: the Jew often does the same thing for three or four reasons. The Gentile can understand thus far why Jewish financiers should seek control of the land in order to prevent widespread Agricultural Independence which, as Protocol Six says, would be "harmful to us." That reason is perfectly clear.

But there is another. It is found in the Twelfth Protocol. It contemplates nothing less than the playing of City against Country in the great game now being exposed. Complete control over the City by the industrial leverage, and over the Country by the debt leverage, will enable the Hidden Players to move first the Country by saying that the City demands certain things, and then move the City by saying that the Country demands certain things, thus splitting Citizens and Farmers apart and using them against one another.

Look at the plainness and the boldness, yet the calm assurance, with which this plan is broached:

> "*Our calculations reach out, especially into the country districts.* There we must necessarily *arouse those interests and ambitions which we can always turn against the city, representing them to the cities as dreams and ambitions for independence on the part of the provinces.* It is clear that the source of this will be precisely the same, and that it will come from us. It will be necessary for us *before we have attained full power* to so arrange

matters that, *from time to time, the cities shall come under the influence of opinion in the country districts*, that is, of the majority *prearranged by our agents* * * *"

The preliminaries of the game are here set forth—to jockey City and Farm against each other, that in the end the Conspirators may use whichever proves the stronger in putting the Plan over. In Russia, both schemes have been worked. The old regime, established in the Cities, was persuaded to lay down power because it was made to believe that the peasants of Russia requested it. Then, when the Bolshevists seized power, they ruled the peasantry on the ground that the Cities wanted it. The Cities listened to the Country, now the Country is listening to the Cities.

If you see any attempt made to divide City and Farm into antagonistic camps, remember this paragraph from the Twelfth Protocol. Already the poison is working. Have you never heard that Prohibition was something which the backwoods districts forced upon the cities? Have you never heard that the High Cost of Living was due to extravagant profits of the farmer?—profits which he doesn't get.

One big dent in this Program of World Control could be made if the Citizen and the Farmer could learn each other's mind, not through self-appointed spokesmen, but directly from each other. City and Farm are drifting apart because of misrepresentation of outsiders, and in the widening rift the sinister shadow of the World Program appears.

Let the Farmers look past the "Gentile fronts" in their villages or principal trading points, past them to the real controllers who are hidden.

---

Issue of September 4, 1920.

XVII.

# Does Jewish Power Control the World Press?

THE purpose of this article is twofold: to set forth what the Protocols have to say about the relation of the Press to the World Program, and to make an introduction to a study of Jewish influence on the Press.

The Jewish race has always been aware of the advantages to be derived from news. This was one of the factors in its control of European commerce from the earliest Christian times. To be informed beforehand, to know what was coming before the Gentiles among whom they lived knew it, was a special privilege of the Jews, made possible by the close communication in which widely separated Jewish groups kept themselves. From the first they were inveterate correspondents. They were the inventors of the news-letter.

This does not imply, however, that the Jews were the forerunners or even the sponsors of the modern Press. It was no part of their purpose to distribute news among the people, but to keep it for themselves as a secret advantage. The political, economic and commercial news which sped with really remarkable facility throughout Europe, from Jewish community to Jewish community, was in reality the official budget by which each community informed all the others of what was transpiring, as to war, trade currents, rising emergencies, or whatever the matter may have been. For centuries the Jews were the best informed people on the continent; from their secret sources in courts and chancellories, from privileged Jews who were placed in every position of vantage, the whole race was informed of the state of the world.

Scouts were kept in motion everywhere. Far down in South America, before the British or Dutch colonies in North America had hardly secured a foothold, there were Jews who served as outposts for European trade interests. The world was spied out in the interests of their race, just as today the entire planet is under the watchful eyes of Jewish agents—mostly Gentiles, it must be said—for any hint of new gold discoveries.

An interesting and historic illustration of the Jews' appreciation of news is to be found in the career of Nathan Rothschild. Rothschild had laid all his plans on the assumption that the Emperor Napoleon, then banished to Elba, was finally eliminated from European affairs. Napoleon unexpectedly returned, and in the "Hundred Days" it seemed as if the Rothschild financial edifice might collapse. Feverishly the financier aided both Prussia and England, and as the Battle of Waterloo approached, no one was more interested in the outcome than he.

Rothschild was a man who shrank from the sight of blood; he was physically a coward, and any sign of violence unnerved him; but so intense was his interest in the battle on which his whole fortune seemed to depend, that he hastened to France, followed the British Army, and when the battle began he hid himself in "some shot-proof nook near Hougomont" where he watched all day the ebb and flow of battle. Just before Napoleon ordered the last desperate charge Rothschild had made up his mind. He said afterward that his exclamation at this point was, "The House of Rothschild has won the battle."

He hurried from the field, galloped wildly to Brussels, communicating not a word of what he knew to the anxious people he met by the way. Hiring a carriage at an exorbitant price, he galloped away to Ostend. Here a fierce storm was raging on the ocean and no sailor was willing to set out for England, about 20 miles away. Rothschild himself, always afraid of danger, forgot his fear in his visions of the stock market. He offered 500, 800, and at length 1,000 francs to the man who would take him across. But no one dared. Finally one sailor proposed that if Rothschild would pay 2,000 francs into his wife's hands, he would attempt it.

Half dead the two men reached the English coast, but without rest Rothschild ordered express post and hurried away to London. Whip and spur were not spared on that journey.

There were no telegrams in those days, no swift communication. England was anxious. The rumors were bad. And on the morning of June 20, 1815, when Nathan Rothschild appeared in his usual place at the

Stock Exchange and leaned against the column, England knew nothing of what he knew. He was pale and broken. The sight of his face led the other financiers to believe that he had received bad news from the front. Then it was seen that he was quietly selling his securities. What? Rothschild unloading? The market dropped disastrously, a very panic seized the financiers, the market was flooded with consols offered for sale—and all that was offered, Rothschild's agents bought!

So it went on, all day the 20th, and all day the 21st. At the close of business the second day, Rothschild's heavy chests were crammed with securities. Then in the evening a courier galloped into London with the news that Wellington had won and Napoleon was a fugitive. But Nathan Rothschild had made $10,000,000 and the men he did business with had lost that much—all as an affair of news!

There was a little incident in Washington during the war—a "leak" of news, it was called. The wise men of Wall Street sometimes whisper that even between 1914-1918 there were men of Rothschild's race who showed his same appreciation of "news," with the same profitable results. And not only the men of "Rothschild's race," but some of their "Gentile fronts," also.

There were times during the war when no Gentile knew what was going on in certain countries. The Jewish leaders always knew. Some very interesting testimony can be presented on that point.

Aside from its own interest, this Rothschild narrative fully illustrates the statement that while the Jews were very early news-gatherers, they were not publicists. They used the news for their own benefit; they did not disseminate it. If it had depended on their influence, there would have been no public Press at all. It was in France, which had no newspapers outside the capital, that the French Revolution was possible. There being no reliable exchange of news and opinion, the people were kept in ignorance. Paris itself did not know that the Bastille had fallen until next day. Where there is no Press, minorities easily gain control—as the Jewish-Bolshevist revolution in Russia illustrates.

One of the most dangerous developments of the time is public distrust of the Press. If the day ever comes when swift, reliable and authoritative communication with the entire people shall be necessary for public action in the interests of public safety, the nation may find itself sadly crippled unless a new confidence in the daily Press can be built up. If for no other reason than that a free press is a safeguard against minority seizure of control, such laws as the zone laws, or any restrictions on the freest and fullest communication between various parts of the country, should be absolutely abolished.

But, the Press being in existence, and being largely an Anglo-Saxon creation, it is a force not to be treated lightly, and that is the point where the World Program and Jewish Control come in contact with it.

The Protocols, which overlook nothing, propose a very definite plan with regard to the Press. As in the multitude of other matters with which these remarkable documents deal, there are the two phases—"what we have done," and "what we will do."

As early as the Second Protocol, the Press comes in for attention. It is significant that it makes its appearance in the same Protocol in which the "No Annexations" program was announced 20 years before the World War, in the same Protocol in which it is announced that Gentile rulers will be allowed to appear before the people for a short period, while Jewish influences were organizing themselves behind the seats of power, and in the same Protocol where Darwinism, Marxism and Nietzscheism are claimed among the most "demoralizing" doctrines which Jewish influence has disseminated. These are very curious statements, but not stranger than the actuality that has come to pass.

Says the Second Protocol:

> "There is one great force in the hands of modern governments, which *creates thought movements among the people, that is, the Press*. The presumed role of the Press is to indicate supposedly indispensable needs, to register popular complaints, and to create discontent. The triumph of 'free speech' (babbling) rests in the Press. But governments are unable to profit by

> this power, *and it has fallen into our hands. Through it we have attained influence while remaining in the shadow. Thanks to it, we have amassed gold, though it has cost us torrents of blood and tears.*"

In the same Protocol "*our* Press" is spoken of as the agency through which are disseminated "those theories of life which we have induced them (the Gentiles) to regard as the dictates of science."

> "To this end *we shall certainly endeavor to inspire blind confidence in these theories by means of our Press.*"

Then follows the claim made concerning the three most revolutionary theories in the physical, economic and moral realms, namely, Darwinism, Marxism and Nietzscheism.

In the Third Protocol the claim is made that this control of the Press is being used to break down respect for authority:

> "*Daring journalists* and audacious pamphleteers *make daily attack upon the personnel of the administration. This abuse of authority is definitely preparing the downfall of all institutions*, and everything will be overturned by blows coming from the infuriated populace."

Again, in the Seventh Protocol, discussing the progress which the World Program has already made, the part played by the Press is indicated:

> "We must force the Gentile governments to adopt measures which will promote *our broadly conceived plan already approaching its triumphal goal, by bringing to bear the pressure of stimulated public opinion*, which has in reality been *organized by us with the help of the so-called 'great power' of the Press. With few exceptions not worth considering, it is already in our hands.*"

Thus twice is the claim made to control of the Press. "It has fallen into our hands," says the Second Protocol. "It is already in our hands," says the Seventh. In the Second Protocol the Press is represented as furthering revolutionary physical, economic and moral philosophies; while in the Seventh it is used to create the "pressure of stimulated public opinion" for the purpose of "forcing Gentile governments to adopt measures which will promote our broadly conceived plan, already approaching its triumphant goal."

A word of comment may be made here upon the claim of the Second Protocol that "thanks to it (the Press), we have amassed gold, though it has cost us torrents of blood and tears."

This is a statement which can be illustrated in many ways. "Though it has cost us torrents of blood and tears" is an admission upon which the Protocols throw light, a light which also shines upon the Jewish argument regarding responsibility for the recent war, namely, that Jewish World Financial Power could not have willed the war seeing that Jews suffered so heavily in Eastern Europe. The Protocols frankly recognize the possibility of Jews suffering during the establishment of the World Program, but it consoles them with the thought that they fall as soldiers for the good of Israel. The death of a Jew, we are told in the Protocols, is more precious in the sight of God than the death of a thousand "seed of cattle," which is one of the delicate names applied to the Gentiles.

The reference to the amassment of gold is very clear. It does not apply to ownership of publications and a share in their profits only, but also the use that may be made of them through silence or outcry to promote International Jewish Financiers' schemes. The Rothschilds bought editors as they bought legislators. It was a preliminary of nearly every scheme they floated to first "fix" the newspapers, either for silence or clacque boosting. In matters of war and peace; in the removal of administrations inimical to Jewish financial or political plans; in the elimination by public exposure of "Gentile fronts" whom their Jewish masters wished to be rid of; in the gradual building up of reputation and influence for "rising men" who had been chosen for work in the future—in these and like matters the Press very greatly aided the International Cabal in attaining its end.

All the details of the foregoing paragraph can be illustrated at length by instances which have occurred in the United States within the past 15 years.

There was once a Senator of the United States who —but that story illustrates another point also, and will be reserved until that point is reached in this series of discussions.

The Twelfth Protocol, however, contains the entire plan of Control of the Press, reaching from the present time into the future when the Jewish World Government shall be established. The reader is invited to read carefully and thoughtfully the deep and wide outreaching of this plan.

Keep also in mind the boast that has been made for generations that no publication that has handled the Jewish Question in a manner distasteful to the Jewish powers has been allowed to live.

> "What role is played at present by the Press? It serves to inflame the passions of selfish partisanship which our interests require. It is shallow, lying and unfair, the most people do not understand what end it serves."

In that quotation we have the same low estimate which was noted when we studied "the estimate of human nature" which the Protocols contain.

Now, for the Plan of Press Control: We separate the points for convenience:

> "*We shall handle the Press in the following manner:*
>
> 1. "We shall saddle it and keep tight rein upon it. We shall do the same also with other printed matter, for of what use is it to rid ourselves of attacks in the Press, if we remain exposed to criticism through pamphlets and books?"
>
> 2. "*Not one announcement will reach the people save under our supervision. We have attained this at the present time to the extent that all news is received through several agencies in which it is centralized from all parts of the world.*"

A sidelight on the first sentence above may be had from this Jewish statement regarding the British Declaration relating to Palestine: "This Declaration was sent *from the Foreign Office to Lord Walter Rothschild.* * * * It came perhaps as a surprise to large sections of the Jewish people * * * But to those who were active in Zionist circles, the declaration was no surprise. * * * *The wording of it came from the British Foreign Office, but the text had been revised in the Zionist offices in America as well as in England. The*

*British Declaration was made in the form in which the Zionists desired it.* * * *" pp. 85-86, "Guide to Zionism," by Jessie E. Sampter, published by the Zionist Organization of America.

> 3. "Literature and journalism are two most important educational forces, and consequently our government will become the owner of most of the journals. * * * *If we permit ten private journals, we shall organize thirty of our own, and so on. This must not be suspected by the public, for which reason all the journals published by us will be EXTERNALLY of the most contrary opinions* and tendencies *thus evoking confidence in them and attracting our unsuspecting opponents*, who thus will be caught in our trap and *rendered harmless*."

This is most interesting in view of the defense now being made by so many Jewish journals. "Look at the newspapers owned and controlled by Jews," they say; "see how they differ in policy! See how they disagree with each other!" Certainly, "externally," as Protocol 12 says, but the underlying unity is never hard to find.

Besides, one way of discovering who are the people that have knowledge of the Jewish World Problem, or who can be convinced of it, or who will write about it, is just to start a paper which "externally" seems to be independent on the Jewish Question. So deeply is this thought shared by even uneducated Jews that a rumor is today widespread in the United States that the reason for the present series of articles in THE DEARBORN INDEPENDENT is the desire of its owner to forward the Jewish World Program! Unfortunately, this scheme of starting a fake opposition in order to discover where the real opposing force is, is not confined to the Jewish Internationalists, although there is every indication that it was learned from them.

This idea of a misrepresentative front for certain secret purposes is expressed at length not only with reference to the Press, but throughout the Protocols in other relations But in Protocol 12 it is fully developed with regard to the Press, as the following quotations show.

(a) In order to force writers into such long productions that no one will read them, a tax on writing is proposed—"on books of less than 30 pages a double tax." Small articles are most feared. Therefore doubly tax the pamphlets of less than 30 pages. The longer articles fewer will read, so the Protocols argue, and the double tax will thus "force writers into such long productions that they will be little read, especially as they will be expensive."

BUT—

"That which we ourselves shall publish for directing the public mind will be cheap and widely read. The tax will discourage mere literary ambition, whereas the fear of punishment will make the writers subservient to us. *Even if there should be those who may desire to write against us, no one will publish their writings.*" (How many American writers know this!)

"Before accepting any work for printing, the publisher or printer must obtain permission from the authorities. *Thus we shall know in advance what attacks are being prepared against us and shall be able to counteract them by coming out beforehand with explanations on the subject.*"

That is largely the situation today. They do know in advance what is being done, and they do seek to disarm it beforehand.

(b) Here are the *Three Degrees of Jewish Journalism* which are not only stated in the Protocols but are observable in the everyday world of the present.

"The leading place will be held by organs of an official character. They will always stand guard over our interests *and consequently their influence will be comparatively small.*

"The second place will be held by semi-official organs whose aim it will be to attract the indifferent and lukewarm.

"In the third category we shall place *organs of apparent opposition.* At least one will be extremely antagonistic. *Our true opponents will mistake this seeming opposition as belonging to their own group and will thus show us their cards.*

"I beg you to notice that *among those who attack us there will be organs founded by us,* and they will attack exclusively those points which we plan to change or eliminate.

"*All our papers will support most diverse opinions:* aristocratic, republican, even anarchist, so long of course as the Constitution lives. * * These fools who believe they are repeating the opinions expressed by their party newspapers will be repeating our opinions or *those things which we wish them to think.*

"By always discussing and contradicting our writings *superficially, and without touching upon their essence, our press* will keep up a blank fire against the official newspapers, only to give us opportunity to express ourselves in greater detail than we could in our first declaration. This will be done when useful to us.

"These attacks will also convince the people of the full freedom of the press, and it will give our agents the opportunity of declaring that the papers opposing us are mere wind-bags, since they cannot find any real arguments to oppose our orders."

Undoubtedly that would be the case were all the papers controlled. In the case of the present series of articles, however, the tables appear to be turned. It is the Jewish Press which has so signally failed to bring forward disproof either by fact or argument.

"When necessary, we shall promulgate ideas in the third section of our Press *as feelers,* and then refute them vigorously in the semi-official press.

"*We shall overcome our opponents without fail because they will not have organs of the Press at their disposal.*

"*The pretext for suppressing a publication* will be that it stirs up the public mind without basis of reason"—a pretext which has already been urged time and again, but without the legal power to effect suppression, although without legal power the Jewish interests in the United States have effected a pretty complete suppression of everything they do not desire.

How far does Jewish influence control the Newspapers of the United States?

In so far as the use of the word "Jew" is concerned, the Press is almost completely dominated. The editor who uses it is certain to hear from it. He will be visited and told—contrary to everything the Jew is told—that the word "Jew" denotes a member of a religious denomination and not a member of a race, and that its use with reference to any person spoken of in the public prints is as reprehensible as if "Baptist," "Catholic," or "Episcopalian" were used.

The Jew is always told by his leaders that regardless of religion or country of birth, he is a Jew, the member of a race by virtue of blood. Pages of this paper could be filled with the most authoritative Jewish statements on this point. But what the Jew is told by his leaders, and what the Gentile editor is told by the Jewish committee are two different and antagonistic things. A Jewish paper may shriek to the skies that Professor So-and-So, or Judge So-and-So, or Senator So-and-So is a Jew; but the secular newspaper that should do that would be visited by an indignant committee bearing threats.

A certain newspaper, as a mere matter of news, published an excerpt from one of THE DEARBORN INDEPENDENT articles. Next day a number of advertising accounts dropped for lack of copy. Inquiry developed the fact that the reticent advertisers were all Jewish firms and the cause of their action was the really unimportant excerpt which the paper published. It developed also that the advertising agent who handled all the advertising for those Jewish firms was himself a Jew who also held an office in a Jewish secret society, which office was concerned exclusively with the control of newspapers in the matter of Jewish publicity. It was this man who dealt with the editor. A lame editorial retraction followed which faintly praised the Jews. The advertising was returned to the paper, and it is just a question whether that editor was rightly handled or not. Certainly he has been made to feel the power. But the diplomacy of it was bad. The editor, along with hundreds of others, has only been given the proper background for estimating the Jewish power in its wider reaches.

This is not to say that every editor should enter upon a campaign to expose the secret power. That is a matter for personal decision. Every editor, however, is so situated that he can see certain things, and he ought to see them, note them, and inwardly digest them.

Jewish publicity in response to these articles is very easy to get in almost any newspaper. Some have fallen most lamentably for lying statements. Others have opened their columns to propaganda sent out from Jewish sources. That is all very well. But the Gentile interest in the question has been largely ignored, even in cases where the editors are awake to the whole Question. This too affords a vantage from which the average editor can view what is transpiring in this country.

If a list of the Jewish owners, bondholders and other interests in our newspapers should be published, the list would be impressive. But it would not account for the widespread control of the Press as observed in this country. Indeed, it would be unfair in such a connection as this to list some of the Jewish-owned newspapers of the United States, because their owners are fair and public-spirited servants of the people.

Actual ownership does not often account for much in a newspaper. Ownership in the newspaper business is not always synonymous with control.

If you wish to know the control of the newspaper, look to its attorney and the interests he serves; look to the social connections of its chief editors; look to the advertising agents who handle the bulk of Jewish advertising; and then look to the matter of the paper's partisanship or independence in politics.

Newspaper control of the Press by the Jews is not a matter of money. It is a matter of *keeping certain things out of the public mind and putting certain things into it.*

One absolute condition insisted upon with the daily Press is that it shall not identify the Jew, mention him, or in any but the most favorable way call the public's attention to his existence.

The first plea for this is based on "fairness," on the false statement that a Jew is not a Jew but a church member. This is the same statement which Jewish agents in the United States Government have used for years to prevent the United States Government from listing the Jews in any racial statistics. It is in direct contradiction to what the Jews themselves are told. A flabby "fairness," a sloppy "broad-mindedness," a cry of "religious prejudice," is the first plea. The second is a sudden cessation of Jewish patronage. The third is withdrawal of patronage by every Gentile concern that is under the grip of Jewish financiers. It is a mere matter of brutal bludgeoning. And the fourth act, in a community thoroughly blinded to the Jewish Question, is the collapse of the offending publication.

Read the Jewish Encyclopedia for a list of some of the papers which dared open up the Question, and ceased!

When old Baron Moses Montefiore said at Krakau:

> "What are you prating about? As long as we do not have the press of the whole world in our hands, everything you may do is vain. We must control or influence the papers of the whole world in order to blind and deceive the people."

—he knew what he was saying. By "blinding" the people he only meant that they should not see the Jew, and by "deceiving" them he only meant that the people should think certain world movements meant one thing when they really meant another. The people may be told what happens: they may not be told what was behind it. The people do not yet know *why* certain occurrences which have affected their whole lives, should have occurred at all. But the "why" of it is very definitely known in certain circles whose news service never sees print, and sometimes not even writing.

Statistics as to the space given the Jews by newspapers concerning the things they want to get into print would also be an eye-opener. A minority nation, they get more publicity than any ten of the important minor nations of Europe—of the kind of publicity they want!

The number of Jewish contributors to the Press of the United States makes another interesting statistical bit. It would be sheer prejudice to make objectionable mention of many Jewish journalists and writers, and they come within the scope of this study only as they have shown themselves to be the watchful agents and active servants of the System. This is what many of them are. Not the ambitious young Jewish reporter who runs around the streets gathering news, perhaps, but the journalist at the seat of news and at the necks of those two or three important international runways through which the news of the world flows.

The whole matter, as far as extent of control is concerned, could be visualized on a map of the United States, by means of colored pins showing the number of Jewish-owned, provably Jewish-controlled papers, and the number of Jewish writers who are directing the majority thought of the various sections of the country.

The Jewish journalist who panders to unrest, whose literary ambition is to maintain a ferment in his readers, whose humor is sordid and whose philosophy is one of negation; as well as the Jewish novelist who extols his or her own people even while the story sows subtle seeds of disruption in Gentile social or economic life must be listed as the agents of that World Program which would break down society through the agency of "ideas". And it is very striking how many there are, and how skillfully they conceal their propaganda in their work.

Here and there in the United States it is now becoming possible to print the word "Jew" in the headlines of an article, and tell the Jewish committee which calls the next day that this as yet is a free country. Quietly a number of newspapers have tested the strength of this assumed control in their communities, and have discounted it.

There is no reason for fear on the part of the editor who has his facts. But the editor who backs down will more and more feel the pressure upon him. The man who courageously and fairly holds his ground will soon learn another thing that is not so generally known, namely, that with all the brilliance there is a lot of bluff, and that the chain of control once broken is felt throughout the whole system as a blow.

There is nothing that the International Jew fears so much as the truth, or any hint of the truth about himself or his plans. And, after all, the rock of refuge and defense, the foundation of endurance for Jew or Gentile must be the Truth.

---

Issue of September 11, 1920.

XVIII.

# Does This Explain Jewish Political Power?

LITTLE has yet been said in this commentary on the Protocols about the political program contained in them. It is desirable that the points be taken separately in order that when our study turns to actual conditions in this country, the reader may be in a position to judge whether the written program agrees with the acted program as it may be seen all about us. The World Program as outlined in these strange documents turns upon many points, some of which have already been discussed. Its success is sought (a) by securing financial control of the world, this having already been secured by the overwhelming indebtedness of every nation through wars, and by the capitalistic (not the manufacturing or managerial) control of industry; (b) by securing political control, which is easily illustrated by the condition of every civilized country today; (c) by securing control of education, a control which has been steadily won under the blinded eyes of the people; (d) by trivializing the public mind through a most complete system of allurement which has just brought us into a period which requires the new word "jazz" to describe it; and (e) by the sowing of seeds of disruption everywhere—not the seeds of progress, but of economic fallacies and revolutionary temper. All of these main objectives entail various avenues of action, none of which has been overlooked by the Protocols.

In leading up to what the Protocols have to say about the selection and control of Presidents, it will be enlightening to take the views which these documents express about other phases of politics.

It may be very interesting to those Jewish apologists, who in all their pronouncements never discuss the *contents* of the Protocols, to know that so far from their being a plea for monarchy, they are a plea for the most drastic and irresponsible liberalism in government. The powers behind the Protocols appear to have absolute confidence in what they can do with the people once the people are made to believe that popular government has really arrived.

The Protocols believe in frequent change. They like elections; they approve frequent revisions of constitutions; they counsel the people to change their representatives often.

Take this from the First Protocol:

"The abstract conception of Liberty made it *possible for us to convince the crowd* that government is only the management for the owner of the country, the people, and that *the steward can be changed like a pair of worn-out gloves. The possibility of changing the representatives of the people has placed them at our disposal* and, as it were, has placed them in our power as creatures of our purposes."

Note also how this Use of Change is buried in this paragraph from the Fourth Protocol which describes the evolution of a Republic:

"Every republic passes through several stages. *The first is that of senseless ravings,* resembling those of a blind man throwing himself from right to left. *The second is that of demagogy* which breeds anarchy and inevitably *leads to despotism,* not of a legal, open and consequently responsible character, but an unseen and unknown despotism, felt none the less because exercised by a secret organization. Such a despotism acts with even less scruple because it is hidden under cover and works behind the backs of *various agents, the shifting and changing of which will not harm its secret power,* but serve it, since such changes will relieve the organization from the necessity of expending its resources on rewards for long service."

This "changing" of servants is not unknown in the United States. A former Senator of the United States could easily testify to this if he only knew who did the "changing." Time was when he was the tool of every Jewish lobbyist in the Senate. His glib tongue lent charm and plausibility to every argument they wished to advance against the government's intentions. Secretly, however, the Senator was receiving "favors" from a very high source, "favors" of a financial character. The time came when it was desirable to "detach" the Senator. The written record of his "favors" was abstracted from its place of supposed secrecy, a newspaper system that has always been the ready organ of American Jewry made the exposure, and an indignant public did the rest. It could not have been done had not the man been compromised first; it could not have been done without certain newspaper connivance; it would never have been done had not the Senator's masters wished it. However, it was done.

In the Fourteenth Protocol, which begins "*When we become rulers*," it is pictured how hopeless the Gentile peoples will have become of any betterment of conditions through changes of government, and therefore will accept the promise of stability which the Protocolists of that time will be prepared to offer:

> "*The masses will become so satiated with the endless changes of administration which we instigated among the Gentiles when we were undermining their governmental institutions*, that they will tolerate anything from us * * *"

The official who is changed most quickly in this country is the man who questions certain matters which come from Jewish sources. There must be a small army of such men in the United States today. Some of them do not know even now how it happened. Some are still wondering why perfectly legitimate and patriotic information should have been lost in an icy silence when they sent it in, and why they should have lost favor for sending it.

Protocol Nine is full of the most amazing claims, of which these may serve as illustration:

> "At the present time, if any government raises a protest against us, it is only for the sake of form, it is under our control, and it is done by our direction, for *their anti-Semitism is necessary for keeping in order our lesser brothers. I will not explain this further as already it has been the subject of numerous discussions between us.*"

This doctrine of the usefulness of anti-Semitism and the desirability of creating it where it does not exist are found in the words of Jewish leaders, ancient and modern.

"In reality there are no obstacles before u

*Our super-government has such an extra-legal status that it may be called by the energetic and strong word*—dictatorship. I can conscientiously say that *at the present time we are the lawmakers.*"

In that Protocol this claim is made:

"*De facto, we have already eliminated every government except our own*, although *de jure* there are still many others left."

That is simple: the governments still exist, under their own names, having authority over their own people; but the super-government has unchallenged influence over all of them in matters pertaining to the Jewish Nation and particularly in matters pertaining to the purpose of The International Jew.

The Eighth Protocol shows how this can be:

"*For the time being, until it will be safe to give responsible government positions to our brother Jews, we shall entrust them to people whose past and whose character are such that there is an abyss between them and the people*; to people, for whom, in case of disobedience to our orders, there will remain only trial or exile (from public life), thus forcing them to protect our interest to their last breath."

In the Ninth Protocol again is this reference to party funds:

"*The division into parties has placed them all at our disposal*, inasmuch as *in order to carry on a party struggle it is necessary to have money, and we have it all.*"

There have been many investigations of campaign funds. None has ever yet gone deep enough to inquire into the "international" sources of these funds.

Now, in the United States during the last five years we have seen an almost complete Judaized administration in control of all the war activities of the American people. The function of the regularly organized United States Government during that time was practically confined to the voting of money. But the administration of the business end of the war was in charge of a government within a government, and this inner, extra government was Jewish.

It is, of course, often asked why this was so. The first answer given is that the Jews who were immediately placed in charge of the business administration of the war were competent men, the most competent men who could be found. This was actually the answer given to an inquiry as to the reason for so large a part of the foreign policy of the United States depending on the counsel of a certain group of Jews—they were the men who knew, no one else knew so much, the officials chosen by the people had a right to select the most efficient and able counsel they could find.

Very well, let that stand. Let the explanation be that in all the United States, Jews were the only persons to be found who could handle the emergency with masterly ease. We shall see more of this phase of the matter at another time. The war is not under discussion in this article, merely the fact that in an emergency the government became distinctly Jewish.

But the Second Protocol would appear to throw a little light on the matter:

> "*The administrators chosen by us* from the masses for their servility *will not be persons trained for government*, and *consequently they will easily become pawns in our game, played by our learned and talented counsellors, specialists educated from early childhood to administer world affairs. As we know, our specialists have been acquiring the necessary knowledge for governing* * * *"

The language is a trifle raw, as it usually is when Gentiles are under discussion. But the same fact, namely, that Jewish specialists have come to the aid of Gentile administrators in an emergency, when uttered for the consideration of the general public, may be very beautifully phrased.

The untrained Gentile administrator must have help; his unpreparedness makes it necessary. And who knows it better than those who have the help to offer? The Gentile public has been taught to suspect the man who has had experience in politics or government. This, of course, makes the whole situation doubly easy for those whose specialty it is to give "aid." Just *what interests* they aid most will give, when discovered, a strong light upon their zeal.

But in all that the Protocols have to say about the political angle of the World Program, nothing is of so great interest as that which concerns the selection and control of Presidents. The whole plan is outlined in the Tenth Protocol. The fact that the President of France seems to have been in mind is a localism; the plan is applicable elsewhere; indeed has elsewhere its most perfect illustration.

This Tenth Protocol, then, leads gradually up to the subject, tracing the evolution of rulers from Autocrat to President, and of nations from Monarchies to Republics.

The language of this passage is particularly objectionable, but no more so than can be found in current Jewish literature where boasting of power is indulged in. Unpleasant as the whole attitude is, it is valuable as showing in just what light the supporters of the Protocol Program view the Gentiles and their dignities. It must be borne in mind that the Jewish ideal is not a President, but a Prince and a *King*. The Jewish students of Russia marched the streets in 1918 singing this hymn—

"We have given you a God;
Now we will give you a *King*."

The new flag of Palestine, now permitted to fly without hindrance, bears insignia, as does every synagogue, of a Jewish *King*. The Jewish hope is that the *Throne* of David shall be set up again, as doubtless it will be. None of these things is to be decried in the least, nor to be regarded with anything but a decent respect, but they should be borne in mind as a side light on the expressed contempt for Gentile Presidents and Legislatures.

The Tenth Protocol reaches the theme of President thus:

> "Then the rise of the republican era became possible, and then in the place of a sovereign we substituted a caricature of him, a President picked from the crowd * * * Such was the foundation of the mine we laid underneath the Gentile people, or more accurately, the Gentile peoples."

It is with something of a shock that onê reads that men with a "past" are specially favored for the presidential office. Men with a "past" have become President in various countries, including the United States, there is no doubt of that. In some instances, the particular scandal that constituted the "past" has been publicly known; in other cases it has been hushed up and lost in a maze of rumor. In at least one case it was made the special property of a syndicate of men who, while protecting the official from public knowledge, compelled him to pay rather stiffly for their service. Men with a "past" are not uncommon, and it is not always the "past" but the concealment of it that concerns them most, and in this lack of frankness, this distrust of the understanding and mercy of the people, they usually fall into another slavery, namely, the slavery of political or financial blackmail.

> "*We will manipulate the election of Presidents whose past contains some undisclosed dark affair,* some 'Panama,' *then they will be faithful executors of our orders from fear of exposure* and from the natural desire of every man who has attained a position of authority to retain the privileges, emoluments and the dignity associated with the position of President."

The use of the word "Panama" here refers to the various scandals which arose in French political circles over the original efforts to construct the Panama Canal. If the present form of the Protocols had been written at a later date they might have referred to the "Marconi wireless" scandals in England—though on second thought, they would not have done so because certain men were involved who were *not* Gentiles. Herzl, the great Jewish Zionist leader, uses the expression in "The Jewish State." Speaking of the management of the business of Palestine he says that the Society of the Jews "will see to it that the enterprise does not become a Panama but a Suez." That the same expression should occur in Herzl and in the Protocols is significant; it has also another significance which will be described at another time. It must be clear to the reader, however, that no one writing for the general public at this day would refer to a "Panama" in a man's past. The reference would not be understood.

It is this practice of holding a man under obligation which makes it needful on the part of the true publicist to tell the truth and the whole truth about aspirants for public office. It is not enough to say of a candidate that he "began as a poor boy" and then became "successful." How did he become successful? How explain the "rise" of his fortunes? Sometimes the clue leads deep into the domestic life of the candidate. It may be told of a man, for example, that he helped another out of a scrape by marrying the woman involved, and received a sum of money for doing so. It may be told of another that he was implicated by his too friendly relations with another's wife, but was relieved of his predicament by the astute diplomacy of powerful friends, to whom thereafter he felt himself in debt of honor. It is strange that, in American affairs at least, the woman-note is predominant. In our higher offices that has more frequently occurred than any other, oftener than the money-note.

In European countries, however, where the fact of a man's being entangled illegitimately with a woman does not carry so heavy a stamp of shame with it, the controlled men have been found to have "pasts" of another character.

The whole subject is extremely distasteful, but truth has its surgical duties to perform, and this is one of them. When, for example, a pivotal assemblage like that of the Peace Conference is studied, and the men who are most subject to Jewish influence are isolated, and their past history is carefully traced, there is almost no difficulty whatever in determining the precise moment when they passed over into that fateful condition which, while it did not hinder them of public honors for one hour, made them unchangeably the servants of a power the public did not see. The puzzling spectacle which the observer sees of the great leaders of Anglo-Saxon races closely surrounded and continuously counseled by the princes of the Semitic race, is explained only by a knowledge of those leaders' "past" and those words of the Protocols—"*We will manipulate the election of Presidents whose past contains some undisclosed dark affair.*"

And where this Jewish domination of officials is glaringly apparent, it may be safely assumed that the custody of the secret is almost entirely with that race. When necessity arises, it may be a public service for those in possession of the facts to make them public—not for the purpose of destroying reputations, but for the purpose of damning for all time a most cowardly practice.

Politically, so the Jewish publicists tell us, Jews do not vote as a group. Because of this so we are told, they have no political influence. Moreover, we are told, they are so divided among themselves that they cannot be led in one direction.

It may be true that when it is a question of being *for* anything, the Jewish community may show a majority and minority opinion—a small minority, it is likely to be. But when it becomes a question of being *against* anything, the Jewish community is always a unit.

These are facts to which any ward politician can testify. Any man in political life can test it for himself by announcing that he will not permit himself to be dominated by Jews or anybody else. Just let him mention Jews in that manner; he will no longer have to read about Jewish solidarity; he will have felt it. Not that, in a vote, this Jewish solidarity can accomplish anything it wishes; the Jew's political strength is not in his vote, but in the "pull" of, say, seven men at the seat of government. The Jews, a political minority so far as *votes* are concerned, were a political majority so far as *influence* was concerned, during the last five years. They ruled. They boast that they ruled. The mark of their rule is everywhere.

The note which everyone observes in politics, as in the Press, is the *fear* of the Jews. This *fear* is such that nowhere are the Jews discussed as are, say, the Armenians, the Germans, the Russians or the Hindoos. What is this *fear* but reflection of the knowledge of the Jews' power and their ruthlessness in the use of it? It is possibly true, as many Jewish publicists say, that what is called anti-Semitism is just a panic-fear. It is a dread of the unknown. The uncanny spectacle of an apparently poor people who are richer than all, of a very small minority which is more powerful than all, creates phantoms before the mind.

It is very significant that those who most assume to represent the Jews are quite content that the *fear* should exist. They wish it to exist. To keep it delicately poised and always *there*, though not too obtrusively, is an art they practice. But once the balance is threatened, their crudeness instantly appears. Then comes the threat, by which it is hoped to re-establish the *fear* again. When the threat fails, there comes the wail of anti-Semitism.

How strange this is, that the Jews should not see that the most abject form of anti-Semitism is just this fear which they are willing to have felt toward them by their neighbors. This fear is "Semitophobia" in its worst form. To inspire fear—what is more dreaded by the normal man, and yet what more delights an inferior race?

Now, a great service is done when the people are emancipated from this fear. It is the process of emancipation that Jewish publicists attack. It is this they call anti-Semitism. It is not anti-Semitism at all; it is the only course that can prevent anti-Semitism.

The process involves several steps. The extent of the Jewish power must be shown. To this, of course, strong Jewish objection is made, though no strong disproof can be made.

Then, the existence of this power must be explained. It can be explained only by the Jewish Will to Power, as it may be called, or by the deliberate program which is followed in the attainment of the power. When the method is explained, half the damage is undone. The Jew is not a superman. He is bright, he is intense, his philosophy of material things leaves him free to do many things from which his neighbor draws back; but, given equal advantages, he is not a superman. The Yankee is more than his equal any time, but the Yankee has an inborn inclination to observe the rules of the game. When the people know by what means this power is gained—when they are informed how, for example, political control is seized, as it has been in the United States, the very method takes all the glamour from the power, and shows it to be a rather sordid thing after all.

This series of articles is attempting to take these orderly steps, and it is believed the complete effort will justify itself to reasonable minds, both Jewish and Gentile.

In the present article one important means of power has been described on the authority of the Protocols. Whether the method laid down by the Protocols is worth considering or not depends entirely on whether it can be found in actual affairs today. It can be found. The two tally. The parallel is complete. It were well for the Jew, of course, if no trace of him could be found in either the written or the actual program. But he is there, and it is illogical for him to blame anyone but himself for being there. Certainly, it is small defense against the fact to heap abuse upon the one who discloses the fact. We have agreed that the Jews are clever, but they are not so clever as to be able to cover their work. There is a certain element of weakness in them which reveals the whole matter in the end. And even the revelation would not mean much if the thing revealed were not wrong. But that is the weakness of the Jewish program—it is wrong. The Jews have never gained any measure of success so great that the world cannot check it. The world is engaged in a great checking tactic now, and if there are still prophets among the Jews they should lead their people in another path.

The proof and the fruit of any exposure of the World Program is the removal of the element of fear from the peoples among whom the Jews live.

*"In a world of completely organized territorial sovereignties he (the Jew) has only two possible cities of refuge; he must either pull down the pillars of the whole national state system, or he must create a territorial sovereignty of his own . . . .In Eastern Europe, Bolshevism and Zionism seem to grow side by side . . . . not because the Jew cares for the positive side of radical philosophy, not because he desires to be a partaker in Gentile nationalism or Gentile democracy, but because no existing Gentile system is ever anything but distasteful to him."*

XIX.

# The All-Jewish Mark on "Red Russia"

WE shall now briefly interrupt the commentary which we have been making on the Protocols, to set at rest once and for all certain misstatements which are made for Gentile consumption.

To learn what the Jewish leaders of the United States or any other country think, do not read their addresses to the Gentiles; read their addresses to their own people. On such matters as these—Whether the Jew regards himself as destined to rule the world; whether he regards himself as belonging to a nation and race distinct from every other nation and race; whether he regards the Gentile world as the legitimate field of his exploitation by a lower moral method than is permissible among his own people; whether he knows and shares the principles of the Protocols—on such matters as these, the only safe guide is to be found in the words which Jewish leaders speak to Jews, not in the words they speak to Gentiles.

The notable Jewish names which appear oftenest in the Press do not represent the spokesmen of Judaism at all, but only a selected few who represent the Department of Propaganda Among the Gentiles. Sometimes that propaganda is in the form of donations for Christian charitable organizations; sometimes it is in the form of "liberal" opinion on religious, social and political questions. In whatever form it comes, you may depend upon it that the real activities of the Jewish hierarchy proceed under cover of that which the Gentile is invited to observe and approve.

The statements offered in this series are never made without the strictest and fullest proof, confirmation and corroboration in the utterances of Jewish leaders. This is one of the strange features of the multitude of Jewish attacks on this series: they are attacking what they themselves stand for, and their only reason for the attack must be their belief that this investigation has not been able to penetrate through to that which has been kept hidden from the world.

The most persistent denials have been offered to the statement that Bolshevism everywhere, in Russia or the United States, is Jewish. In these denials we have perhaps one of the most brazen examples of the double intent referred to above. The denial of the Jewish character of Bolshevism is made to the Gentile; but in the confidence and secrecy of Jewish communication, or buried in the Yiddish dialect, or obscurely hidden in the Jewish national press, we find the proud assertion made—to their own people!—that Bolshevism is Jewish.

Jewish propaganda has only two straws to grasp in the terrible tale of murder, immorality, robbery, enforced starvation and hideous humanism which make the present Russian situation impossible to describe and all but impossible to comprehend.

One of these straws is that Kerensky, the man who eased in the opening wedge of Bolshevism, is not a Jew. Indeed, one of the strongest indications that Bolshevism is Jewish is that the Jewish press emphasizes so fiercely the alleged Gentilism of at least *two* of the revolutionary notables. It may be cruel to deny them two among hundreds, but merely saying so cannot change Kerensky's nationality. His name is Adler. His father was a Jew and his mother a Jewess. Adler, the father, died, and the mother married a Russian named Kerensky, whose name the young child took. Among the radicals who employed him as a lawyer, among the forces that put him forward to drive the first nail into Russia's cross, among the soldiers who fought with him, his Jewish descent and character have never been doubted.

"Well, but there is Lenin," our Jewish publicists say—"Lenin the head of it all, the brains of it all, and Lenin is a Gentile! We've got you there—Lenin is a Gentile!"

Perhaps he is, but why do his children speak Yiddish? Why are his proclamations put forth in Yiddish? Why did he abolish the Christian Sunday and establish by law the Jewish Saturday Sabbath?

The explanation of all this may be that he married a Jewess. The fact is that he did. But another explanation may be that he himself is a Jew. Certainly he is not the Russian nobleman he has always claimed to be. The statements he has made about his identity thus far have been lies. The claim that he is a Gentile may be unfounded too.

No one has ever doubted Trotsky's nationality—he is a Jew. His name is Braunstein. Recently the Gentiles were told that Trotsky had said he wasn't much of anything—in religion. That may be. But still he must be something—else why are the Russian Christian churches turned into stables, slaughter houses and dancing halls, while *the Jewish synagogues remain untouched*? And why are Christian priests and ministers made to work on the roads, *while Jewish rabbis are left their clerical privileges*? Trotsky may not be much of anything in religion, but he is a Jew nevertheless. This is not mere Gentile insistence that he shall be considered a Jew whether or no; it is straight Jewish teaching that he is. In a future discussion on "religion or race?" we shall show that even without religion, Trotsky is, and is considered by all Jewish authorities to be, a Jew.

An apology must be made here for repeating well-known facts. Yet, so many people are not even now aware of the true meaning of Bolshevism, that at the risk of monotony, we shall cite a few of the salient facts. The purpose, however, is not alone to explain Russia, but to throw a warning light on conditions in the United States.

The Bolshevik Government, as it stood late this summer when the latest report was smuggled through to certain authorities, shows up the Jewish domination of the whole affair. It has changed very slightly since the beginning. We give only a few items to indicate the proportion. It must not be supposed that the non-Jewish members of the government are Russian.

Very few Russians have anything to say about their own country these days. The so-called "Dictatorship of the Proletariat," in which the proletariat has nothing whatever to say, is Russian only in the sense that it is set up in Russia; it is not Russian in that it springs from or includes the Russian people. It is the international program of the Protocols, which might be "put over" by a minority in any country, and which is being given a dress-rehearsal in Russia.

## Table Showing Jewish Control of Russia

| | Number of Members | Number of Jewish Members | Jewish Percentage |
|---|---|---|---|
| The Council of the Commissaries of the People | 22 | 17 | 77.2% |
| The Commissariat of War | 43 | 33 | 76.7% |
| The Commissariat of Foreign Affairs | 16 | 13 | 81.2% |
| The Commissariat of Finance | 30 | 24 | 80.0% |
| The Commissariat of Justice | 21 | 20 | 95.2% |
| The Commissariat of Public Instruction | 53 | 42 | 79.2% |
| The Commissariat of Social Assistance | 6 | 6 | 100.0% |
| The Commissariat of Work | 8 | 7 | 87.5% |
| Delegates of the Bolshevik Red Cross to Berlin, Vienna, Varsovie, Bucharest, Copenhagen | 8 | 8 | 100.0% |
| Commissaries of the Provinces | 23 | 21 | 91.3% |
| Journalists | 41 | 41 | 100.0% |

These are enlightening figures. The reader will note that the Jewish percentage is high at all times, never lower than 76 per cent in any case. (Curiously enough, the lowest percentage of Jews is found in the Commissariat of War.) But in those committees which deal most closely with the mass of the people, as well as in the committees of defense and propaganda, Jews fill literally all the places.

Remember what the Protocols say about Press Control: remember what Baron Montefiore said about it, and then look at the Government Journalists. That committee comprises 41 men, and the 41 are Jews. Only Jewish pens are trusted with Bolshevist propaganda.

And then the so-called "Red Cross delegates," which are merely Red Revolutionary delegates to the cities named—of the 8, there are 8 Jews.

The Commissariat of Social Assistance, upon whose word the life and privilege of tens of thousands hang—there are 6 members, and the 6 are Jews. And so on through the list.

Out of the 53 members of the Commissariat of Public Instruction, 11 are noted as non-Jews. But what kind of non-Jews is not stated. They may be "non-Jews like Lenin" whose children speak the Yiddish as their native tongue. Whatever they are, there is a sidelight upon their attitude in the fact that the Bolsheviki immediately took over *all the Hebrew schools* and continued them as they were and laid down a rule that *the ancient Hebrew language* should be taught in them. The ancient Hebrew language is the vehicle of the deeper secrets of the World Program.

And for the Gentile Russian children—? "Why," said these gentle Jewish educators, "we will teach them sex knowledge. We will brush out of their minds the cobwebs. They must learn the truth about things!"—with consequences that are too pitiable to narrate. But this can be said: unquestionably there were deaths among innocent Jews when Hungary wrested itself free from the Red Bolshevism of Bela Kun (or Cohen). The Jews may well call it the "White Terror" that followed their failure to re-enact the tragedy of Russia in Hungary. But there are mountains of evidence to show that nothing had so potent an effect in producing the bloodshed of the "White Terror" as the outraged minds of parents whose children had been compulsorily drawn through sloughs of filth during the short time the Jewish Bolsheviki had charge of the schools.

American Jews do not like to hear this. Their shrinking from it would be greatly to their honor did they not immediately return to the defense of the people who do these things. It is well enough known that the chastity of Christians is not so highly regarded by the orthodox male Jew as is the chastity of his own people, but it would be pleasant to be certain that all of them condemn what went on in Russia and Hungary in the matter of education. However, as most of the influences which destroy Gentile youth today—in America—are in the hands of the Jews, and as it is plainly stated in the Protocols that one of the lines of campaign is "to corrupt the youth of the Gentiles," the situation is one that calls for something more than mere hard feelings and angry denials whenever these facts are referred to.

It is not the economic experiment, so-called, tnat one objects to in Russia; it is not the fallacies, the sad delusion of the people. No. It is the downright, dirty immorality, the brutish nastiness of it all; and the line which the immorality and nastiness draws between Jew and Gentile. The horrible cruelty involved we will not deal with, leaving it merely with the explanation which has found utterance in the Jewish press that "it *may* be that the Jew in Russia is taking an *unconscious* revenge for his centuries of suffering."

"But," asks some reader, "how may we know that all this is true?"

Bearing in mind that we are speaking of Russia, not for the interest of the Russian situation at all, but to indicate the international character of those who are responsible for conditions there, and to identify them for the protection of the United States, we shall look at the evidence.

There is, of course, the evidence brought to light by our own United States Senate and printed in a Report of the Committee on the Judiciary. We do not wish to spend much time on this, because we prefer in these articles to use Jewish testimony instead of Gentile. But we shall pause long enough to show the nature of the testimony brought out by our own government.

Dr. George A. Simons, a clergyman in charge of an American congregation in Petrograd at the time the Bolshevik terror broke out, was a witness. Parts of his testimony are given here:

> "'There were hundreds of agitators who followed in the trail of Trotsky-Bronstein, these men having come over from the lower East Side of New York * * * A number of us were impressed by the strange Yiddish element in this thing right from the start, and it soon became evident that more than half the agitators in the so-called Bolshevik movement were Yiddish.'
>
> "Senator Nelson—'Hebrews?'
>
> "Dr. Simons—'They were Hebrews, apostate Jews. I do not want to say anything against the Jews, as such. I am not in sympathy with the anti-Semitic movement, never have been, and do

not ever expect to be * * * But I have a firm conviction that this thing is Yiddish, and that one of its bases is found in the East Side of New York.'

"Senator Nelson—'Trotsky came over from New York during that summer, did he not?'

"Dr. Simons—'He did.'

"Later Dr. Simons said: 'In December, 1918 * * * under the presidency of a man known as Apfelbaum * * * out of 388 members, only 16 happened to be real Russians, and all the rest Jews, with the exception possibly of one man, who is a Negro from America, who calls himself Professor Gordon * * * and 265 of this northern commune government that is sitting in the Old Smolny Institute came from the lower East Side of New York—265 of them. * * *

" 'I might mention this, that when the Bolsheviki came into power, all over Petrograd we at once had a predominance of Yiddish proclamations, big posters, and everything in Yiddish. It became very evident that now that was to be one of the great languages of Russia; and the real Russians, of course, did not take very kindly to it.' "

William Chapin Huntington, who was commercial attache of the United States Embassy at Petrograd, testified:

"The leaders of the movement, I should say, are about two-thirds Russian Jews * * * The Bolsheviks are internationalists, and they were not interested in the particular national ideals of Russia."

William W. Welch, an employe of the National City Bank, New York, testified:

"In Russia it is well known that three-fourths of the Bolshevik leaders are Jewish * * * There were some—not many, but there were some—real Russians; and what I mean by real Russians is Russian-born, and not Russian Jews."

Roger E. Simmons, Trade Commissioner connected with the United States Department of Commerce, also testified. An important anonymous witness, whom the committee permitted to withhold his name, told the same things.

The British White Book, Russia, No. 1—"A Collection of Reports on Bolshevism in Russia, presented to Parliament by Command of His Majesty, April, 1919," contains masses of the same testimony from many sources, all of them eyewitnesses.

In that very highly respected magazine *Asia* for February-March, 1920, is an article which contains, among other important ones, these statements: (the italics are ours)

> "In all the Bolshevist institutions the heads are Jews. The Assistant Commissar for Elementary Education, Grunberg, *can hardly speak Russian*. The Jews are successful in everything and obtain their ends. They know how to command and get complete submission. But they are proud and contemptuous toward everyone, which strongly excites the people against them * * * *At the present time there is a great national religious fervor among the Jews.* They believe that the promised time of the rule of God's elect on earth is coming. *They have connected Judaism with a universal revolution.* They see in the spread of revolution the fulfilling of the Scriptures: 'Though I make an end of all the nations, whither I have scattered thee, yet will I not make an end of thee.' "

Now, if Gentile proof were wanted, the files of THE DEARBORN INDEPENDENT for a whole year would not begin to contain it. But Jewish proof is better.

There has been a strange vacillation in Jewish opinion concerning Bolshevism. At first it was hailed with delight. There was no concealment whatever in the early days of the new regime as to the part which Jewry had in it. Public meetings, interviews, special articles poured forth in which very valuable elements of truth were mingled. There was no attempt at concealment of names.

Then the horror of the thing began to take hold upon the world, and for just a breathing space Jewish opinion fell silent. There was a spasmodic denial or two. Then a new burst of glorification. The glorification continues within Judaism itself, but it now carries on the Gentile side of its face a very sad expression labeled "persecution."

We have lived to see the day when to denounce Bolshevism is to "persecute the Jews."

In the *American Hebrew*, for September 10, 1920, an article appears which not only acknowledges and explains the part which the Jew plays in the present unrest and upheaval, but justifies it—and justifies it, curiously enough, by The Sermon on the Mount.

The writer says that *"the Jew evolved organized capitalism with its working instrumentality, the banking system."*

This is very refreshing, in view of the numerous Jewish denials of this economic fact.

"One of the impressive phenomena of the impressive time is the revolt of the Jew against the Frankenstein which his own mind conceived and his own hand fashioned * * *" If this is true, why is Jewish "organized capital with its working instrumentality, the banking system" supporting the revolt?

"That achievement (referring to the Russian overthrow), destined to figure in history as the overshadowing result of the World War, *was largely the outcome of Jewish thinking, of Jewish discontent, of Jewish effort to reconstruct.*"

"This rapid emergence of the Russian revolution from the destructive phase and its entrance into the constructive phase is a conspicuous expression of the constructive genius of *Jewish discontent.*"

(This, of course, requires proof that the constructive phase has appeared. The implication here is sheer propaganda. The Protocols, however, have a reconstructive program. We have not reached it as yet in this series of articles, but it is clearly outlined in the Protocols—destroy Gentile society, and then reconstruct it according to "our" plans.)

Now read carefully:

*"What Jewish idealism and Jewish discontent have so powerfully contributed to accomplish in Russia, the same historic qualities of the Jewish mind and heart ARE TENDING TO PROMOTE IN OTHER COUNTRIES."*

Read that again. "What Jewish idealism and Jewish discontent have so powerfully contributed to accomplish in Russia!" Just what was that? And just how did it "powerfully contribute?" And why are

"Jewish idealism" and "Jewish discontent" always linked together? If you read the Protocols it is all very clear. Jewish idealism is the destruction of Gentile society and the erection of Jewish society. Was it not so in Russia?—Yiddish proclamations on the walls, the ancient Hebrew in the schools, Saturday substituted for Sunday, and the rabbis respected while the priests were put to work on the roads! All "powerfully contributed" to by murder, rapine, theft and starvation.

Our author is more candid than he realizes. He calls this linked idealism and discontent *"the historic qualities of the Jewish mind."* THE DEARBORN INDEPENDENT is indebted to him for this clear confirmation of what it has been saying for some time.

But even that is not all. "These same historic qualities of the Jewish mind" which "contributed so powerfully to accomplish in Russia" the Red Terror still existing there, are declared by this author to be tending to promote the same sort of thing in other countries. He says so in so many words—"tending to promote in other countries."

But we knew that. The only difference is that when Gentiles said it, they were overwhelmed with the wildest abuse; but now a pro-Jewish writer says it in a leading Jewish publication. And he says it apologetically—listen to him:

"It was natural that * * * *discontent in other parts of the world* should find expression in overemphasis of issues and overstatement of aims."

What discontent? Jewish discontent, of course. Discontent with what? With any form of Gentile rule. And how did it find expression? "In overemphasis of issues and overstatement of aims." What were these issues and aims? To bring the Bolshevik revolution to the United States.

No, they did not overstate their aims; they exactly stated them—they simply selected the wrong country, that's all.

There are Russian Bolshevists in this country now, hawking about the streets of New York the gold cigaret cases which they stole from Russian families, and the family jewels, the wedding and birthday rings, which they filched from Russian women. Bolshevism never got further than the pawnshop and burglar's "fence" idea. The proof of this traffic in stolen property is going to drive some people into hiding before long. It will be a long, long time before America will be taking orders in Yiddish, or American women will be giving up their jewels to "the chosen race."

However, that happens to be only the most recent acknowledgement that has come to hand. It is significant for its confession that "Jewish discontent" was "tending to promote" in "other countries" what it has "so powerfully contributed to accomplish in Russia."

And with such a link between the American Hebrew, Russian Bolshevism and the Protocols, there are still Jewish publicists with the crust to say that only crazy people could see the connection. Only blind people will not see it. But that is only a minor connection. This series of articles does not rest on anything so accidental as this Jewish New Year's apology for Bolshevism in the great Hebrew weekly of the United States.

Issue of September 25, 1920.

*"Out of the economic chaos, the discontent of the Jew evolved organized capital with its working instrumentality, the banking system . . . .*

*"One of the impressive phenomena of the impressive time is the revolt of the Jew against the Frankenstein which his own mind conceived and his own hand fashioned. . . .*

*"That achievement (Russian Bolshevik revolution-Ed.), destined to figure in history as the overshadowing result of the World War, was largely the outcome of Jewish thinking, of Jewish discontent, of Jewish effort to reconstruct . . . .*

*"What Jewish idealism and Jewish discontent have so powerfully contributed to accomplish in Russia, the same historic qualities of the Jewish mind and heart are tending to promote in other countries . . . .*

*"Shall America, like the Russia of the Czars, overwhelm the Jew with the bitter and baseless reproach of being a destroyer, and thus put him in the position of an irreconcilable enemy?*

*"Or shall America avail itself of Jewish genius as it avails itself of the peculiar genius of every other race? . . . .*

*"That is the question for the American people to answer."*

*—From an article in The American Hebrew, Sept. 10, 1920.*

XX.

# Jewish Testimony in Favor of Bolshevism

THE American people will answer that question, and their answer will be against the disruptive genius of dissatisfied Jews.

It is very well known that "what Jewish idealism and Jewish discontent have so powerfully contributed to accomplish in Russia" is also being attempted in the United States. Why did not the writer in the *American Hebrew* say the United States, instead of saying "the same historic qualities of the Jewish mind and heart are tending to promote *in other countries*."

"Jewish idealism and Jewish discontent" are not directed against capital. Capital is enlisted in their service. The only governmental order the Jewish effort is directed against is Gentile governmental order; and the only "capital" it attacks is Gentile capital.

Lord Eustace Percy who, if one may judge by the full and appreciative quotations of his words in the Jewish press, has the sanction of thinkers among the Jews, settles the first point. Discussing the Jewish tendency to revolutionary movements he says:

> "In Eastern Europe Bolshevism and Zionism often seem to grow side by side, just as Jewish influence molded Republican and Socialist thought throughout the nineteenth century down to the Young Turk revolution in Constantinople hardly more than a decade ago—*not because the Jew cares for the positive side of radical philosophy, not because he desires to be a partaker in Gentile nationalism or Gentile democracy, but because no existing Gentile system of government is ever anything but distasteful to him.*"

And that analysis is absolutely true. In Russia, the excuse was the czar; in Germany, the kaiser; in England it is the Irish question; in the numerous South American revolutions, where the Jews always had a ruling hand, no particular reason was thought necessary to be given; in the United States it is "the capitalistic class;" but always and everywhere it is, by the confession of their own spokesman, a distaste for any form whatsoever of Gentile government. The Jew believes that the world is his by right; he wants to collect his own, and the speediest way of doing so is the destruction of order by revolution—a destruction which is made possible by a long and clever campaign of loose and destructive ideas.

As to the second point, every reader can verify the fact from his own experience. Let him recall to his mind the capitalists who have been held up to public scorn in the Jew-controlled press of the United States—and whom does he find them to be? Whose forms have you seen caricatured with the dollar-mark in Hearst's papers? Are they Seligman, Kahn, Warburg, Schiff, Kuhn, Loeb & Company, or any of the others? No. These are Jewish bankers. The attack is never made on them. The names made most familiar to you by newspaper denunciation are the names of Gentile industrial and banking leaders—and Gentile leaders only—the principal ones being Morgan and Rockefeller.

It is a well-known fact that during the French Commune when men of wealth suffered severe losses in property, the Jewish Rothschilds were not injured to the extent of one pennyworth. It is also a well-known fact, capable of proof satisfactory to any ordinary mind, that the connections between Jewish financiers and the more dangerous revolutionary elements here in the United States are such that it is most unlikely that the former stand to lose anything in any event. Under cover of the disorder in Russia at the present time, Jewish financiers are taking advantage of the stress of the people to gain control of all the strategic natural resources and municipal property, by methods which they fully expect to be legalized by Jewish courts when the present "Bolshevik regime" announces that it will give way to a "modified communism." The world hasn't seen the end of Bolshevism yet. Like the World War, Bolshevism cannot be interpreted until it is seen who profits most by it, and the profiteering is in full sway now. The enemy is Gentile capital. Not any other. And "all the wealth of the world in our hands" is the unspoken slogan of every Jewish outbreak in the world today.

The quotation at the head of this article represents the position which the Jews are now ready to take with reference to the Russian Revolution. They have always been charged with responsibility for what has occurred in that unhappy country, but at first their spokesmen denied it. The denials were most indignant, and were usually accompanied by the typical plaint that the charge was "persecution." But the facts have been so overwhelming, and the government investigations have been so revealing, that denials have been abandoned.

For a while an attempt was made to distract attention from Russia by a tremendously powerful propaganda concerning the Jews in Poland. There are many indications that the Polish propaganda was undertaken as a "cover" for the immense immigration of Jews into the United States. It may be that some of our readers do not know it, but an endless stream of the most undesirable immigrants pours daily into the United States, tens of thousands of the same people whose presence has been the problem and menace of the governments of Europe.

Well, the Polish propaganda and the immigration movement are sailing along smoothly, and the United States Government is assured by the Jewish ring at Washington that everything is quiet along the Potomac (it *is* quiet there, quiet as the Jewish ring could wish), but still the Russian fact persists in calling for explanation.

And here is the explanation: The Jews created capitalism, we are told. But capitalism has proved itself ill-behaved. So now, the Jewish creators are going to destroy their creation. They have done so in Russia. And now, will the American people be good and let their Jewish benefactors do the same in America?

That is the new explanation, and, typically Jewish again, it is coupled with a proposal for the United States—and a threat! If America refuses this particular service of the Jew, we "put him in the position of an irreconcilable enemy." See quotation at the head of this article.

But the Jews have *not* destroyed capitalism in Russia. When Lenin and Trotsky make their farewell bow and retire under the protective influence of the Jewish capitalists of the world, it will be seen that only Gentile or Russian capital has been destroyed, and that Jewish capital has been enthroned.

What is the record? Documents printed by the United States Government contain this letter: Please note the date, the Jewish banker and the Jewish names:

"Stockholm, Sept. 21, 1917.

"To Mr. Raphael Scholan:

"Dear Comrade:—The banking house, M. Warburg, opened an account for the enterprise of Comrade Trotsky upon receipt of a telegram from the Chairman of the 'Rhein-Westphalian Syndicate.' A lawyer, probably Mr. Kestroff, obtained ammunition and organized the transportation of same, together with that of the money * * * to whom the sum demanded by Comrade Trotsky is to be handed.

"Fraternal Greetings!

"Furstenberg."

Long before that, an American Jewish financier was supplying the funds which carried revolutionary propaganda to thousands of Russian prisoners of war in Japanese camps.

It is sometimes said, by way of explaining the Bolshevik movement, that it was financed from Germany, a fact which was seized upon to supply war propaganda. It is true that part of the money came from Germany. It is true that part of the money came from the United States. It is the whole truth that Jewish finance in all the countries was interested in Bolshevism as an All-Jewish investment. For the whole period of the war, the Jewish World Program was cloaked under this or that national name—the blame being laid on the Germans by the Allies, and on the Allies by the Germans, and the people kept in ignorance of who the real personages were.

It was stated by a French official that two millions of money was contributed by one Jewish banker alone.

When Trotsky left the United States to fulfill his appointed task, he was released from arrest at Halifax upon the request of the United States, and everyone knows who constituted the War Government of the United States.

The conclusion, when all the facts are considered, is irresistible, that the Bolshevik revolution was a carefully groomed investment on the part of International Jewish Finance.

It is easy to understand, then, why the same forces would like to introduce it to the United States. The real struggle in this country is not between labor and capital; the real struggle is between Jewish capital and Gentile capital, with the I. W. W. leaders, the Socialist leaders, the Red leaders and the labor leaders almost a unit on the side of the Jewish capitalists.

Again recall which financiers these men most attack. You cannot recall a single Jewish name.

The main purpose in these two articles, however, is to introduce the Jewish testimony which exists as to the Jewish nature of Bolshevism.

The Jewish *Chronicle*, of London, said in 1919:

> "There is much in the fact of Bolshevism itself, in the fact that so many Jews are Bolsheviks, in the fact that the ideals of Bolshevism at many points are consonant with the finest ideals of Judaism."

In the same paper, of 1920, is a report of an address made by Israel Zangwill, a noted Jewish writer, in which he pronounced glowing praise on "the race which has produced a Beaconsfield, a Reading, a Montagu, a Klotz, *a Kurt Eisner, a Trotsky*." Mr. Zangwill, in his swelling Semitic enthusiasm, embraced the Jews in the British Government in the same category with the Jews of the Hungarian and Russian Bolshevik governments. What is the difference? They are all Jewish, and all of equal honor and usefulness to "the race."

Rabbi J. L. Magnes, in an address at New York in 1919, is reported to have said:

> "When the Jew gives his thought, his devotion, to the cause of the workers and of the dispossessed, of the disinherited of the world, the radical quality within him goes to the roots of things, and in Germany he becomes a Marx and a Lassalle, a Haas and an Edward Bernstein; in

Austria he becomes a Victor Adler and a Friedrich Adler; *in Russia, a Trotsky.* Just take for a moment the present situation in Russia and in Germany. The revolution set creative forces free, and *see what a large company of Jews was available for immediate service.* Socialist Revolutionaries and Mensheviki, and Bolsheviki, Majority and Minority Socialists—whatever they be called—*Jews are to be found among the trusted leaders and the routine workers of all these revolutionary parties.*"

"See," says the rabbi, "what a large company of Jews are available for immediate service." One ought to see where he points. There are as many Jewish members of revolutionary societies in the United States, as there were in Russia; and here, as there, they are "available for immediate service."

Bernard Lazare, a Jewish writer who has published a work on anti-Semitism, says:

"The Jew, therefore, *does take a part in revolutions, and he participates in them in so far as he is a Jew, or more correctly, in so far as he remains a Jew.*"

He says also—"The Jewish spirit is essentially a revolutionary spirit, and consciously or otherwise, the Jew is a revolutionist."

There is hardly any country in the world, except the United States, where denials of this could be made in such a way as to require proof. In every other country the fact is known. Here we have been under such a fear of mentioning the word "Jew" or anything pertaining to it, that the commonest facts have been kept from us—facts which even a superficial knowledge of Jewish writing would have given us. It was almost a pathetic spectacle to see American audiences go to lectures about the Russian situation, and come away from the hall confused and perplexed because the Russian situation is so un-Russian, all because no lecturer thought it politic to mention "Jew" in the United States, for, as some day we shall see, the Jew has contrived to gain control of the platform too.

Not only do the literary lights of Jewry acknowledge the Jew's propensity to revolution generally, and his responsibility for the Russian situation particularly, but the lower lights also have a very clear idea about it. The Jew in the midst of the revolution is conscious that somehow he is advancing the cause of Israel. He may be a "bad Jew" in the synagogue sense, but he is enough of a Jew to be willing to do any thing that would advance the prestige of Israel. Race is stronger than religion in Jewry.

The Russian paper, *On to Moscow*, in September, 1919, said:

> "It should not be forgotten that *the Jewish people*, who for centuries were oppressed by kings and czars, *are the real proletariat, the real Internationale, which has no country.*"

Mr. Cohan, in the newspaper, *Communist*, in April, 1919, said:

> "Without exaggeration, it may be said that *the great Russian social revolution was indeed accomplished by the hands of the Jews.* Would the dark, oppressed masses of the Russian workmen and peasants have been able to throw off the yoke of the bourgeoisie by themselves? No, *it was precisely the Jews who led the Russian proletariat to the dawn of the Internationale and not only have led, but are also now leading the Soviet cause* which remains in their safe hands. We may be quiet as long as the chief command of the Red Army is in the hands of Comrade Leon Trotsky. It is true that *there are no Jews in the ranks of the Red Army as far as privates are concerned, but in the committees and Soviet organizations, as commissars, the Jews are gallantly leading the masses* of the Russian proletariat to victory. It is not without reason that during the elections to all Soviet institutions the Jews are winning by an overwhelming majority * * * *The symbol of Jewry,* which for centuries has struggled against capitalism, *has become also the symbol of the Russian proletariat,* which can be seen even in the adoption of the Red five-pointed *star,* which in former times, as it is well known, *was the symbol of Zionism and Jewry.* With this sign comes victory, *with this sign comes the death*

*of the parasites of the bourgeoisie * * * Jewish tears will come out of them in sweat of drops of blood."*

This confession, or rather boast, is remarkable for its completeness.

The Jews, says Mr. Cohan, are in control of the Russian masses—the Russian masses who have never risen at all, who only know that a minority, like the czar's minority, is in control at the seat of government.

The Jews are not in the Red Army, Mr. Cohan informs us, that is, in the ranks where the actual fighting is done; and this is strictly in line with the Protocols. The strategy of the World Program is to set Gentiles to kill Gentiles. This was the Jewish boast during the various French social disasters, that so many Frenchmen had been set killing each other.

*In the World War just passed, there were as many Gentiles killed by Gentiles as there are Jews in the world.* It was a great victory for Israel. "Jewish tears will come out in sweat of drops of blood."

But the Jews are in the places of control and safety, says Mr. Cohan, and he is absolutely right about it. The wonder is that he was so honest as to say it.

As to the elections, so-called, at which the Jews are so unanimously chosen, the literature of Bolshevism is very explicit. Those who voted against the Jewish candidates were adjudged "enemies of the revolution" and executed. It did not require many executions at a voting place to make all the elections unanimous.

Mr. Cohan is especially instructive on the significance of the Red Star, the five-pointed emblem of Bolshevism. "The symbol of Jewry," he says, "has become also the symbol of the Russian proletariat."

The Star of David, the Jewish national emblem, is a six-pointed star, formed by two triangles, one standing on its base, the other on its apex. Deprived of their base lines, these triangles approximate the familiar Masonic emblem of the Square and Compass. It is this Star of David of which a Jewish observer in Palestine remarks that there are so few among the graves of the British soldiers who won Palestine in the recent war; most of the signs are the familiar wooden

Cross. These Crosses are now reported to be objectionable to the new rulers of Palestine, because they are so plainly in view of the visitor who approaches the new Jewish university. As in Soviet Russia, so in Palestine, not many Jews laid down their lives for the cause: there were plenty of Gentiles for that purpose.

As the Jew is a past master in the art of symbolism, it may not be without significance that the Bolshevik Star has one point less than the Star of David. For there is still one point to be fulfilled in the World Program as outlined in the Protocols—and that is the enthronement of "our leader." When he comes, the World Autocrat for whom the whole program is framed, the sixth point may be added.

The Five Points of the Star now apparently assured are the Purse, the Press, the Peerage, Palestine and Proletarianism. The sixth point will be the Prince of Israel.

It is very hard to say, it is hard to believe, but Mr. Cohan has said it, and revolutions especially since the French Revolution confirm it, that "with this sign comes the death of the parasites of the bourgeoisie * * * Jewish tears will come out of them in sweat of drops of blood." The "bourgeoisie," as the Protocols say, are always Gentile.

The common counterargument to the invincible fact of the Jewish character of the Russian revolution—an argument which is destined to disappear now that Jewish acknowledgment is coming thick and fast—is that the Jews in Russia suffer too. "How can we favor a movement which makes our own people suffer?" is the argument put up to the Gentile.

Well, the fact is this: they *are* favoring that movement. Today, this very moment, the Bolshevik Government is receiving money from Jewish financiers in Europe, and if in Europe, then of course from the International Jewish bankers in America also. That is one fact.

Another fact is this: the Jews of Russia are not suffering to anywhere near the extent we are told by the propagandists. It is now a fact admitted by Jews themselves that upon the first sweep of the Bolshevists across Poland, the Polish Jews were friendly with the invaders and helped them. The fact was explained by American Jews in this manner: since Bolshevism came to Russia, the condition of the Jews there has greatly improved—therefore the Polish Jews were friendly. And it is true—the condition of Russian Jews is good.

One reason is: they have Russia. Everything there belongs to them.

The other reason is: The Jews of Russia are the only ones receiving help there today.

Did that second statement ever strike you as significant? Only the Jews of Russia have food and money sent to them. It is one form, of course, of the support which the Jewish world is giving Bolshevism. But if the suffering among the Jews is what the propagandists say it is, what must it be among the Russians? Yet no one is sending food or money to *them*. The probable truth of the whole situation is that Jewish Bolshevism is laying a tax on the world. Any time it may be required, there is plenty of evidence as to the good condition of the Jews in Russia. They have all there is.

Another source of confusion is revealed in the question: "How can Jewish capitalists support Bolshevism when Bolshevism is against capitalism?"

Bolshevism, as before stated, is only against Gentile capitalism. Jewish financiers who remained in Russia are very useful to the Bolsheviki. Read this description by an eyewitness: "A Jew is this Commissary of the Bank, very elegant, with a cravat of the latest style, and a fancy waistcoat. A Jew is this District Commissary, former stockbroker, with a double bourgeois chin. Again a Jew, this inspector of taxes: he understands perfectly how to squeeze the bourgeoisie."

These agents of Jewry are still there. Other agents are among the Russians who fled, getting their lands away from them on mortgage loans. When the curtain lifts, most of the choice real estate will be found to have passed into Jewish control by perfectly "legal" means.

That is one answer to the question, Why the Jewish capitalists support Bolshevism. The Red Revolution is the greatest speculative event of human history. Besides, it is for the exaltation of Israel;

it is a colossal revenge, which the Jews always take where they can, for wrongs real or imaginary.

Jewish capitalism knows exactly what it is doing. What are its gains?

1. It has taken a whole rich country, without the cost of war.

2. It has demonstrated the necessity of gold. Jewish power rests on the fiction that gold is wealth. By the premeditated clumsiness of the Bolshevik monetary system, the unthinking world has been made to believe still more strongly that gold is necessary, and this belief gives Jewish capitalism another hold on the Gentile world. If the Bolshevists had been honest, they could have dealt Jewish capitalism its death blow. No! Gold is still on its throne. Destroy the fiction that gold has value, and you leave the Jewish International Financiers sitting forlorn on heaps of useless metal.

3. It has demonstrated its power to the world. Protocol Seven says: "To demonstrate our enslavement of the Gentile governments of Europe, *we will show our power to one of them* by crimes of violence, that is, a reign of terror." Has Europe been sufficiently "shown"? Europe has, and is afraid! That is a great gain for Jewish capitalists.

4. Not the least of the gains is the field practice in the art of revolution which Russia has offered. Students in that Red school are coming back to the United States. The technique of revolution has been reduced to a science according to the details laid down in the Protocols. To use Rabbi Magnes's words again: "See what a large company of Jews was available for immediate service." The available company is now much larger.

---

Issue of October, 2, 1920.